Aris and Phillips Classical Texts

ULPIANUS

On the Duty of the Proconsul

Edited with an Introduction, Translation, and Commentary by

Ido Israelowich

LIVERPOOL UNIVERSITY PRESS

First published 2025
Liverpool University Press
4 Cambridge Street
Liverpool, L69 7ZU

British Library Cataloguing-in-Publication Data
A British Library CIP Record is available.

ISBN 978-1-83624-428-8
eISBN 978-1-83624-409-7

Typeset by Carnegie Book Production, Lancaster
Printed and bound by CPI Group (UK) Ltd, Croydon CR0 4YY

In memory of Nissim

CONTENTS

INTRODUCTION

1. THE AUTHOR

Cn. Domitius Annius Ulpianus was born in the city of Tyre *circa* 170 CE and suffered a violent death before the end of 224 CE.[1] He was a prolific author and a prominent jurist.[2] About 40 per cent, or *circa* 300,000 words, of the *Digest* is composed of his work. Furthermore, Justinian chose Ulpian's definition of law (*ius*) as the opening paragraph of the *Digest*: *Iuri operam daturum prius nosse oportet, unde nomen iuris descendat. est autem a iustitia appellatum: nam, ut eleganter Celsus definit, ius est ars boni et aequi.*[3] Ulpian was also a high-ranking official, holding posts as distinguished as *praetorian prefect*, *procurator*, *a libellis*,[4] and *praefectus annonae.* He was a member of the inner circle of the Roman emperor, actively participating in high politics and intrigues.[5]

---

1 That name is attested in *CIL* xi, 3587. The time of his murder by a certain M. Aurelius Epagathus is conjectured based on P. *Oxy.* 2565, dated 224 CE, which mentioned the now deceased Ulpian, hence providing a *terminus ante quem*. The main sources on Ulpian's career are his own works, as well as mentions in Dio Cassius, the Scriptores Historiae Augustae, Herodian, and later authors. Ulpian is mentioned in two rescripts of Alexander Severus as prefect: *CJ* 8.37.4; 4.65.4.1. The name of Ulpian is also recorded in an inscription from Tyre, which also mentioned his two prefectures: *AE* 1988, 1051.

2 Standard studies of Ulpian's life and work include the entry of Jörs in the *RE*; Crifò 1976; Honoré 2002; Syme 1972; Liebs 1984; Millar 1986.

3 'It is appropriate to know, before giving the function of the law, where the name of the law descended from. It is named after justice (*iustitia*): indeed, Celsus defined it elegantly, the law is the art of the good and the just', *Dig.* 1.1.1.pr (translations, unless otherwise stated, are my own).

4 SHA, *Pescennius Niger* 7.3–4, with Festus 22 and Eutropius 9.33 dating Ulpian's procuratorship to the reign of Alexander Severus, with the reservations of Honoré 2002: 18.

5 Ulpian attested that he was part of the *consilium* of the praetor of Rome (*me adsidente*; *Dig.* 4.2.9.3); a rescript of Alexander Severus named him as a praetorian

Ulpian was appointed as a praetorian prefect during the reign of Alexander Severus, which was to become, from the age of Septimius Severus onwards, the most important of magistracies, with responsibilities over all legal matters in Rome and its vicinity.[6] He was not the only jurist to assume this post, succeeding Tarrutienus Paternus, Papinian, and Marcian. It is clear that the Severan dynasty encouraged the rise of prominent jurists to senior magistracies.[7] Similarly, like other prominent Severan jurists, Ulpian was part of the mechanism of producing imperial responses to queries of both officials and individuals known as *rescripta*.[8] These responses to legal questions were later published, bearing the force of law.[9] An imperial magistracy entitled *a libellis*, the holder of which was responsible for the petitions (*libelli*) addressed to the emperor, attracted prominent jurists such as Ulpian.[10]

After the death of Septimius Severus (193–211 CE),[11] the murder of Geta (26 December 211), and the ascent of Caracalla (211) to the position of sole emperor, Ulpian found his place within the inner circle of the new ruler. It was during this time (213–17) that the bulk of his

---

prefect (*CJ* 8.37.4) Modern scholars, while unanimous in their appreciation of Ulpian's skills as a jurist, are divided in their judgement of his willingness to participate in government (cf. Honoré 2002; Liebs 1997, who saw it positively) and (cf. Syme 1972; 1980 who perceived Ulpian as an opportunist).

6 On the praetorian prefecture see Howe 1942; Schiller 1953; Absil 1997.

7 See in this context the invaluable work of Corriat 1997. For a prosopography of this post Pflaum 1950 is essential.

8 On the rescript system see Honoré 1994: chap. 2. On the authority of selected jurists to formulate such replies in the name of the emperor (*ius respondendi*) see Tuori 2004.

9 Connolly 2010: chapters 2–3.

10 The *a libellis* administered the handling of petitions – both private and public – arriving in the imperial court. The *a libellis* also decided which cases would be heard by the emperor himself, notably cases of *maledictio Caesaris* ('slander of the Caesar'; *CJ* 9, 8, 4; 9, 7, 1. By the time of Nero, the post of *a libellis* was already public, cf. Tac. *Ann.* 15, 35. Furthermore, the *a libellis* also published the adjudications (*decreta*) of the imperial *consilium*; Hirschfeld 1877: 327ff; Mommsen 1887/8: 838ff., 980ff.

11 On Severus see Birley 1999.

work was written.[12] He was probably involved in the formulation of the *Constitutio Antoniniana*, perhaps with Paul.[13] Honoré wrote:

> Up to 212 the customary law of various ethnic groups, the *ius gentium*, had been an element on which Roman law drew for certain purposes, which might include criticism of existing civil law institutions. Now the Roman law *became* the *ius gentium*, the law of peoples. Once that step had been taken, it was crucial to provide for the citizens of the empire, new and old, a clear exposition of the common law to which they were subject and in doing so to bring out its universal and rational character. This, Ulpian, with his deep understanding of the problems of the provincial administration,[14] was uniquely well qualified to do.[15]

Ulpian himself mentioned the universal bestowal of Roman citizenship, attributing it to Caracalla.[16]

The treatise on the duty of the proconsul (*de officio proconsulis*) was composed and published during this period. It is tempting to conjecture that Ulpian envisaged this work to meet the needs of those who recently became Roman citizens on account of the *Constitutio Antonianina*. It is also tempting to speculate that Ulpian himself was involved in its formulation, publication, and implementation. However, there is no conclusive evidence to support this claim. In fact, in his *de officio proconsulis*, Ulpian discussed the merits of a clear proconsular edict and the importance of being conscious of local habits. Both are incongruent with an attempt to enforce a universal legal system.

---

12 Millar 1986: 274; Liebs 1997: § 424 A; Honoré 2002: 23.

13 Birley 1999: 190; Honoré 2002: 24.

14 Millar 1986: 275.

15 Honoré 2002: 24.

16 *In orbe Romano qui sunt ex constitutione imperatoris Antonini cives Romani effecti sunt* ('those who are in the Roman world became Roman citizens out of a constitution of the emperor Antoninus (i.e., Caracalla)', Ulpianus libro 22 ad edictum, *Dig.* 1.5.17). According to Dio Cass. the edict was designed to raise revenues, Dio Cass. 78.9.4–5. P. *Giessen* could offer support for associating the *Constitutio Antoniniana* with the aftermath of Geta's death. The edict is dated to 11 June 212.

2. THE WORK

An Ephesian inscription, dating probably to the tetrarchy, records a letter of an unnamed proconsul to the city of Ephesus on the matter of the city's privileges (δικαιώματα) and instructs it to present the things said based on the old laws in the *de officio* of Ulpian: τά τε ἐκ τῶν παλαιῶν νόμων ἐν τοῖς Δὴ ὀφφι[κίω παρ'] Οὐλπιανῷ εἰρημένα, alongside relevant constitutions (διατάξεις) and *consulta* of the senate.[17] It appears that, within half a century, Ulpian's *de officio proconsulis* became authoritative enough for a proconsul-designate to see it as abiding and assume that the city of Ephesus shares this view and has access to the text.[18] Indeed, Ulpian urged his proconsul to show reverence towards provincial and municipal institutions and habits (§ 2142).[19] The treatise on the duty of the proconsul discusses all aspects of the proconsul's *officium*, from the assumption of the post, *en route* to his allocated province,[20] while governing,[21] and until the termination of duty (§ 2251). Its main concern is the administration of justice.[22]

---

17 *AE* 1966, 436 = *I.K. Ephesos* ii 1979: 46. For dating see Robert 1967: 46.

18 Ulpian's text would have been accessible in one of the many public libraries in the Roman world; cf. Nicholls 2005.

19 References of this form refer to the edition of Lenel, in his *Palingenesia*. The image of a perfect governor is commonplace in provincial inscriptions, cf. *CIL* ii, 4111; *CIL* viii, 2753; *AE* 1917/18, 71; *ILS* 9488; *CIL* iii, 1177; *CIL* viii, 9359; *CIL* iii, 781 (*epistula Severi et Caracallae ad Tyranos* = *FIRA* I2, 86.

20 Cf. *Dig.* 1.16.2.pr. (Marcian).

21 *Proconsul ubique quidem proconsularia insignia habet statim atque urbem egressus est: potestatem autem non exercet nisi in ea provincia sola, quae ei decreta est* ('the proconsul has proconsular insignia as soon as he departs from Rome. However, he does not exercise his power unless he is in the province allocated to him by decree', *Dig.* 1.16.1 (Ulp. *Libero primo disputationum*). Cf. *Dig.* 1.18.3.pr. (Paul. *libro 13 ad Sabinum*): *Praeses provinciae in suae provinciae homines tantum imperium habet, et hoc dum in provincia est: nam si excesserit, privatus est* ('a provincial governor has full imperium in his province, and as long as he is in his province, for if he would leave his province he would be a private person').

22 For a general study of the role of the provincial governor under the High Empire see Bérenger 2014.

Hence, upon arrival, the proconsul must issue an edict (§ 2142).[23] He should delegate jurisdiction to his legate(s) (§ 2143),[24] hold court, and maintain the assizes system intact (§ 2175).[25] He should also inspect public works and sacred places to ensure that they are well maintained. If needs be, the proconsul will allocate resources for reparations (§ 2147). As the bearer of *imperium maius*,[26] the proconsul appoints tutors and curators if he encounters a ward, a woman, a lunatic, or a spendthrift who lacks one (§ 2158). Furthermore, as the curator of the Roman judiciary system, the proconsul must guarantee that every person has access to an *advocatus* when he has his day in court (§ 2152). He must also safeguard that his province is peaceful, lawful, and free from crime: *Congruit bono et gravi praesidi curare, ut pacata atque quieta provincia sit quam regit* ('It is fitting for a good and serious governor to ensure that the province he governs is peaceful and calm', § 2181).[27] He is in charge of interrogating

23 The nature, extent, and variability of such provincial edicts are highly debated. A work entitled *Ad edictum provinciale* by Gaius has been used by Justinian for the preparation of the *Digest*. It is the only treatise bearing this title currently known. As such, the edict of the provincial governor presented his attitude towards non-Romans in his court. It is unclear what a provincial edict would/could have contained after the enactment of the *Constitutio Anroniniana* because, at least in theory, all provincials would have been subjected to Roman law, hence rendering a provincial edict redundant. Cf. Buckland 1934; Katzoff 1969; Marshall 1964.

24 For the Republican origins of this habit cf. Cic. *Q. fr.* 1.1.20 and, more generally, Fanizza 1994.

25 Cf. Fournier 2007: 41–100. However, the decision of whether a certain case merits his own *cognitio* or that of a person appointed by him or by a municipal institution was left to the governor; Fournier 2007: 327.

26 The first piece of legislation that defined the role of the provincial governor is the *lex de provinciis praetoriis*, otherwise known as the *lex de piratis persequendis* or the *lex de Cilicia Macedoniaque provinciis*, dated to 101 or 99 BCE (*RS* § 12). It defines the authority of the provincial governor (ἐξουσία πάντων πραγμάτων). Furthermore, while originally a senatorial committee would have supervised the exercise of the governor's *imperium*, on a model similar to that outlined in the *lex Rupilia*, the *imperium* itself was unconditioned.

27 Cf. *Dig.* 1.18.3.pr. (Paul. *libro 13 ad Sabinum*): *nam et in mandatis principum est, ut curet is, qui provinciae praeest, malis hominibus provinciam purgare, nec*

suspects of crime, and when and how torture should be implemented is left to his discretion (§ 2209). The proconsul must protect slaves who are abused by their owners (§ 2213) but should not infringe on the property rights of slave owners, or their *vitae necisque potestas*. In short, Ulpian offers in this treatise a complete (and unique) manual of Roman criminal law.[28]

Ulpian composed his treatise on the duty of the proconsul, alongside the vast majority of his written works, during the years 213–17, and probably in 213.[29] It is a medium-sized work, in comparison to his commentaries on the praetorian edict and on the work of the jurist Sabinus. Composed and published shortly after the enactment of the so-called *Constitutio Antoniniana*, Ulpian's *de officio proconsulis* does not bear clear traces of a need for institutional revision after the universal grant of citizenship.[30] As a governor and the highest judicial authority in his province, Ulpian's proconsul worked in tandem with local institutions.[31] This, of course, is not a novelty. The aforementioned *lex de provinciis praetoriis* encouraged the governor to rely not only on his legates, on whom he bestowed jurisdiction, but also to appoint local judges (*recuperatores*): [κ]ριτὰς ξενοκρίτας διδόναι. An early attestation of provincial criminal courts, independent of the governor's jurisdiction/*cognitio*, is found in the first Edict of Cyrene and depicts

---

distinguuntur unde sint ('for it is of the first principles in the imperial mandates that he who governs a province must attend that it is purged of evil men without any distinction as to where they come from').

28 Cf. Nogrady 2006.

29 For dating see Honoré 2010: chapters 7–9, accepted by Rodger 1983; Birks 1983; Liebs 1984; and Millar 1986.

30 On the (limited) impact of the *Constitutio Antoniniana* on private legal practice in the East see Alonso 2020 and, more broadly (even if somewhat dated), Mitteis 1891.

31 A juxtaposition with relevant items in the so-called municipal laws, such as the *lex Irnitana*, shows how far this interdependence went. For an edition and commentary of the *lex Irnitana* see González and Crawford 1986. For a study of municipal jurisdiction in light of the *lex Irnitana*, which bears upon that of the proconsul, see Simshäuser 1989; Johnston 1989; Rodger 1990; 1991; 1996.

a hierarchical interdependence between the duty of the governor and local judicial institutions.[32] These local courts were modelled after the criminal courts in Rome (*quaestiones perpetuae*).[33] However, even when holding court himself under the *cognitio* process, the provincial governor habitually relied on local jurists as members of his *consilium*.[34] While Ulpian does not discuss it explicitly in the *de officio proconsulis*, he emphasises the importance of being attentive to local laws, customs, and habits both generally (§ 2147) and particularly in holding court (§ 2234).[35] Furthermore, Ulpian's governor superintends the rightful composition of municipal councils under his jurisdiction (§ 2161), the nomination of municipal magistrates (§ 2163), excuses from liturgies (§ 2166), and the record of those suitable to act as *iudices* or *recuperatores* on albums (§ 2162).

Ulpian's *de officio proconsulis* is one of four works bearing this title and cited in the *Digest*.[36] It is part of a broader genre of treatises on particular magistracies, like ones on the consul; proconsul; praeses; praefectus urbi; praefectus vigilum; praefectus praetorio; quaestor; curator rei publicae; adsessor; consularis; astynomos; and praetor tutelarius.[37] They correspond to two titles in the Digest, *de officio proconsulis et legati* (Dig. 1.16) and *de officio praesidis* (Dig. 1.1.8).

---

32 Oliver 1989: § 8.

33 For the Cyrene Edict see De Visscher 1964. Sherwin-White 1966: 640 assumed that this institution is the one referred to in Plin. *Ep.* 10.58: *Cum citarem iudices, domine, conventum incohaturus, Flavius Archippus vacationem petere coepit ut philosophus* ('When, Sir, I was summoning jurors and preparing to hold assizes, Flavius Archippus tried to claim exemption on the grounds that he was a teacher of philosophy').

34 Fournier 2007: 25; Bérenger 2014: 171–236.

35 Aulus Gellius 12.13.2 highlighted the importance of experts in local law in the governor's *consilisum*. *IGR* iv, 618 is an honourary attestation for such a service. Cf. Fournier 2007: 27.

36 Three works bore the title *de officio proconsulis* (Ulpian, Venuleius Saturninus, and Iulius Paulus). Aemilius Macer composed a treatise entitled *de officio praesidis*.

37 For a literary survey see Peachin 1996: 58–9.

Modern scholars, such as Dell'Oro, Nogari, and Mantovani, assumed that Ulpian composed this work for the use of provincial governors.[38] This stands to reason. It could be stated beyond dispute that Ulpian's *de officio proconsulis* is the single most important source for the role, function, and *officia* of the provincial governor.

3. THE ROMAN PROVINCIAL SYSTEM: FOUNDATION, ADMINISTRATION, AND ADJUDICATION

The term province itself alludes to the extent of the jurisdiction (or *imperium*) of a Roman magistrate. Thus, Italy was the *provincia* of the consuls, and the praetor superintended the *provincia urbana*. With the territorial expansion of Rome and the institution of additional praetors, the term *provincia* became quintessentially geographic. The first Roman provinces of Sicilia and Sardinia were subjected to the *imperium* of a pro-magistrate. In the aftermath of the Second Punic War two additional provinces were created in Spain, and the Third Macedonic War resulted in the foundation of the province of Macedonia. The creation of additional provinces soon followed. These provinces were governed by an ex-consul or praetor. A *lex Pompeia de provinciis* of 53 BCE made it mandatory for every senior magistrate to assume the responsibility of governing a province after his term in office.[39] These provincial governors relied on a very limited staff, including a quaestor, with responsibilities for tax collection, and one or more legates, on whom the governor could bestow some of his responsibilities.[40]

Once in office, the provincial governor administered all civic, fiscal,

38 Dell'Oro 1960; Mantovani 1993/4; Marotta 2004; Nogrady 2006; Crews 2016.

39 Marshall 1972; Gruen 1974: 457–60; Ferrary 2001; Steel 2012.

40 In a recent synthesis Clifford Ando stated that, during the first two imperial centuries, there were *circa* 160 provincial governors, who ruled over an estimated 55 million inhabitants; Ando 2006: 179. Governors arrived in their allocated provinces with lictors, heralds, messengers, scribes, and a personal guard; cf. Cic. *Q. fr.* 1.1.10–14; Oliver 1966; Brunt 1990: 271; Nelis-Clément 2000.

and judicial duties as an embodiment of the sovereign power of Rome.[41] However, from the time of Augustus onwards, a distinction existed between the judicial and administrative authority of the governor and the fiscal responsibilities, which lay with either an imperial procurator or an imperial legate.[42] An assizes system, which meant a pre-scheduled annual visit to judicial centres to hold court, allowed the provincial governor to offer access to this form of arbitration to all inhabitants of the province.[43] During the Republican era this proved particularly challenging concerning the local population whose legal status depended on its particular type of treaty with Rome, as well as relevant acts of legislation. These included items of law relevant to all provinces as well as provincial laws that regulated the status of the inhabitants of single communities or provinces, and magisterial edicts, issued by a military commander and ratified by the Roman senate when the province was established.

The Augustan Revolution introduced the division of the Roman provinces into two groups. The first, in which there was a large military presence, was governed by a representative of Augustus himself (mostly *legati augusti pro praetore*, but also *praefecti* or *procuratores*, depending on the nature of the province). A second group of provinces, in which there was no military presence, or a very limited one, were governed by proconsuls, chosen by lot and appointed by the senate.[44] However, this division had little effect on the *modus operandi* of provincial governors and no effect on the lives of the inhabitants of the provinces.[45] We learn from the letters of Pliny that jurisdiction demanded most of the governor's time and effort. Furthermore, the governor's limited staff required a heavy reliance

41 During the Republican era, the jurisdiction of the provincial governor included several areas, often defined in an edict he published upon entering his allocated province. Cases not included in this list were adjudicated in Rome.

42 Brunt 1990: 53–95, 487–506; Ando 2006: 179.

43 Scholarship on the assizes system is vast but see Marshall 1966 (Republican era); Burton 1975 (imperial era); Haensch 1997b; Meyer-Zwiffelhoffer 2002; Fournier 2010.

44 De facto, the emperor had a decisive voice here too.

45 Ando 2000: 152–74; Millar 2002: 271–320.

on local institutions, particularly municipal ones, such as councils for administration, adjudication, and collection of taxes.[46] In the Greek East the Romans relied on pre-existing municipal institutions, even if they soon became *de facto* oligarchies.[47] In the West Rome had to create these civic institutions herself.[48] Provinces were often divided into *conventus* for administrative purposes. The creation of a province meant a process of *in formam provinciam*, which means putting it in the form of a province. This required (i) an inventory of the cities, (ii) a census, and (iii) a survey of the land. The information gathered was subsequently put in *formulae* (records of people and land) and *formae* (maps).[49] It is based on these documents that the province has been governed and the assizes system has been laid.

4. THE TEXT

With the exception of the *Institutes* of Gaius, none of the works of the classical jurists survived intact or unmediated. The vast majority of these are known exclusively through Justinian's *Digest*. While the collation of Ulpian's *de officio proconsulis* (untypically) benefits from three other sources (the *Fragmenta Vaticana*, the *Collatio Legum Mosaicarum et Romanarum*, and the *Institutiones Divinae* of the Christian author Lactantius) most of the existing fragments of Ulpian's original work derive from the *Digest*. Thus, an edition of Ulpian's *de officio proconsulis* rests on three sets of editorial questions: 1. what is the relation between the medieval manuscripts of the *Digest* (predominantly, but not exclusively, that of the *Codex Florentinus*)[50]

---

46 For the early history of the province of Macedon, recorded by Liv. 45, see Derow 1989. This pattern became ubiquitous.

47 Although popular elections soon diminished, municipal councils remained active and seminal. Plutarch, for example, composed a manual for the young politician (*Mor.* 799c–f, 814a–b, 815a–b) and Dio of Prusa often discusses events from the assemblies of the Greek East (cf. *Or.* 48).

48 Hanson 1988.

49 Nicolet 1991.

50 Although no original manuscript of the *Digest* survived, a near contemporary manuscript, known as *Codex Florentinus* or *Littera Florentina*, is extant. The

and Justinian's text itself; 2. What is the relation between the excerpts included in the *Digest* and the texts of the Roman jurists available to Tribonian and his committee? 3. What is the relation between these texts and the original works themselves? As a critical edition of any text aspires to produce the most accurate version of it – that is, the one closest to the work produced by the author himself/herself – a preface of an edition of Ulpian's *de officio proconsulis* must emphasise the hazards *en route* of achieving this goal.[51]

The codification of Roman law, which denotes a systematic collation of individual works of Roman jurists to offer a comprehensive guidebook for the use of jurists, magistrates, and laymen, can be traced back to third-century works such as the *Sententiae* of Paul,[52] the *Regularum Liber Singularis* attributed to Ulpian (but composed by an anonymous posterior jurist),[53] and the *Epitome Iuris* by Hermogenianus.[54] Two fourth-century collections, the *Fragmenta Vaticana*[55] and the *Collatio*

---

scribe of the *Littera Florentina* must have had access to the original text, which makes it paramount for any future edition. However, the manuscript includes many clear errors, which have been amended. Following Mommsen, they are signed as F^1. The corrections are assigned F^2. They are important because they are derived from the different manuscripts that were available to the scribe.

51 It is noteworthy that Mommsen's edition of the *Digest* explicitly aimed to produce an accurate image of the medieval manuscripts, and that Mommsen himself confessed that such an edition should enable a future edition of Justinian's *Digest*, which is to be distinguished from the original works of the jurists used; Mommsen 1870: LXXVIII. Lenel, in his *Palingenesia*, had a different objective – namely, to produce the texts of the jurists themselves.

52 For a brief exposition see Schiller 1978: 46–8. Standard edition is that of Baviera 1940. For a revised text see Liebs 1996.

53 The standard edition is Mommsen 1890. For the relation between this work and Gaius see Buckland 1924.

54 The *epitome iuris* followed the scheme of the praetorian edict. One hundred and six excerpts are preserved in the *Digest* and collated in Lenel's *Palingenesia*. For a revised text see Liebs 1964.

55 This collection of fragments originated from a late antique (fourth-century) legal work by an anonymous author. The text currently available is a palimpsest of a fifth-century manuscript. The original work was typical of its age. It is a collection of thematically organised abridged legal principles. The *Vatican*

Legum Mosaicarum et Romanarum,[56] offer the novelty of thematic arrangement of past jurists' authoritative opinions (in the case of the *FV*) and a comparison between Mosaic law and esteemed representatives of the Roman judiciary (the *Collatio Legum Mosaicarum et Romanarum*) can equally be seen as antecedents of the enterprises of Theodosius II and Justinian.[57]

Justinian commissioned the *Digest* to include excerpts of eminent Roman jurists, arranged thematically in a single volume of fifty books. It was designed to form a new law syllabus and for the use of practising jurists and courts.[58] For that purpose, a committee chaired by Tribonian had been appointed.[59] Tribonian was instructed to collate, excerpt, and present the entire law in a way that was elegant, conclusive, and free from inner disputes.[60] The outcome was to be approved and ratified by Justinian himself.[61] However, as Tribonian and the members of his committee were given the power to shorten, correct, and slightly modify the works of the jurists they used, it became highly challenging to trace the original wording of the jurists themselves.[62] Justinian also instructed in the *Constitutio Deo Auctore* (*de conceptione digestorum*) of 15 December 530 that the book that will emerge from the work of Tribonian's committee will be entitled

---

Fragments hold excerpts from classical jurists, such as Paul, Ulpian, and Papinian, as well as third-century constitutions taken from the *Codex Gregorianus* and the *Codex Hermogenianus*. The fragments currently available cover matters of private law under original headings, which include sale, usufruct, exemptions, and gifts between husband and wife, where this fragment is located. Modern scholars, such as Mommsen, Schiller, and Corcoran, assume that the work was aimed at legal practitioners and that it was composed in the first half of the fourth century in Italy. The edition hereby used is the critical edition of Mommsen 1890.

56 See below.

57 Honoré 1978: 138–9.

58 Honoré 1978: 147–8.

59 *C. Deo Auctore* 4 (15 December 530).

60 *C. Deo Auctore* 5 (15 December 530).

61 *C. Deo Auctore* 6 (15 December 530).

62 *C. Deo Auctore* 7.

Digesta or *Pandectus*, and allocated three years for its completion. Indeed, the work was completed within this time and on 16 December 533 Justinian published the *Constitutio Tanta* (*de confirmatione digestarum*), which sanctioned the *Digest* as an ultimate authority and equated its content with Roman law.[63] Furthermore, and particularly relevant for any edition of Ulpian's work, the Greek indirect tradition presented by the *Basilika* and the *Scholia Basilicorum* is paramount where the text of the *Digest* is obscure.[64]

Another source that excerpts Ulpian's *de officio proconsulis* is the intriguing late antique *Collatio Legum Mosaicarum et Romanarum*.[65] It is a legal treatise of sixteen sections concerning various aspects of criminal law, such as homicide, adultery, stuprum [which means for the collator homosexuality], incest, theft, perjury, and inheritance. Each of the sections begins with a quote from the Old Testament (in Latin) and is followed by an excerpt from a Roman jurist, intending to demonstrate the superiority and originality of the Old Testament. The identity of its author (*collator*) is unknown, as is his religious identity (Jewish, Christian, or pagan) and the aim and prospective readership of the work.[66] Internal evidence suggests a composition date between the end of the fourth century and the middle of the fifth century.[67]

63 The *modus opernadi* of Tribonian's committee, and its ability to produce the *Digest* in just three years, has long intrigued Romanists at least since Bluhme's monumental *Die Ordnung der Fragmente in den Pandectentitel. Ein Beitrag zur Entstehungsgeschichte der Pandecten* of 1820. For a history of this debate (which exceeds the scope of this introduction) see the authoritative monograph Honoré 2010.

64 For Mommsen, concurrence between the *Codex Florentinus* and the *Basilika* amounts to certainty in the text of the *Digest*.

65 The first edition of the *Collatio* is that of Pithou 1573: 1–54 for text and 66–112 for commentary. In 1833 F. Bluhme published *Lex Dei sive Mosaicarum et Romanarum legum collatio*, followed by Huschke 1860; and Mommsen 1890: 107–98, but see Schulz 1951 for textual criticism and the establishment of a reliable textual transmission, and Frakes 2011 for uncertainty concerning MSS traditions.

66 For a review of existing speculations see Frakes 2011: chapter 2.

67 *Coll.* 5.3.1 referred to a constitution from the *CTh* 9.7.6 which was enacted after 390 CE. Frakes (2011: 59) suggested a publication date of either 422 or 395 CE.

The sources available to the *collator*, other than the Bible, include works of Gaius, Papinian, Modestinus, Ulpian, and Paulus, the *Codex Gregorianus*, and the *Codex Hermogenianus*.[68] It is the reason why the *Collatio* is invaluable for an edition of Ulpian's *de officio proconsulis*, as it quotes both parts of the work not included in the *Digest* as well as excerpts that were also included in the *Digest*. This gives a rare opportunity to compare two independent textual traditions and learn about the way juristic works of classical jurists were handled by Tribonian and his committee.

Finally, an edition of Ulpian's *de officio proconsulis*, which relies on posterior sources for its collation, must be attentive to the hazards of interpolations. These could be identified based on content or style. The collation hereby offered is based on Lenel's *Palingenesia* (vol. II, cols 966–91; §§ 2142–251). The paragraphs are numbered according to Lenel's collation. Lenel relied solely on explicit references in the sources that cite Ulpian's work. However, the study of interpolations, particularly in the *Digest*, has come a long way since Lenel published his *opus magnum* in 1889. Companions such as the *Index Interpolationum quae in Iustiniani Codice inesse dicuntur* and the *Vocabularium iurisprudentiae Romanae*, as well as works such as Wieacker's *Textstufen klassischer Juristen*, offer general guidelines. Other works will be cited and used as appropriate.

5. THE PRESENT EDITION

In one of many illuminating works, Fergus Millar pointed out how absent legal texts are from classical studies and the study of ancient literature.[69] While the past four decades have seen a welcome improvement in the incorporation of legal texts in the study of classical literature, this edition is, to the best of my knowledge, the first of its kind. It is meant to be easy to use. The commentary focuses on both

68 These five jurists were declared most authoritative in *CTh* 1.4.3 both during their lifetime and probably within the cultural milieu where the collator composed his work. The works used are discussed in Frakes 2011: 66–79.

69 Millar 1986.

legal matters and textual criticism. Particular attention is given to textual issues particular to legal texts. In addition, an appendix with the fragments of the three other works bearing an identical or similar title is presented.[70]

70 There are three treatises entitled *de officio proconsulis* (Ulpian, Aemilius Macer, and Venuleius Saturninus), and a fourth is entitled *de officio praesidis* (Iulius Paulus).

De Officio Proconsulis

DE OFFICIO PROCONSULIS

LIBER I.

[De ingressu].[1]

2142.[2] Observare autem proconsulem oportet, ne in hospitiis praebendis oneret provinciam, ut imperator noster cum patre Aufidio Severiano rescripsit. Nemo proconsulum stratores suos habere potest, sed vice eorum milites ministerio in provinciis funguntur. Proficisci autem proconsulem melius quidem est sine uxore: sed et cum uxore potest, dummodo sciat senatum Cotta et Messala consulibus censuisse futurum, ut si quid uxores eorum qui ad officia proficiscuntur deliquerint, ab ipsis ratio et vindicta exigatur. Antequam vero fines provinciae decretae sibi proconsul ingressus sit, edictum debet de adventu suo mittere continens commendationem aliquam sui, si qua ei familiaritas sit cum provincialibus vel coniunctio, et maxime excusantis,[3] ne publice vel privatim occurrant ei: esse enim congruens, ut unusquisque in sua patria eum exciperet. Recte autem et ordine faciet, si edictum decessori suo miserit significetque, qua die fines sit ingressurus: plerumque enim incerta haec et inopinata turbant provinciales et actus impediunt. Ingressum[4] etiam hoc eum observare oportet, ut per eam partem provinciam ingrediatur, per quam ingredi moris est, et quas Graeci ἐπιδημίας appellant sive *κατάπλουν* observare, in quam primum civitatem veniat vel applicet: magni enim facient provinciales servari sibi consuetudinem istam et huiusmodi praerogativas. Quaedam provinciae etiam hoc habent, ut per mare in eam provinciam proconsul veniat, ut Asia, scilicet usque adeo, ut imperator noster Antoninus Augustus ad desideria asianorum rescripsit[5] proconsuli necessitatem impositam per mare Asiam applicare *καὶ τῶν μητροπόλεων ἔφεσον* primam attingere.

---

1 Titles are in square brackets because they were, in all likelihood, added not by Ulpian himself but by a later hand, probably during late antiquity, in what Mantovani (2021: 256) referred to as the 'passage from scroll to codex'.

2 *Dig.* 1.16.4 pr.-§ 5; cf. *Bas* 6.2.6.

3 excusans, Mommsen 1870 *ad loc.*

4 ingressurum (*u. i.*) *vel* in ingressu (Brenchmann)? Mommsen 1870 *ad loc.*

5 rescripserit? Mommsen 1870 *ad loc.*

ON THE DUTY OF THE PROCONSUL

Book 1.

[On having arrived].
2142. The proconsul must ensure not to burden the province with mandatory lodging, as our emperor, together with his father, wrote in a rescript to Aufidius Servianus. No proconsul may have personal attendants; instead, soldiers serve in that capacity in the provinces. It is preferable for the proconsul to travel without a wife; however, if accompanied by one, he must be aware that during the consulship of Cotta and Messala the Senate decreed that any misconduct by the wives of magistrates would require explanation and punishment from the magistrates themselves. Before entering his assigned province, the proconsul should issue an edict announcing his arrival, with a brief introduction if he has any prior acquaintance or connection with the provincials, and, importantly, excusing them from formal or informal visits. It is proper for everyone to receive him in his own homeland. He would act correctly and in order by sending a letter to his predecessor, indicating the day he plans to cross into the province, as such uncertainties and unforeseen events disturb the provincials and hinder administrative matters. Upon entering, the proconsul should ensure he enters the province through the customary route and observes what the Greeks call 'ἐπιδημία' (arrival) or 'κατάπλους' (landing), arriving or docking first in that civitas. The provincials greatly value the preservation of their customs and privileges. Indeed, in some provinces like Asia, our emperor Antoninus Augustus [Caracalla] wrote in a rescript responding to the desires of the Asians that the proconsul must approach Asia by sea and first dock at Ephesus of the metropoleis.

[De iurisdictione mandata].
2143.[6] Post haec ingressus provinciam mandare iurisdictionem legato suo debet nec hoc ante facere, quam fuerit provinciam ingressus; est enim perquam absurdum, antequam ipse iurisdictionem nanciscatur (nec enim prius ei competit, quam in eam provinciam venerit) alii eam mandare, quam non habet. Sed si et ante fecerit et ingressus provinciam in eadem voluntate fuerit, credendum est videri legatum habere iurisdictionem, non exinde ex quo mandata est, sed ex quo provinciam proconsul ingressus est.

2144.[7] Solent etiam custodiarum cognitionem mandare legatis, scilicet ut praeauditas custodias ad se remittant, ut innocentem ipse liberet. Sed hoc genus mandati extraordinarium est: nec enim potest quis gladii potestatem sibi datam vel cuius alterius coercitionis ad alium transferre, nec liberandi igitur reos ius, cum accusari apud eum non possint. Sicut autem mandare iurisdictionem vel non mandare est in arbitrio proconsulis, ita adimere mandatam iurisdictionem licet quidem proconsuli, non autem debet inconsulto principe hoc facere. Legatos non oportet principem consulere, sed proconsulem suum, et is ad consultationes legatorum debebit respondere.

[De xeniis].
2145.[8] Non vero in totum Xeniis abstinere debebit proconsul, sed modum adicere, ut neque morose in totum abstineat neque avare modum xeniorum excedat. Quam rem divus Severus et imperator Antoninus elegantissime epistula sunt moderati, cuius epistulae verba haec sunt: 'quantum ad Xenia pertinet, audi quid sentimus: vetus proverbium est: *οὔτε πάντα οὔτε πάντοτε οὔτε παρὰ πάντων*. Nam valde inhumanum est a nemine accipere, sed passim vilissimum est et omnia avarissimum.' Et quod mandatis continetur, ne donum vel munus ipse proconsul vel qui in alio officio erit accipiat ematve quid nisi victus cottidiani causa, ad xeniola non pertinet, sed ad ea quae edulium excedant usum. Sed nec Xenia producenda sunt ad munerum qualitatem.

2146.[9] Diuturna consuetudo pro iure et lege in his quae non ex scripto descendunt observari solet.

---

6 *Dig.* 1.16.4.6; cf. *Bas* 6.2.6.
7 *Dig.* 1.16.6.pr.-2; cf. *Bas* 6.2.8.
8 *Dig.* 1.16.6.3; cf. *Bas* 6.2.8.
9 *Dig.* 1.3.33; cf. *Bas* 2.1.42.

[On bestowed jurisdiction].
2143. After entering the province, the proconsul should delegate jurisdiction to his legate, but he should not do this before having entered the province. For it is indeed very absurd to delegate jurisdiction to another before he himself has acquired it (since it does not belong to him until he has entered that province). However, if he has done this beforehand and then entered the province with the same intent, it should be considered that the legate holds jurisdiction, not from the time it was delegated, but from the time the proconsul entered the province.

2144. Proconsuls are also accustomed to delegating to their legates the investigation of prisoners, specifically so that the examined detainees can be sent back to them, allowing the proconsul himself to release the innocent. However, this type of delegation is extraordinary: for no one can transfer to another the power of the sword (capital authority) or any other coercive power given to them, nor the authority to release the accused, as they cannot be prosecuted before the legate. Just as the proconsul has the discretion to delegate jurisdiction or not, he is also permitted to revoke delegated jurisdiction, but he should not do so without consulting the emperor. Legates should not consult the emperor but their proconsul, and the proconsul must respond to the inquiries of his legates.

[On presents].
2145. The proconsul should not abstain from gifts altogether but should exercise moderation, so as not to abstain entirely in a peevish manner, nor to greedily exceed the proper measure of gifts. The deified Severus and our emperor Antoninus elegantly moderated this in a letter, the words of which are: 'As far as gifts are concerned, listen to what we think: there is an old proverb: οὔτε πάντα οὔτε πάντοτε οὔτε παρὰ πάντων ("neither everything, nor always, nor from everyone"). For it is very inhumane to accept from no one, but to receive from everyone indiscriminately is cheap and avaricious.' It is contained in the mandates that neither the proconsul himself nor anyone else in office shall receive or purchase any gift or service except for daily sustenance. This does not pertain to small gifts but only to those which exceed normal consumption. Furthermore, gifts must not be extended to the level of more substantial presents.

2146. A long-established custom is usually observed as if it were a right and a law in matters that are not derived from written sources.

LIBER II.

[De provincia circumvenda].

2147.[10] Si in aliam quam[11] celebrem civitatem vel provinciae caput advenerit, pati debet commendari sibi civitatem laudesque suas non gravate audire, cum honori suo provinciales id vindicent: et ferias secundum mores et consuetudinem quae retro optinuit dare. Aedes sacras et opera publica circumire inspiciendi gratia, an sarta tectaque sint vel an aliqua refectione indigeant, et si qua coepta sunt ut consummentur, prout vires eius rei publicae permittunt, curare debet curatoresque operum diligentes sollemniter praeponere, ministeria quoque militaria, si opus fuerit, ad curatores adiuvandos dare.

[De iure dicundo].

2148.[12] Cum plenissimam autem iurisdictionem proconsul habeat, omnium partes, qui Romae vel quasi magistratus vel extra ordinem ius dicunt, ad ipsum pertinent,[13]

nec quicquam est in provincia, quod non per ipsum expediatur. Sane si fiscalis pecuniaria causa sit, quae ad procuratorem principis respicit, melius fecerit, si abstineat.

2149.[14] Ubi decretum necessarium est, per libellum id expedire proconsul non poterit: omnia enim, quaecumque causae cognitionem desiderant, per libellum non possunt expediri.

2150.[15] Circa advocatos patientem esse proconsulem oportet, sed cum ingenio, ne contemptibilis videatur, nec adeo dissimulare, si quos causarum concinnatores vel redemptores deprehendat, eosque solos pati postulare, quibus per edictum eius postulare permittitur.

---

10 *Dig.* 1.16.7.pr.-1; cf. *Bas* 6.2.9.

11 si in aliquam (dett.)? Mommsen 1870 *ad loc.*

12 *Dig.* 1.16.7.2; cf. *Bas* 6.2.9.

13 Libro primo *insect. F.*; secondo *recte inscr. Dig.* 50.17.71; § 2149 (Lenel). The break in text is due to the two independent sources (*Dig.* 1.16.7.2 and *Dig.* 50.1.7.71) which make § 2148.

14 *Dig.* 1.16.9.1; cf. *Bas* 6.2.11.

15 *Dig.* 1.16.9.2; cf. *Bas* 6.2.11.

Book 2.

[On travelling around the province].
2147. If he arrives in a city other than the most celebrated one or the capital of the province, he must allow the city to be recommended to him and listen to its commendations willingly, as the provincials assert this in his honour. He should grant holidays according to the customs and traditions that have prevailed in the past. He should inspect the sacred buildings and public works to see whether they need repairs or any other maintenance and, if any projects have been started, he should ensure they are completed and for this purpose his men should be offered to the public cause. He must appoint diligent curators of the works solemnly and, if necessary, provide military assistance to help the curators.

[On holding court].
2148. Since the proconsul possesses the fullest jurisdiction, all matters which at Rome are judged either by magistrates or by special procedure pertain to him, and there is nothing in the province which is not settled by him. Certainly, if it involves a fiscal pecuniary case that falls under the responsibility of the imperial procurator, it would have been better if he refrained.

2149. Where a decree is necessary, the proconsul could not resolve the matter by a letter; indeed, all cases that require investigation cannot be expedited by letter.

2150. The proconsul must be patient with advocates, and he should not appear contemptuous, nor, by nature, should he conceal whether he would allow those who prepare or buy cases alone to bring them to court, and those alone are permitted to plead, to whom it is permitted by his edict to prosecute.

2151.[16] De plano autem proconsul potest expedire haec: ut obsequium parentibus et patronis liberisque patronum exhiberi iubeat: comminari etiam et terrere filium a patre oblatum, qui non ut oportet conversari dicatur, poterit de plano: similiter et libertum non obsequentem emendare aut verbis aut fustium castigatione.

[17] Levia crimina audire et discutere de plano proconsulem oportet et vel liberare eos, quibus obiciuntur, vel fustibus castigare vel flagellis servos verberare.

2152.[18] Observare itaque eum oportet, ut sit ordo aliquis postulationum, scilicet ut omnium desideria audiantur, ne forte dum honori postulantium datur vel improbitati ceditur, mediocres desideria sua non proferant, qui aut omnino non adhibuerunt, aut minus frequentes neque in aliqua dignitate positos advocatos sibi prospexerunt. Advocatos quoque petentibus debebit indulgere plerumque: feminis vel pupillis vel alias debilibus vel his, qui suae mentis non sunt, si quis eis petat: vel si nemo sit qui petat, ultro eis dare debebit. Sed si qui per potentiam adversarii non invenire se advocatum dicat, aeque oportebit ei advocatum dare. Ceterum opprimi[19] aliquem per adversarii sui potentiam non oportet: hoc enim etiam ad invidiam eius qui provinciae praeest spectat, si quis tam impotenter se gerat, ut omnes metuant adversus eum advocationem suscipere. Quae etiam omnium praesidum communia sunt et debent et ab his observari.

2153.[20] Praeses provinciae minorem in integrum restituere potest etiam contra suam vel decessoris sui sententiam: quod enim appellatio interposita maioribus praestat, hoc beneficio aetatis consequuntur minores.

2154.[21] Maiores viginti annis ita demum ad libertatem proclamare[22] non possunt, si pretium ad ipsum qui veniit pervenerit: ex ceteris autem causis, quamvis maior viginti annis se venum dari passus sit, ad libertatem ei proclamare[23] licet. Minori autem viginti annis ne quidem ex causa supra scripta debet denegari

---

16 *Dig.* 1.16.9.3; cf. *Bas* 6.2.11.
17 *Dig.* 48.2.6; cf. *Bas* 60.34.6.
18 *Dig.* 1.16.9.4–6; cf. *Bas* 6.2.11.
19 oprimi, Mommsen 1870 *ad loc.*
20 *Dig.* 4.4.42; cf. *Bas* 10.4.42.
21 *Dig.* 40.13.1. pr.-1.
22 in libertatem adseri Ulp. Lenel, *ad loc.*
23 in libertatem emu adserere Ulp. Lenel, *ad loc.*

2151. Moreover, the proconsul can promptly resolve these matters: he can command that respect and obedience be shown to parents, patrons, and the children of patrons; he can also threaten and intimidate a son brought forward by his father, who is reported not to behave as expected; similarly, he can correct a disobedient freedman either with words or with the punishment of the rod.

The proconsul should promptly hear and adjudicate minor offences, and either acquit those accused or punish slaves with rods or lashes.

2152. Therefore, he must ensure that there is a certain order in the processing of petitions: namely, that the desires of all are heard. It should not happen that while favour is shown to the high standing of certain petitioners, or dishonesty is accommodated, those more humble do not present their needs at all or less frequently–those who either did not apply at all or did not choose advocates of sufficient standing for themselves. He should generally grant advocates to those who seek them: to women, wards, or other vulnerable individuals, or to those who are not of sound mind, if someone requests them. Or if no one requests, he should offer them voluntarily. But if someone claims not to seek an advocate due to the power of their opponent, he [i.e., the proconsul] should equally provide them with an advocate. Furthermore, he should not allow anyone to be oppressed by the power of their adversary, for such behaviour would also reflect poorly on the governor of the province if someone behaves so tyrannically that all fear taking an advocate against him. These are matters common to all governors and should be observed by them.

2153. The governor of the province can restore a minor to their original status even against their own judgement or that of their predecessor: for, just as an appeal benefits adults, minors benefit from this privilege due to their age.

2154. A person twenty years of age or older cannot become free if the price of his sale comes to the vendor. However, in all other cases, even if they allowed themselves to be sold before reaching twenty years of age, they may be libertatis proclamatio,[24] nisi maior annis viginti factus duravit in servitute: tunc enim si pretium partitus sit, dicendum erit denegari ei debere libertatis proclamationem.[25]

2155.[26] Si quis actionem, quae ex maleficiis oritur, velit exsequi: si quidem pecuniariter agere velit, ad ius ordinarium[27] remittendus erit nec cogendus erit in crimen subscribere: enimvero si extra ordinem eius rei poenam exerceri velit, tunc subscribere eum in crimen oportebit.

2156.[28] De custodia reorum proconsul aestimare solet, utrum in carcerem recipienda sit persona an militi tradenda vel fideiussoribus committenda vel etiam sibi. Hoc autem vel pro criminis quod obicitur qualitate vel propter honorem aut propter amplissimas facultates vel pro innocentia personae vel pro dignitate eius qui accusatur facere solet.

2157.[29] Impp. Augg. Iulio Iuliano rescripserunt – [18] – ream factam dotem recte reddi sibi desiderare diuusque – [18] – quod etiam in patre seruabitur, qui consentiente filia repetit – [18] nec moratoriae dilationi locus erit, quod mal – [18] – .

24 minori … libertatis proclematio] minoris … libertatis adsertio Ulp. Lenel *ad loc.*

25 ei … libertatis proclamationem] élus … libertatis adsertionem Ulp. Lenel *ad loc.*

26 *Dig.* 47.1.3; cf. *Bas* 60.11.3.

27 ius ordinarium] forum *Ulp.* Lenel *ad loc.*

28 *Dig.* 48.3.1; cf. *Bas* 60.35.1. Fortasse pro libro secundo (II) inscr. Libro septimo (VII), cf. fr. 2187; Lenel.

29 *FV.* 119. The repeated number 18 indicates the (approximate) number of missing characters, due to a corrupt manuscript. For a critical edition, see Mommsen 1890.

proclaimed free. Moreover, those under twenty must not be denied freedom for the reasons stated above, unless they reached twenty years of age while in servitude; then, if the price has been divided, it must be argued that the proclamation of freedom should be denied to them.

2155. If someone wishes to pursue an action that arises from a crime, if he wants to proceed for a monetary remedy, he should be referred to the ordinary law and should not be compelled to sign the criminal charge. However, if he wishes to seek an extraordinary punishment for that matter, then he must sign the criminal charge.

2156. Regarding the custody of the accused, the proconsul usually decides whether the person should be detained in prison, handed over to the army, committed to guarantors, or even left to his own custody. He makes this decision according to the seriousness of the alleged crime, the honour, the considerable means, the innocence of the person, or the dignity of the accused.

2157. The Emperors Augusti responded to Julius Julianus in a rescript: [18] – that it is right for a dowry, having become subject to litigation, to be returned to him, and the deified [18] – this will also be upheld in the case of a father who reclaims it with the consent of his daughter. [18] – there will be no room for postponement, because [18] –.

LIBER III.

[De tutoribus et curatoribus].
2158.[30] His qui in ea causa sunt, ut superesse rebus suis non possint, dare curatorem proconsulem oportebit. Nec dubitabit filium quoque patri curatorem dare: quamvis enim contra sit apud Celsum et apud alios plerosque relatum, quasi indecorum sit patrem a filio regi, attamen divus Pius Insteio Celeri, item divi fratres rescripserunt filium, si sobrie vivat, patri curatorem dandum magis quam extraneum. Divus Pius matris querellam de filiis prodigis admisit, ut curatorem accipiant, in haec verba: 'Non est novum quosdam, etsi mentis suae videbuntur ex sermonibus compotes esse, tamen sic tractare bona ad se pertinentia, ut, nisi subveniatur is, deducantur in egestatem. Eligendus itaque erit, qui eos consilio regat: nam aequum est prospicere nos etiam eis, qui quod ad bona ipsorum pertinet, furiosum faciunt exitum.'

2159.[31] Si disceptetur, ubi morari, vel ubi educari pupillum oporteat, causa cognita id praesidem statuere oportebit. In causae cognitione evitandi sunt, qui pudicitiae impuberi possunt insidiari.

2160.[32] Si praedia minoris viginti quinque annis distrahi desiderentur, causa cognita praeses provinciae debet id permittere. Idem servari oportet et si furiosi vel prodigi vel cuiuscumque alterius praedia curatores velint distrahere.

[De decurionibus].
2161.[33] Generaliter id erit defendendum, ut qui clementiorem sententiam passus est ob hoc quod ad tempus relegatur, boni consulere debeat humanitatis sententiae nec decurionatum recipiat. Sed si quis ob falsam causam vel aliam de gravioribus non ad tempus sit relegatus, sed ad tempus ordine motus, in ea est causa, ut possit in ordinem redire. Imperator enim Antoninus[34] edicto proposito statuit, ut cuicumque aut quacumque causa ad tempus ordine vel advocationibus vel quo alio officio fuisset interdictum, completo tempore nihilo minus fungi honore vel officio possit. Et hoc recte: neque enim exaggeranda fuit sententia, quae modum interdictioni fecerat. Spurios posse in ordinem

30 *Dig.* 26.5.12; cf. *Bas* 37.5.12.
31 *Dig.* 27.2.5; cf. *Bas* 38.2.5.
32 *Dig.* 27.9.11; cf. *Bas* 38.9.11.
33 *Dig.* 50.2.3.
34 Cf. *CJ* 10.61.1.

Book 3.

[On tutors and curators]
2158. For those who are in such a situation that they cannot manage their own affairs, it will be necessary for the proconsul to appoint a curator. He will not hesitate to appoint a son as a curator of his father, albeit an opposing view is found in Celsus and many others, as if it is indecorous that a father is governed by his son. Nevertheless, the deified Pius confirmed to Insteius Celer, and the deified brothers wrote in a rescript that a son – if he lives soberly – should be given as a curator to his father in preference to an outsider. The deified Pius accepted a plea of a mother concerning her spendthrift children that they should get a curator in these words: 'It is not new that those, even if they seem to be sound of mind by their utterances, nonetheless manage their property in such a way that unless he [i.e. the proconsul] intervenes, they will lead themselves into poverty. A curator should therefore be appointed, to govern them by *consilium*: for it is reasonable that we make sure that people remove madness from that which pertains to their property.'

2159. If it is debated where a ward should reside, or where he should be educated, the governor must resolve it, having held an inquiry into the case. In the resolution of the case, the people who could ambush the virtue of the youth must be avoided.

2160. If the estates of a person younger than twenty-five years of age should be divided, the governor should allow it upon examination. Similarly, it should be applied if the curators want to divide the estates of a mad person, a spendthrift, or any other person under their care.

[on decurions].
2161. Generally, it must be maintained that someone who has suffered a more lenient sentence, for which he has been temporarily relegated, should accept the humanity of the sentence with good grace and not reclaim his position as a decurion. But if someone has been relegated temporarily or removed from the order for forgery or another of the more serious crimes, he is in such a position that he may return to his office. For Emperor Antoninus, in an edict, decreed that anyone who had been temporarily prohibited from holding office, advocacy, or any other duty for any cause, upon the completion of the time,

allegi nulla dubitatio est: sed si habeat competitorem legitime quaesitum, praeferri eum oportet, divi fratres Lolliano Avito Bithyniae praesidi rescripserunt. Cessantibus vero his etiam spurii ad decurionatum et re et vita honesta recipientur: quod utique non sordi erit ordini, cum ex utilitate eius sit semper ordinem plenum habere. Eis, qui iudaicam superstitionem sequuntur, divi[35] Severus et Antoninus honores adipisci permiserunt, sed et necessitates eis imposuerunt, qui superstitionem eorum non laederent.

2162.[36] Decuriones in albo ita scriptos esse oportet, ut lege municipali praecipitur: sed si lex cessat, tunc dignitates erunt spectandae, ut scribantur eo ordine, quo quisque eorum maximo honore in municipio functus est: puta qui duumviratum gesserunt, si hic honor praecellat, et inter duumvirales antiquissimus quisque prior: deinde hi, qui secundo post duumviratum honore in re publica functi sunt: post eos qui tertio et deinceps: mox hi qui nullo honore functi sunt, prout quisque eorum in ordinem venit. In sententiis quoque dicendis idem ordo spectandus est, quem in albo scribendo diximus.

LIBER IV.

[Ad municipalem I.]

2163.[37] Rescripto divorum fratrum ad Rutilium Lupum ita declaratur: 'Constitutio, qua cautum est, prout quisque decurio creatus est, ut ita et magistratum apiscatur, totiens servari debet, quotiens idoneos et sufficientes omnes contingit. Ceterum si ita quidam tenues et exhausti sunt, ut non modo publicis honoribus pares non sint, sed et vix de suo victum sustinere possint: et minus utile et nequaquam honestum est talibus mandari magistratum, praesertim cum sint qui convenienter ei et suae fortunae et splendori publico

35 divi *gloss.* Lenel.

36 *Dig.* 50.3.1.

37 *Dig.* 50.4.6.pr.-§ 2.

could nonetheless resume their honour or office. And this is right: for the sentence that had set a limit on the prohibition should not be exaggerated. There is no doubt that illegitimate children (spurii) can be enrolled in the order (of decurions); but if there is a legitimate competitor, he ought to be preferred, as the divine brothers (Emperors Marcus Aurelius and Lucius Verus) wrote in a rescript to Lollianus Avitus, governor of Bithynia. However, if these legitimate competitors are absent, illegitimate children who are reputable in both conduct and life will be admitted to the decurionate; this will not be disgraceful to the order, since it is in its interest always to have the order fully staffed. The divine Severus and Antoninus permitted those who follow the Jewish religion to obtain honours but also imposed upon them obligations, provided that they did not harm their religion.

2162. Decurions should be listed in the register as prescribed by the municipal law; but if the law is absent, then their ranks should be considered so that they are listed in the order according to the highest office each of them has held in the municipality. For example, those who have held the office of duumvir should be listed first if this is the highest honour, and among the duumvirs, the most senior should be placed first. Then those who have held the second highest office after the duumvirate should be listed, followed by those who have held the third highest office, and so on. Finally, those who have held no office should be listed according to the order in which they joined the decurionate. This order, which we have mentioned pertaining to the listing of names, should equally be maintained when holding court is due.

Book 4.

[On municipal law(?)[1]]

2163. It is thus declared in a rescript of the deified brothers to Rutilius Lupus: 'The constitution, which stipulates that as soon as someone is created a decurion, he should thus obtain a magistracy, can stay in office as long as they are capable and possess sufficient resources. However, if some are so poor and destitute that they are not only unsuitable for public offices but can scarcely support themselves, it is neither useful nor proper to bestow a magistracy on such persons, especially when there are others who, due to their means and public distinction, can be suitably appointed. Therefore, the wealthy should

1 The title has only the adjective *municipalem*, without a noun to qualify. I assume a missing *lex*, but without textual evidence to support it.

possint creari. Sciant igitur locupletiores non debere se hoc praetextu legis uti et de tempore, quo quisque in curiam allectus sit, inter eos demum esse quaerendum, qui pro substantia sua capiant honoris dignitatem.' Debitores rerum publicarum ad honores invitari non posse certum est, nisi prius in id quod debetur rei publicae satisfecerint. Sed eos demum debitores rerum publicarum accipere debemus, qui ex administratione rei publicae reliquantur: ceterum si non ex administratione sint debitores, sed mutuam pecuniam a re publica acceperint, non sunt in ea causa, ut honoribus arceantur. Plane vice solutionis sufficit, ut quis aut pignoribus aut fideiussoribus idoneis caveat: et ita divi fratres Aufidio Herenniano rescripserunt. Sed et si ex pollicitatione debeant, quae tamen pollicitatio recusari non potest, in ea sunt condicione, ut honoribus arceantur. Si quis accusatorem non habeat, non debet honoribus prohiberi, quemadmodum non debet is, cuius accusator destiterit. Ita enim imperator noster cum divo patre suo rescripsit.

2164.[38] Sciendum est quaedam esse munera aut personae aut patrimoniorum, itidem quosdam esse honores. Munera, quae patrimoniis iniunguntur, vel intributiones talia sunt, ut neque aetas ea excuset neque numerus liberorum nec alia praerogativa, quae solet a personalibus muneribus exuere.[39] Sed enim haec munera, quae patrimoniis indicuntur, duplicia sunt: nam quaedam possessoribus iniunguntur, sive municipes sunt sive non sunt, quaedam [quadam] non nisi municipibus vel incolis. Intributiones, quae agris fiunt vel aedificiis, possessoribus indicuntur: munera vero, quae patrimoniorum habentur, non aliis quam municipibus vel incolis.

2165.[40] *Modestinus libro secundo excusationum.* Nam et Ulpianus libro quarto de officio proconsulis ita scribit: sed et reprobari medicum posse a republica, quamvis semel probatus sit, imperator noster cum patre Laelio Basso rescripsit.

38 *Dig.* 50.4.6.3–5; cf. *Bas* 54.4.5.

39 Mommsen 1870 *ad loc.*: excusare (edd.)?

40 *Dig.* 27.1.6.6. Mommsen directed readers to Mod. apud *Dig.* 50.4.11.3, which also uses this phrase.

not use this legal pretext to avoid responsibility, and the matter of when each person was elected to the municipal council should be considered only among those who, according to their means, deserve the honour of the position.' It is certain that those who are in debt to the city cannot be invited to hold public offices unless they have first settled what they owe to the city. However, we should only consider those as debtors to the city who have incurred debt through the administration of public affairs; if they are debtors for other reasons, such as having borrowed money from the city, they are not in the category that should be barred from magistracies. Indeed, it is sufficient for them to provide adequate pledges or sureties, as the deified brothers wrote in a rescript to Aufidius Herennianus. Those who owe debts due to an undertaking (*pollicitatio*) that cannot be refused are also in a condition where they should be barred from public office. If someone has no accuser, he should not be barred from honours, just as one whose accuser has withdrawn should not be. Thus, our emperor wrote in a rescript together with his deified father.

2164. It should be known that some *munera* are personal and some are patrimonial, much like offices. *Munera* which are attached to the patrimony are levies, so age cannot be used as an excuse, or the number of children, or any other prerogative, which is used to excuse from personal *munera*. But the *munera* which are indicated by patrimony are twofold. Some are attached to possessors, whether *municipes* or not, while others are associated only with *municipes* and *incolae*. Levies, which originate from fields or buildings, are charged to possessors: *munera*, however, which are of the patrimony are imposed only on *municipes* and *incolae*.

2165. Modestinus in his Second Book on Excuses: Ulpian, in his fourth book *On the Duty of the Proconsul* thus wrote: a *medicus* can be disapproved by the city, even if he has once been approved, as our imperator, alongside his father, wrote in a rescript to Laelius Bassus.

2166.[41] Viae sternendae immunitatem veteranos non habere Iulio Sossiano veterano rescriptum est. Nam nec ab intributionibus, quae possessionibus fiunt, veteranos esse excusatos palam est. Sed et naves eorum angariari posse Aelio Firmo et Antonino[42] Claro veteranis rescriptum est.

2167.[43] Si qui certa condicione muneribus vel honoribus se adstrinxerunt, cum alias compelli non possent inviti suscipere istum honorem: fides eis servanda est condicioque, qua ad munera sive honores applicare se passi sunt.

2168.[44] Impuberes, quamvis necessitas penuriae hominum cogat, ad honores non esse admittendos rescripto ad Venidium Rufum legatum Ciliciae declaratur.

2169.[45] Filio propter patrem legationis vacatio ne concedatur, imperator noster cum patre Claudio Callisto rescripsit in haec verba: 'Quod desideras, ut propter legationem patris tui a legatione tu vaces, in intervallis honorum, qui sumptum habent, recte observatur: in impendiis[46] legationum, quae solo ministerio obeuntur, diversa causa est.'

2170.[47] Cum de consuetudine civitatis vel provinciae confidere quis videtur, primum quidem illud explorandum arbitror, an etiam contradicto aliquando iudicio consuetudo firmata sit.

---

41 *Dig.* 49.18.4; cf. B 57.6.
42 Antonio? Mommsen 1870 *ad loc.*
43 *Dig.* 50.6.2.
44 *Dig.* 50.6.3.
45 *Dig.* 50.7.7.
46 in intercapedine? Mommsen 1870 *ad loc.*
47 *Dig.* 1.3.34; cf. *Bas* 2.1.43. Cf. Dig. 50.2.11. Lenel.

2166. It is stated in a rescript to the veteran Iulius Sossianus that veterans do not have immunity from paving roads. Indeed, it is clear that veterans are not exempt from levies that originate from their possessions. And it is written in a rescript to Aelius Firmus and Antoninus Clarus, the veterans, that their ships [i.e., the veterans'] can be requisitioned.

2167. Those who have bound themselves by a specific stipulation to perform certain duties or assume certain offices, when otherwise they could not be compelled to accept such an office unwillingly, their commitment and the condition by which they allowed themselves to be appointed to duties or offices must be respected.

2168. It is declared by a rescript addressed to Venidius Rufus, legate of Cilicia, that *impuberes*, although necessity due to a shortage of men might compel, are not to be admitted to offices.

2169. Immunity should not be granted to a son from the service as an ambassador on account of his father, as our imperator, alongside his father, wrote in a rescript of Claudius Callistus in these words: 'that which you seek, that because the service of your father on an embassy you will be exempt from an ambassadorship is rightfully observed [i.e., the right to immunity] in the intervals of offices which entail expenses: on the issue of the outlay of ambassadorship, which only requires service, it is a different case'.

2170. If someone seems to rely on a municipal or provincial practice, I think it should first be examined whether this practice has ever been confirmed by a legal dispute.

LIBER V.

[ad municipalem 2.]
2171.[48] Si quis a pluribus manumissus sit, omnium patronorum originem sequitur.

2172.[49] Maiores septuaginta annis a tutelis et muneribus personalibus vacant. Sed qui ingressus est septuagensimum annum, nondum egressus, hac vacatione non utetur, quia non videtur maior esse septuaginta annis qui annum agit septuagensimum.

2173.[50] Tutor vel curator, cuius iniusta appellatio pronuntiata erit cuiusve excusatio recepta non sit, ex quo accedere ad administrationem debuit erit obligatus.[51]

2174.[52] Totiens locum habet deminutio pollicitationis in persona heredis, quotiens non est pollicitatio ob honorem facta. Ceterum si ob honorem facta sit, aeris alieni loco habetur et in heredum persona non minuitur. Si quis ob honorem promiserit coeperitque solvere, eum debere quasi coepto opere imperator noster Antoninus rescripsit. Non tantum masculos, sed etiam feminas, si quid ob honores pollicitatae sunt, debere implere sciendum est: et ita rescripto imperatoris nostri et divi patris eius continetur. Si cui res publica necessitatem imposuerit statuarum principi ponendarum, qui non promisit, non esse ei necesse obtemperare rescriptis imperatoris nostri et divi patris eius continetur.

[de conventu].
2175.[53] Eum, quem temere adversarium suum in iudicium[54] vocasse constitit, viatica litisque sumptus adversario suo reddere oportebit. Iudicibus de iure dubitantibus praesides respondere solent: de facto consulentibus non debent praesides consilium impertire, verum iubere eos prout religio suggerit sententiam proferre: haec enim res nonnumquam infamat et materiam gratiae vel ambitionis tribuit.

---

48 *Dig.* 50.1.7; cf. *Bas* 54.1.n.
49 *Dig.* 50.6.4; cf. *Bas* 54.6.n.
50 *Dig.* 26.7.20; cf. *Bas* 37.7.19.
51 *similiter hi qui res civitatium administrant.* Lenel *ad loc.*
52 *Dig.* 50.12.6.
53 *Dig.* 5.1.79; cf. *Bas* 7.5.72.
54 ius *Ulp.* Lenel *ad loc.*

Book 5.

[On municipal law(?) 2]
2171. If a person is manumitted by many, he will ensue the origin of all [his new] patrons.

2172. Persons who are older than seventy years of age are exempt from tutelage and personal duties. However, a person who has entered his seventieth year but has not yet completed it cannot use this exemption, because one who is in his seventieth year is not considered by law to be seventy years old.

2173. A tutor or a curator, whose appeal has been declared unjust or whose excuse has not been accepted is obliged to approach the administration of his duty.

2174. A reduction in the scale of a promise made by an heir can occur as often as the promise was not made for the sake of honour. However, if the promise was made for the sake of honour, it is regarded as a debt and cannot be reduced for the heirs. If someone has promised something for the sake of honour and has begun to pay, our Emperor Antoninus wrote in a rescript that he must pay as if he had begun a project. It must be understood that not only men but also women, if they have pledged something for the sake of honour, must fulfill their promise: and this is stated in a rescript by our Emperor and his deified father. If the city imposes the obligation of setting up statues of the emperor on someone who did not promise (to set up a statue of the emperor), it is stated in rescripts by our Emperor and his deified father that he is not required to comply.

[On judicial assembly]
2175. It behooves a person who has heedlessly summoned his adversary to court to reimburse his adversary for travel expenses and legal costs. Provincial governors should respond to queries from judges who are uncertain about matters of law; however, provincial governors should not provide advice to judges regarding matters of fact. Instead, they should instruct the judges to render a decision according to their conscience: for this matter often brings ill-repute and provides grounds for favouritism or ambition.

2176.[55] In eum, cuius instinctu ad infamandum dominum servus ad statuam confugisse compertus erit, praeter corrupti servi actionem, quae ex edicto perpetuo competit, severe animadvertitur.

LIBER VI.

[De collegiis].
2177.[56] Quisquis illicitum collegium usurpaverit, ea poena tenetur, qua tenentur, qui hominibus armatis loca publica vel templa occupasse iudicati sunt.

[De bonorum possessionibus].
2178.[57] Bonorum ventris nomine curatorem dari oportet eumque rem salvam fore viri boni arbitratu satisdare proconsul iubet: sed hoc, si non ex inquisitione detur: nam si ex inquisitione, cessat satisdatio.

2179.[58] Cum heres instituta furiosa hereditatem esset rogata restituere, curatorem eius secundum tabulas bonorum possessione accepta posse transferre actiones divus Pius decrevit.

[De manumissionibus].
2180.[59] Si minor annis viginti manumittit, huiusmodi solent causae manumissionis recipi: si filius filiave frater sororve naturalis sit, si collactaneus, si educator,[60] si paedagogus ipsius, si nutrix,[61] vel filius filiale cuius forum, vel alumnus, vel capsarius (id est qui portat libros), vel si in hoc manumittatur, vel procurator sit, dummodo non minor annis decem et octo sit. Praeterea et illud exigitur, ut non unique unum servum habeat, qui manumittit. Item si matrimonii causa virgo vel mulier manumittatur, exacto prius iureiurando, ut intra sex mensem uxorem eam duci oporteat: ita enim senatus censuit.

---

55 *Dig.* 47.11.5; cf. *Bas* 60.22.5. libro octavo (viii pro v) *inscr.* (cf. § 2213 sq.)? Lenel.
56 *Dig.* 47.22.2; cf. *Bas* 60.32.2.
57 *Dig.* 27.10.8; cf. *Bas* 38.10.8.
58 *Dig.* 36.1.35; cf. *Bas* 35.11.36.
59 *Dig.* 40.2.11.11; cf. *Bas* 48.2.11.
60 educator *F*[1].
61 nutrix sit *F*[2].

2176. Against a person at whose instigation a slave is found to have taken refuge at a statue of the emperor for the purpose of defaming his master, a severe punishment shall be inflicted, in addition to the action for corrupting a slave, which is available under the perpetual edict.

Book 6.

[on associations]
2177. Anyone who has usurped an illicit association is subjected to the same penalty as those who have been found guilty of occupying public places or temples with armed men.

[on possession of property]
2178. A curator should be appointed for the property of an unborn child, and the proconsul demands that he [the curator] gives assurances that the property will be preserved according to the judgement of a good man: however, this security should be provided if the curatorship is not appointed through an inquiry; for if it is appointed through an inquiry, the security is unnecessary.

2179. The deified Pius decreed that when an heiress who has been instituted as a lunatic is requested to restore the inheritance, her curator can transfer the actions after taking possession of the property according to the will.

[On manumission].
2180. If a person under the age of twenty manumits a slave, the following grounds for manumission are usually accepted: if the person manumitted is his natural son or daughter, brother or sister; if it is a foster sibling, a foster father, the manumitter's pedagogue, a wet-nurse, or the son or daughter of the aforementioned, or a ward, or a capsarius (that is, a person who carries books), or if the person is manumitted for the purpose of becoming a procurator, provided they are not younger than eighteen years of age. Furthermore, it is required that the person manumitting must not own more than one slave. Also, if a virgin or woman is manumitted for the purpose of marriage, an oath must first be taken that he will marry her within six months. Indeed, the senate so ordered.

LIBER VII.

[De disciplina publica].
2181.[62] Congruit bono et gravi praesidi curare, ut pacata atque quieta provincia sit quam regit. Quod non difficile optinebit, si sollicite agat, ut malis hominibus provincia careat eosque conquirat: nam et sacrilegos, latrones, plagiarios, fures conquirere debet et prout quisque deliquerit, in eum animadvertere, receptoresque eorum coercere, sine quibus latro diutius latere non potest.

[De fugitivis].
2182.[63] Divus Pius rescripsit eum, qui fugitivum vult requirere in praediis alienis, posse adire praesidem litteras ei daturum et, si ita res exegerit, apparitorem quoque, ut ei permittatur ingredi et inquirere, et poenam eundem praesidem in eum constituere, qui inquiri non permiserit. Sed et divus Marcus oratione, quam[64] in senatu recitavit, facultatem dedit ingrediendi tam Caesaris quam senatorum et paganorum praedia volentibus fugitivos inquirere scrutarique[65] cubilia atque vestigia occultantium.

[De furiosis].
2183.[66] Furiosis, si non possint per necessarios contineri, eo remedio per praesidem obviam eundum est: scilicet ut carcere contineantur. Et ita divus Pius rescripsit. Sane excutiendum divi fratres putaverunt in persona eius, qui parricidium admiserat, utrum simulato furore facinus admisisset an vero re vera compos mentis non esset, ut si simulasset, plecteretur, si fureret, in carcere contineretur.

[De accusationibus et subscriptionibus].
2184.[67] Si cui crimen obiciatur, praecedere debet crimen subscriptio. Quae res ad id inventa est, ne facile quis prosiliat ad accusationem, cum sciat inultam sibi accusationem non futuram. Cavent itaque singuli, quod crimen obiciant, et praeterea perseveraturos se in crimine usque ad sententiam. Isdem criminibus, quibus quis liberatus est, non debet praeses pati eundem accusari, et ita divus

---

62 *Dig.* 1.18.13.pr.; cf. *Bas* 6.1.46.
63 *Dig.* 11.4.3; cf. *Bas* 60.7.8.
64 quam] qua *F.*
65 scrutandique *(Hal.)?* Mommsen 1870 *ad loc.*
66 *Dig.* 1.18.13.1.
67 *Dig.* 48.2.7.pr.-3; cf. *Bas* 60.34.7.

Book 7.

[On public order].
2181. It is fitting for a good and serious governor to ensure that the province he governs is peaceful and calm. This he will achieve without difficulty if he acts diligently to ensure the province is free from evildoers and actively seeks them out. Indeed, he ought to apprehend sacrilegious individuals, bandits, kidnappers, and thieves, and punish each according to their offences, while also restraining those giving them shelter, without whom a bandit cannot long remain hidden.

[On fugitives]
2182. The deified Pius responded in a rescript that anyone wishing to seek a fugitive on another's property can approach the governor, who will provide him with letters. Moreover, if circumstances require, the governor will also send an official so that he may be allowed to enter and investigate, and the governor will impose a penalty on anyone who prevents the investigation. Furthermore, the deified Marcus, in a speech delivered in the senate, granted permission for those desiring to search for fugitives to enter both imperial and senatorial estates and thoroughly examine the hiding places and traces of those concealed.

[On lunatics].
2183. As for the insane, if they cannot be restrained by their relatives, the governor must intervene with this remedy: namely, that they be confined in prison. This is what Antoninus Pius decreed in a rescript. Indeed, the deified brothers deemed it necessary to examine in the case of a person who became guilty of patricide whether he perpetrated the crime under feigned madness or was genuinely of unsound mind. If he feigned madness, he should be punished; if genuinely mad, he should be confined in prison.

[On accusations and indictments]
2184. If a crime is to be charged against someone, the accusation must be preceded by a formal statement of the charge (subscriptio). This requirement was introduced to prevent people from making accusations lightly, knowing that unfounded accusations will not go unpunished. Therefore, individuals should be cautious about the accusations they bring and should be prepared to see the case through to judgement. A governor should not allow a person to be accused again of the same charges from which they have been acquitted,

Pius Salvio Valenti rescripsit: sed hoc, utrum ab eodem an nec ab alio accusari possit, videndum est. Et putem, quoniam res inter alios iudicatae alii non praeiudicant, si is, qui nunc accusator exstitit, suum dolorem persequatur doceatque ignorasse se accusationem ab alio institutam, magna ex causa admitti eum ad accusationem debere. Si tamen alio crimine postuletur ab eodem, qui in alio crimine eum calumniatus est, puto non facile admittendum eum qui semel calumniatus sit: quamvis filium accusatoris admitti oportere aliam accusationem instituentem adversus eum, quem pater accusaverat divus Pius Iulio Candido rescripsit.

2185.[68] Divus Hadrianus Salvio Caro proconsuli Cretae rescripsit tutorem, qui pupilli causa instituerat accusationem, defuncto pupillo, cuius causa accusare coeperat, non esse cogendum accusationem implere.

2186.[69] Idem imperator rescripsit servos ibi puniendos, ubi deliquisse arguantur, dominumque eorum, si velit eos defendere, non posse revocare in provinciam suam, sed ibi oportere defendere, ubi deliquerint. Cum sacrilegium admissum esset in aliqua provincia, deinde in alia minus crimen, divus Pius Pontio Proculo rescripsit, postquam cognoverit de crimine in sua provincia admisso, ut reum in eam provinciam remitteret, ubi sacrilegium admisit.

[De custodia reorum].
2187.[70] Divus Pius ad epistulam Antiochensium Graece rescripsit non esse in vincula coiciendum eum, qui fideiussores dare paratus est, nisi si tam grave scelus admisisse eum constet, ut neque fideiussoribus neque militibus committi debeat, verum hanc ipsam carceris poenam ante supplicium sustinere.

2188.[71] Divus Traianus Minicio Natali rescripsit ferias a forensibus tantum negotiis dare vacationem, ea autem, quae ad disciplinam militarem pertinet, etiam feriatis diebus peragenda: inter quae custodiarum quoque cognitionem esse.

---

68 *Dig.* 48.16.14; cf. *Bas* 60.1.23.
69 *Dig.* 48.2.7.4–5; cf. *Bas* 60.34.7.
70 *Dig.* 48.3.3; cf. *Bas* 60.35.3.
71 *Dig.* 2.12.9; cf. *Bas* 7.17.9.

and the deified Pius confirmed this in a rescript to Salvius Valens. However, whether this applies to the same accuser or another should be considered. I believe that since matters adjudicated between certain parties should not prejudice another, if a new accuser, pursuing his own grievance, demonstrates that he was unaware of the previous accusation, he should be allowed to bring forth the accusation. Nonetheless, if a person faces another accusation from someone who previously made a false accusation, I think that the one who previously made a false accusation should not be easily admitted to accuse again. However, the deified Pius wrote in a rescript to Iulius Candidus that the son of an accuser should be allowed to bring a new accusation against the person his father accused.

2185. The deified Hadrian wrote in a rescript to Salvius Carus, proconsul of Crete, that a tutor who had instituted an accusation on behalf of a ward is not to be compelled to complete the accusation if the ward, on whose behalf he began the accusation, has died.

2186. The same emperor wrote in a rescript that slaves must be punished where they are accused of having committed the offence, and their master if he wishes to defend them, cannot recall them to their own province but must defend them where they committed the offence. When sacrilege has been committed in one province, and then a lesser crime in another, the deified Pius wrote in a rescript to Pontius Proculus that after he has investigated the crime committed in his province, he should send the accused back to the province where he committed sacrilege.

[On the detention of the accused].
2187. The deified Pius wrote in a rescript in Greek, in reply to a letter from the people of Antioch, that a person who is prepared to provide sureties should not be cast in chains unless it is established that he has committed such a serious crime that he should not be entrusted either to sureties or to soldiers, but rather should endure this very punishment of imprisonment before execution.

2188. The deified Trajan wrote in a rescript to Minicius Natalis that holidays shall exempt only from court proceedings, but those things which pertain to military discipline must be carried out even on holidays: among these is also the prosecution of persons in custody.

[De absentibus].
2189.[72] Absentem in criminibus damnari non debere divus Traianus Iulio Frontoni rescripsit. Sed nec de suspicionibus debere aliquem damnari divus Traianus Adsidio Severo rescripsit: satius enim esse impunitum relinqui facinus nocentis quam innocentem damnari. Adversus contumaces vero, qui neque denuntiationibus neque edictis praesidum obtemperassent, etiam absentes pronuntiari oportet secundum morem privatorum iudiciorum. Potest quis defendere haec non esse contraria. Quid igitur est? Melius statuetur in absentes pecuniarias quidem poenas vel eas, quae existimationem contingunt, si saepius admoniti per contumaciam desint, statui posse et usque ad relegationem procedi: verum si quid gravius irrogandum fuisset, puta in[73] metallum[74] vel capitis poenam, non esse absentibus irrogandam. In accusatorem autem absentem nonnumquam gravius statuendum, quam Turpilliani senatus consulti poena irrogatur,[75] dicendum est.

[De sacrilegis].
2190.[76] Sacrilegii poenam debebit proconsul pro qualitate personae proque rei condicione et temporis et aetatis et sexus vel severius vel clementius statuere. Et scio multos et ad bestias damnasse sacrilegos, nonnullos etiam vivos exussisse, alios vero in furca suspendisse. Sed moderanda poena est usque ad bestiarum damnationem eorum, qui manu facta templum effregerunt et dona dei in noctu tulerunt. Ceterum si qui interdiu modicum aliquid de templo tulit, poena metalli coercendus est, aut, si honestiore loco natus sit, deportandus in insulam est.

[De Christianis].
2191.[77] *Domitius de officio proconsulis libro septimo rescripta principum nefaria collegit, ut doceret, quibus poenis affecti oporteret eos qui se cultores dei confiterentur.*

---

72 *Dig.* 48.19.5; cf. *Bas* 60.51.5.
73 om. *F*[1].
74 metallum] *Hal.*, metallo *F*[1].
75 irrogata? Mommsen 1870 *ad loc.*
76 *Dig.* 48.13.7(6); cf. *Bas* 60.45.15; *Collect.* p. 1307.
77 Lactant. *div. inst.* 5.11.

[On absentees].
2189. An absentee should not be condemned in criminal cases, as the deified Trajan wrote in a rescript to Iulius Frontinus. Nor should anyone be condemned based on suspicions, as the deified Trajan wrote to Adsidius Severus in a rescript: for it is better that a guilty person's crime goes unpunished than that an innocent person be condemned. However, against the contumacious, who obey neither the summons nor the edicts of the governors, it is appropriate to pronounce judgement even in their absence according to the custom of private judgements. One can argue that these are not contradictory. What then? It is better to impose pecuniary penalties or those affecting reputation on absentees if they repeatedly abscond out of contumacy, and to proceed to exile; however, if something more severe were to be imposed, such as sending to the mines or capital punishment, it should not be imposed on absentees. However, it should be said that sometimes an absent accuser should be subjected to harsher penalties than those imposed by the Senatus Consultum Turpillianum.

[On sacrilege].
2190. A punishment for sacrilege the proconsul shall set more severely or more clemently, according to the culprit's nature, the circumstances of the matter, the culprit's age, and sex. And I know that many sacrilegious were condemned to fight wild beasts, some were burned alive, while others were hanged on the gallows. However, the punishment should be moderated up to condemnation to fighting wild beasts for those who stormed into temples using armed force and took the donations of the god by night. As for the rest, if someone took something modest during the daytime, he should be confined to the mines, or, if he is of noble birth, he should be deported to an island.

[On Christians].
2191. Domitius [i.e., Ulpian] in the seventh book on the duties of the proconsul collected nefarious rescripts of emperors, in order to demonstrate by what punishments those who confess to be worshippers of God should be treated.

De mathematicis et vaticinatoribus.

2192.[78] Praeterea interdictum est mathematicorum callida impostura et obstinata persuasione. Nec hodie primum interdici eis placuit, sed vetus haec prohibitio est denique extat senatus consultum Pomponio et Rufo conss. factum quo cavetur, ut mathematicis Chaldaeis ariolis et ceteris, qui simile inceptum fecerunt, aqua et igni interdicatur omniaque bona eorum publicentur, et si externarum gentium quis id fecerit, ut in eum animadvertatur. Sed fuit quaesitum, utrum scientia huiusmodi hominum puniatur an exercitio et professio. Et[79] quidem apud veteres dicebatur professionem eorum, non notitiam esse prohibitam: postea variatum. Nec dissimulandum est nonnumquam inrepsisse in usum, ut etiam profiterentur et publice se praeberent. Quod quidem magis per contumaciam et temeritatem eorum factum est, qui visi erant vel consulere vel exercere, quam quod fuerat permissum. Saepissime denique interdictum est fere ab omnibus principibus, ne quis omnino huiusmodi ineptiis se inmisceret, et varie puniti sunt hii[80] qui id exercuerunt,[81] pro mensura scilicet consultationis. Nam qui de principis salute, capite puniti sunt vel qua alia poena graviore adfecti; enimvero si qui de sua suorumque, levius. Inter hos habentur vaticinatores, quamquam hii[82] quoque plectendi sunt, quoniam nonnumquam contra publicam quietem imperiumque populi Romani inprobandas artes exercent. Extat denique decretum divi Pii ad Pacatum, legatum provinciae Lugudunensis, cuius rescripti verba quia multa sunt, de fine eius ad locum haec pauca subieci. Denique divus Marcus eum, qui motu Cassiano vaticinatus erat et multa quasi instinctu deorum dixerat, in insulam Syrum relegavit. Et sane non debent inpune ferre huiusmodi homines, qui sub obtentu ex monito deorum quaedam vel enuntiant vel iactant vel scientes confingunt.

[Ad legem Iuliam maiestatis].

2193.[83] [Proximum sacrilegio crimen est, quod maiestatis dicitur]. Maiestatis autem crimen illud est, quod adversus populum Romanum vel adversus securitatem eius committitur. Quo tenetur is, cuius opera dolo malo consilium initum erit, quo obsides iniussu principis interciderent: quo armati homines cum telis lapidibusve in urbe sint conveniantve adversus rem publicam,

78 *Coll.* 15.2.

79 *et om. libri.* Mommsen 1870 *ad loc.*

80 Following Frakes. Mommsen = ii.

81 Following Frakes. Mommsen = exercuerint.

82 Following Frakes. Mommsen = ii.

83 *Dig.* 48.4.1; cf. *Bas* 60.36.1.

On astrologers and soothsayers.

2192. Also prohibited is the crafty imposture and persistent persuasion of the astrologers. The decision to outlaw them is no recent innovation but is of long standing. In fact, there is an extant decree of the Senate, made in the consulship of Pomponius and Rufus, which provides that astrologers, Chaldaeans, soothsayers, and others who have embarked on similar activities shall be denied fire and water and that all their property shall be confiscated, and that if anyone of a foreign nation does the like, he shall be capitally punished. It has, however, been questioned whether the knowledge possessed by persons of this kind is punishable or only its use and profession. It was indeed said by the ancients that it was their profession, not their knowledge, that was prohibited; later authorities take varying views on this matter. Nor should we pretend that this art has not sometimes crept into common use, with men openly professing it and openly offering their services – though this was more due to the contumacy and audacity of those who had been seen either to practise the art or to consult its practitioners than to any formal permission. At any rate, it has very frequently been formally ordained, by almost every emperor, that no person whatever should meddle in nonsense of this sort, and various punishments have been inflicted on the practitioners, according to the importance of the subject on which they were consulted. If it was about the life or health of the emperor, they were put to death or subjected to some other severe penalty, with lighter punishments for those who asked about their own or their families' fortunes. Reciters of prophecies are considered to belong to the latter class, though they also can merit severe punishment when they practise their reprehensible arts contrary to public peace and Roman imperial power. There is indeed extant a decree of the deified Antoninus Pius addressed to Pacatus, legate of Gallia Lugdunensis; since this rescript is lengthy, I have simply added, in the appropriate place, these few words about its objective. And also, the deified Marcus Aurelius banished to the island of Syros the man who had uttered prophecies at the time of Cassius' rebellion and said many things allegedly by divine inspiration. And certainly, one ought not to allow men of this sort to go unpunished, men who under pretence of divine instruction utter this sort of proclamation, boast, or wilfully invented fiction.

[On the Julian Law concerning treason]

2193. The crime closest to sacrilege is that which is called *maiestas* (treason). The crime of treason is that which is committed against the Roman people or their security. The following is liable: one whose actions, with malicious intent, initiate a plan whereby hostages are killed without the emperor's command;

locave occupentur vel templa, quove coetus conventusve fiat hominesve ad seditionem convocentur: cuiusve opera dolo malo consilium initum erit, quo quis magistratus populi Romani quive imperium potestatemve habet occidatur: quove quis contra rem publicam arma ferat: quive hostibus populi Romani nuntium litterasve miserit signumve dederit feceritve dolo malo, quo hostes populi Romani consilio iuventur adversus rem publicam: quive milites sollicitaverit concitaveritve, quo seditio tumultusve adversus rem publicam fiat.

[Ad legem Corneliam] de sicariis et veneficis.
2194.[84] Capite primo legis corneliae de sicariis cavetur, ut is praetor iudexve quaestionis, cui sorte obvenerit quaestio de sicariis eius quod in urbe Roma propius<ve> mille passus factum sit, uti quaerat cum iudicibus, qui ei ex lege sorte obvenerint de capite eius, qui cum telo ambulaverit hominis necandi furtive faciendi causa, hominemve occiderit, cuiusve id dolo malo factum erit. Et reliqua. Relatis verbis legis modo ipse loquitur Ulpianus: Haec lex non omnem, qui cum telo ambulaverit, punit, sed eum tantum, qui hominis necandi furtive faciendi causa telum gerit, coercet. Compescit item eum, qui hominem occidit, nec adiecit cuius condicionis hominem, ut et ad servum et peregrinum pertinere haec lex videatur.

2195.[85] Lege Cornelia de sicariis tenetur, qui, cum in magistratu est esset, eorum quid fecerit contra[86] hominis necem, quod legibus permissum non sit.

2196.[87] Distinctionem, casus et voluntatis in homicidio servari rescripto Hadriani[88] confirmatur. Verba rescripti: 'Et qui hominem occidit absolvi solet, sed si non occidendi animo[89] id admisit: et qui non occidit, sed voluit occidere, pro homicida damnatur. E re itaque constituendum est: ex quo[90] ferro percussit Epafroditus?[91]

---

84 *Coll.* 1.3.
85 *Dig.* 48.8.4.pr; cf. *Bas* 60.39.4.
86 contra] circa (*Krueger*)? Mommsen 1870 *ad loc.*
87 *Coll.* 1.6.
88 Cf. Marcian *fr.* 169 § 3. Lenel = *Dig.* 48.8.1.3. For the slight variation between the rescript, as it is quoted by Marcian and Ulpian, see Wieacker 1960: 402–4.
89 The term *animus* has a wide variety of meanings. I translate *occidendi animo* as intention to kill, denoting the mental component of the act.
90 I follow Frakes' reading (who follows the MSS), Mommsen = ecquo.
91 The identity of Epafroditus is perplexing. The name is not mentioned by Marcian, who also quoted this rescript in his treatise *on Institutions*, and which has been excerpted as *Dig.* 48.8.1.3. As noted by Mommsen, the two versions display

one who has armed men with weapons or stones in the city, or assembles them against the Republic, or occupies places or temples; one who forms an assembly or a gathering, or summons people for the purpose of insurrection; one whose actions, with malicious intent, initiate a plan whereby a magistrate of the Roman people or someone who holds imperium or power is killed; one who bears arms against the Republic; one who sends a message or letters to the enemies of the Roman people, gives them a sign, or acts with malicious intent to aid the enemies of the Roman people with counsel against the Republic; one who solicits or incites soldiers, causing sedition or commotion against the Republic.

[On the Cornelian law concerning assassins].
2194. In the first chapter of the Cornelian law concerning assassins it is stipulated that the praetor or judge of the inquiry, to whom the investigation of assassins will have fallen by lot, concerning a crime that has been committed in Rome or within one mile of it, should conduct the inquiry with the judges assigned to him by lot according to the law, concerning the capital case of the person who has walked around with a weapon with the intent to kill a man or commit a robbery, or has killed a man, or has done such an act with criminal intent. And other similar things. Ulpian himself, in recounting the words of the law, says: This law does not punish everyone who has walked around with a weapon, but only the person who carried the weapon with the intent to kill a man or commit a robbery. It also punishes those who killed a man, without specifying the condition of the man, so that this law seems to apply to both slaves and foreigners.

2195. Liable under the Cornelian law concerning assassins is he, who, while in office, has done anything against a person's life, which is not permitted by law.

2196. It is confirmed by a rescript of Hadrian that a distinction should be maintained between chance and premeditation in homicide. The words of the rescript: 'he who kills a man should be absolved if he commits it without intention to kill and he who does not kill, but wants to kill, is condemned for homicide. This should be constituted out of this: with which iron Epafroditus stabbed?

Nam si gladium instrinxit aut telo percussit, quid dubium est, quin occidendi animo percusserit? Si clave[92] percussit aut cucuma, aut, cum forte rixaretur, ferro percussit, sed non occidendi mente. Ergo hoc exquirite et si voluntas occidendi fuit, ut homicidam servum supplicio summo iure iubete affici.'

2197.[93] Cum quidam per lasciviam causam mortis praebuisset, conprobatum est factum Taurini Egnati proconsulis Baeticae a divo Hadriano, quod eum in quinquennium relegasset.[94] Verba consultationis et rescripti ita se habent: 'Inter Claudium, optime imperator, et Evaristum cognovi, quod Claudius Lupi filius in convivio, dum sago iactatur, culpa Mari Evaristi ita male acceptus fuerit, ut post diem quintum moreretur. Atque adparebat nullam inimicitiam cum Evaristo ei[95] fuisse. Tamen cupiditatis culpa coercendum credidi, ut ceteri eiusdem aetatis iuvenes emendarentur. Ideoque Mario Evaristo urbe Italia provincia Baetica in quinquennium interdixi et decrevi, ut impendi causa duo milia patri eius persolveret Evaristus, quod manifesta eius fuerat paupertas.' V(erba) r(escripti): 'Poenam Mari Evaristi recte, Taurine, moderatus es ad modum culpae; refert enim et in maioribus delictis, consulto aliquid admittatur an casu.' Et sane in omnibus criminibus distinctio haec poenam aut iustam provocare[96] debet aut temperamentum admittere.[97]

---

slight discrepancies. I quote *Dig.* 48.8.1.3 in full: *Divus Hadrianus rescripsit eum, qui hominem occidit, si non occidendi animo hoc admisit, absolvi posse, et qui hominem non occidit, sed vulneravit, ut occidat, pro homicida damnandum: et ex re constituendum hoc: nam si gladium strinxerit et in eo percusserit, indubitate occidendi animo id eum admisisse: sed si clavi percussit aut cuccuma in rixa, quamvis ferro percusserit, tamen non occidendi animo. Leniendam poenam eius, qui in rixa casu magis quam voluntate homicidium admisit.*

92 Although the MSS has *lapis* here, Mommsen et al. print *clavis* on the basis of a comparison with *Dig.* 48.8.1.3: *Divus Hadrianus rescripsit eum, qui hominem occidit, si non occidendi animo hoc admisit, absolvi posse, et qui hominem non occidit, sed vulneravit, ut occidat, pro homicida damnandum: et ex re constituendum hoc: nam si gladium strinxerit et in eo percusserit, indubitate occidendi animo id eum admisisse: sed si clavi percussit aut cuccuma in rixa, quamvis ferro percusserit, tamen non occidendi animo. Leniendam poenam eius, qui in rixa casu magis quam voluntate homicidium admisi.*

93 *Coll.* 1.11.1.

94 = *Dig.* 48.8.4.1.

95 cum Evaristo ei] *scripsi.* Mommsen 1870 *ad loc.*

96 Provocare] *Dig.* 48.19.5.2.

97 = *Dig.* 48, 19, 5, 2.

If he employed a sward or stabbed with a spear, what doubt is there that he did not stab to kill? If he stabbed with a nail or with a cooking utensil, while in an intensive conflict, he did stab with an iron, but not to kill. Therefore, it is this that you must seek diligently, and if there has been a will of killing you should order that the slave is punished by the most severe punishment for murder.'

2197. When someone had caused a death through wantonness, the action taken by Taurinus Egnatius, proconsul of Baetica, was approved by the deified Hadrian, who had exiled him for five years. The words of the consultation and the rescript are as follows: 'I have judged a case, excellent emperor, between Claudius and Evaristus, because Claudius, the son of Lupus, was injured at a banquet when a cloak was thrown, due to the fault of Marius Evaristus, and he died five days later. It was clear that there was no animosity between Evaristus and him. However, I believed that the fault of negligence must be restrained so that other youths of the same age would be corrected. Therefore, I have banned Marius Evaristus from the city of Rome, Italy, and the province of Baetica for five years and decreed that Evaristus should pay 2000 sestertii to his [Claudius's] father for expenses, given the manifest poverty of his father.' The words of the rescript: 'You have rightly moderated the punishment of Marius Evaristus, Taurinus, according to the degree of his fault; for it matters, even in more serious offences, whether something is committed deliberately or by chance.' And indeed, in all crimes, this distinction should either provoke a just punishment or allow for moderation.

2198.[98] Idem divus Hadrianus rescripsit: ‘Constitutum quidem est, ne spadones fierent, eos autem, qui hoc crimine arguerentur, Corneliae legis poena teneri eorumque bona merito fisco meo vindicari debere, sed et in servos, qui spadones fecerint, ultimo supplicio animadvertendum esse: et qui hoc crimine tenentur, si non adfuerint, de absentibus quoque, tamquam lege Cornelia teneantur, pronuntiandum esse. Plane si ipsi, qui hanc iniuriam passi sunt, proclamaverint, audire eos praeses provinciae debet,[99] qui virilitatem amiserunt: nemo enim liberum servumve invitum sinentemve castrare debet, neve quis se sponte castrandum praebere debet. At si quis adversus edictum meum fecerit, medico quidem, qui exciderit, capitale erit, item ipsi qui se sponte excidendum praebuit.’

2199.[100] Et eum, qui puerum ingenuum rapuit, puniendum divus Pius rescripsit in haec verba: ‘Exemplum libelli dati mihi a Domitio Silvano nomine Domitii Silvani patrui subici iussi, motus querella eius, qua significavit filium suum ingenuum, iuvenem admodum, raptum atque conclusum, mox verberibus ac tormentis usque ad summum periculum adflictum, Gemine carissime: velim audias eum et, si compereris haec ita admissa, rem severe exequaris.’

[Ad legem Iuliam peculatus].
2200.[101] Qui, cum in moneta publica operarentur, extrinsecus sibi signant pecuniam forma publica vel signatam furantur, hi non videntur adulterinam monetam exercuisse, sed furtum publicae monetae fecisse, quod ad peculatus crimen accedit. Si quis ex metallis caesarianis aurum argentumve furatus fuerit, ex edicto divi Pii exilio vel metallo, prout dignitas personae, punitur. Is autem, qui furanti signum praebuit, perinde habetur, atque si manifesti furti condemnatus esset, et famosus efficitur. Qui autem aurum ex metallo habuerit illicite et conflaverit, in quadruplum condemnatur.

---

98 *Dig.* 48.8.4.2.

99 Exciderunt quaedam; Lenel. Mommsen has the following note: sed item animadvertere, etsi tacebunt ipsi similiave ins. (u.i). Mommsen offered (*ut infra*) (“as [noted] below”) a phrase from the Nomocanon: εἰ γέ αὐτοὶ οἱ ταύτην τὴν ἀδικίαν παθόντες ἀναφωνοῦσιν, ὀφείλει αὐτῶν ἀκούειν ὁ ἄρχων τῆς ἐπαρχίας τῶν ἀπολεσάντων τὴν ἀνδρείαν (‘If indeed those who have suffered this injustice cry out, the governor of the province is obliged to listen to those who have lost their manliness’, BS 60.3.27 sch 86 = vol. 6, p. 46 Heimb.).

100 *Dig.* 48.6.6; cf. *Bas* 60.18.6.

101 *Dig.* 48.13.8; cf. *Bas* 60.45.7.

2198. The same deified Hadrian has written in a rescript: 'It is indeed established that eunuchs should not be made. Those accused of this crime should be held accountable under the Cornelian law and their property should rightly be confiscated by my treasury. Slaves who make eunuchs must be subjected to the ultimate punishment, and those who are charged with this crime, even if they are not present, should be convicted in their absence as if under the Cornelian law. Clearly, if those who have suffered this injury cry out, the governor of the province must hear them, those who have lost their manhood: for no one should emasculate a free man or a slave against their will, nor should anyone offer himself to be castrated willingly. If anyone acts against my edict, it will be a capital offence for the doctor who performs the procedure and also for the person who willingly underwent it.'

2199. And he who kidnapped a free-born boy must be punished, the deified Pius wrote in a rescript in these words: 'I have ordered that a copy of the petition presented to me by Domitius Silvanus, in the name of his uncle Domitius Silvanus, be submitted, moved by his complaint in which he indicated that his free-born son, a very young boy, had been kidnapped and imprisoned, and then afflicted by scourges and torments to the point of extreme danger. My dear Geminus, I would like you to hear him, and if you find that these things have occurred, pursue the matter severely.'

[On the Julian law of peculate].

2200. Those who, while employed in the public mint, create for themselves money with the official design or steal already minted money, are not seen as having engaged in counterfeiting but as having committed theft of public funds, which amounts to the crime of peculation. If someone steals gold or silver from an imperial mine, he will be punished, following an edict of the deified Pius, by relegation to the mines or exile, according to his social status. He who provides a thief with a die will be considered in the same manner as one condemned for manifest theft, and he becomes infamous. Anyone who illicitly possesses gold from a mine and melts it down will be liable to a fourfold penalty.

2201.[102] Quicumque nummos aureos partim raserint, partim tinxerint vel finxerint: si quidem liberi sunt, ad bestias dari, si servi, summo supplicio adfici debent.

LIBER VIII.

Ad legem Iuliam de vi publica et privata.
2202.[103] Lege Iulia de vi publica tenetur, qui, cum imperium potestatemve haberet, civem Romanum adversus provocationem necaverit verberaverit iusseritve quid fieri aut quid in collum iniecerit, ut torqueatur. Item quod ad legatos oratores comitesve attinebit, si quis eorum pulsasse et sive iniuriam fecisse arguetur.

2203.[104] Eadem lege quibusdam testimonium omnino, quibusdam interdicitur invitis capite octogesimo septimo et capite octogesimo octavo. in haec verba his hominibus: 'hac lege in reum testimonium dicere ne liceto, qui se ab eo parenteve eius libertove cuius eorum libertive libertave liberaverit, quive inpubes erit, quive [iudicio publico damnatus est, qui] eorum in integrum restitutus non est, quive in vinculis custodiaque publica erit, quive depugnandi causa auctoratus erit, quive ad bestias depugnare se locavit locaverit, praeterquam qui iaculandi causa ad urbem missus est erit, palamve corpore quaestum faciet feceritve, quive ob testimonium dicendum [vel non dicendum] pecuniam accepisse iudicatus erit.' Nec volens quis eorum hac lege in reum testimonium dicit. Capite octogesimo septimo his: '[Homines] inviti in reum testimonium ne dicunto qui sobrinus est ei reo propioreve cognatione coniunctus, quive socer gener vitricus privignusve eius erit.' Et reliqua.

[Ad legem Pompeiam de Parricidiis].
2204.[105] Utrum qui occiderunt parentes an etiam conscii poena parricidii adficiantur, quaeri potest. Et ait Maecianus etiam conscios eadem poena adficiendos, non solum parricidas. Proinde conscii etiam extranei eadem poena adficiendi sunt.

---

102 *Dig.* 48.10.8; cf. *Bas* 60.41.8.
103 *Dig.* 48.6.7; cf. *Bas* 60.18.7.
104 *Coll.* 9.2.
105 *Dig.* 48.9.6; cf. *Bas* 60.40.5.

2201. Whoever has partly shaved, partly gilded, or counterfeited gold coins: if they are free persons, they shall be thrown to the beasts, and if they are slaves, they shall be subjected to the highest punishment.

Book 8.

On the Julian law on public and private violence.
2202. A person is accountable under the Julian law concerning public violence if, while holding *imperium*, he kills a Roman citizen despite an appeal (*provocatio*), or whips him, or orders something to be done, or places something around his neck to torture him. Similarly, it pertains to legates, orators, and their companions if any of them are accused of having struck or caused an injury (*iniuria*).

2203. By the same law, testimony is entirely forbidden to some individuals, while for others it is forbidden if given unwillingly, as stated in the eighty-seventh and eighty-eighth chapters of the law. The law states for these people: 'By this law, it shall not be allowed to give testimony against a defendant if the witness has been freed by the defendant, his parent, his freedman, or any of their freedmen or freedwomen; anyone who is under age; anyone who has been condemned by a public court and not been fully reinstated; anyone in chains or public custody; anyone contracted for fighting; anyone who has hired or will hire himself to fight wild beasts in the arena, except those who have been sent or will be sent to a city to throw javelins; anyone who has openly engaged in prostitution; or anyone judged to have received money for giving (or not giving) testimony.' No one among these may give testimony against an accused if unwilling, according to this law. In the eighty-seventh chapter, it is stated: 'Unwilling persons shall not give testimony against an accused who is their maternal cousin or a closer relative; or against an accused who is a father-in-law, son-in-law, stepfather, or stepson.' And other matters.

[On the Pompeian law on parricide].
2204. Those who killed their parents or also those who were privy to the act should be afflicted with the punishment of parricide. And Maecianus said that those who were privy should also be afflicted with the same punishment, not merely the parricides. Therefore, those who were privy, even if they were not blood-related, should be equally punished.

De poena legis Corneliae testamentariae.

2205.[106] Lege Cornelia cavetur, ut, qui in aurum vitii quid addiderit, qui argenteos nummos adulterinos flaverit, falsi crimine teneri. Eadem poena adficitur etiam is qui, cum prohibere tale quid posset, non prohibuit. Eadem lege exprimitur, ne quis nummos stagneos plumbeos emere vendere dolo malo vellet.

2206.[107] Praeterea factum est senatus consultum Statilio et Tauro consulibus, quo poena legis Corneliae inrogatur ei, qui quid aliud quam testamentum sciens [dolo malo falsum] signaverit signarive curaverit, item qui ad falsas testationes faciendas testamentave falsa invicem dicenda aut consignanda dolo malo coierint, <Licinio V et Tauro conss. >[108] Item qui ob instruendam advocationem testimoniave pecuniam acceperit pactusve fuerit societatemve coierit, aut aliquam de ea re pactionem interposuerit, item si quis coierit ad occisionem innocentium, senatus consulto quod Cotta et Messalla factum est coercetur. Sed et si quis ob denuntiandum vel non denuntiandum remittendumve testimonium pecuniam acceperit, senatus consulto quod duobus Geminis conss. factum est poena legis Corneliae adficitur. Et reliqua.

2207.[109] Qui delatorem summisit in causa pecuniaria, eadem poena tenetur, qua tenentur hi qui ob instruendas lites pecuniam acceperunt.

[De testibus].

2208.[110] Inviti testimonium non dicunt publicani, item is qui non detractandi testimonii causa aberit, item is qui quid exercitui praebendum conduxerit. Sed nec pupillis testimonium denuntiari potest.

---

106 *Dig.* 48.10.9.pr.-2; cf. *Bas* 60.41.8.

107 *Coll.* 8.7; cf. *Dig.* 48.10.9.3.

108 Following Wieacker 1960: 396, and Frakes *ad loc.*

109 *Dig.* 48.10.9.4.

110 *Dig.* 22.5.19; cf. *Bas* 21.1.18.

On the punishment of the Cornelian law concerning testimonies.
2205. It is provided by the Lex Cornelia that anyone who adds any impurity to gold, or who forges silver coins, is guilty of the crime of falsification. The same punishment is applied to anyone who, though able to prevent such an act, did not do so. The same law specifies that no one should knowingly and deceitfully buy or sell coins made of pewter or lead. The penalty of the Lex Cornelia is imposed on anyone who, with fraudulent intent, knowingly signs or arranges for the signing of anything false in a will, as well as on those who, with fraudulent intent, conspire to create false wills or give false testimony. Anyone who brings forward an informer in a financial case is held to the same penalty as those who receive money to support lawsuits.

2206. In addition, the *Senatus consultum* from the consulate of Statilius and Taurus stated that the punishment of the Cornelian law shall be imposed on anyone, who knowingly and fraudulently sealed something other than a testimony or arranged for it to be sealed. Similarly, those who shall come together to produce false evidence or false wills or to approve or seal a document fraudulently. Similarly, he who shall receive wages for furnishing legal assistance or advocacy, or shall agree to do it, or shall enter an alliance to do it, or shall interpose another agreement of this sort. Similarly, if anyone shall assemble for the massacre of an innocent person, by the *Senatus consultum* enacted under the consulship of Cotta and Messalla, he shall be restrained. And if someone shall receive a pay for denouncing, or not denouncing, or for remitting a testimony, he shall be afflicted by the punishment of the Cornelian law, which had been enacted during the consulship of the two Gemini. And the rest.

2207. Anyone who has suborned an informer in a pecuniary case shall be subjected to the same punishment as those who have accepted money for instigating lawsuits.

[On witnesses].
2208. Publicani do not give testimony unwillingly, nor does someone who is absent not for the purpose of avoiding testimony, nor someone who has contracted to provide something for the army. Furthermore, a ward cannot be summoned to give testimony.

[De quaestionibus].

2209.[111] In criminibus eruendis quaestio adhiberi solet. Sed quando vel quatenus id faciendum sit, videamus. Et non esse a tormentis incipiendum et divus Augustus constituit neque adeo fidem quaestioni adhibendam, sed et epistula divi Hadriani ad Sennium Sabinum continetur. Verba rescripti ita se habent: 'Ad tormenta servorum ita demum veniri oportet, cum suspectus est reus et aliis argumentis ita probationi admovetur, ut sola confessio servorum deesse videatur.' Idem divus Hadrianus Claudio Quartino rescripsit: quo rescripto illud expressit a suspectissimo incipiendum et a quo facillime posse verum scire iudex crediderit. Ad quaestionem non esse provocandos eos, quos accusator de domo sua produxit, nec facile credendum subiectam eam, quam ambo parentes dicuntur caram filiam habuisse rescripto divorum fratrum ad Lucium Tiberianum emisso declaratur. Idem Cornelio Proculo rescripserunt non utique in servi unius quaestione fidem rei constituendam, sed argumentis causam examinandam. Divus Antoninus, et divus Hadrianus Sennio Sabino, rescripserunt, cum servi pariter cum domino aurum et argentum exportasse dicerentur, non esse de domino interrogandos: ne quidem, si ultro aliquid dixerint, obesse hoc domino. Divi fratres Leliano Longino rescripserunt de servo heredum non esse habendam quaestionem in res hereditarias, quamvis suspectum fuisset, quod imaginaria venditione dominium in eo quaesisse heres videretur. Servum municipum posse in caput civium torqueri saepissime rescriptum est, quia non sit illorum servus, sed rei publicae. Idemque in ceteris servis corporum dicendum est: nec enim plurium servus videtur, sed corporis. Si servus bona fide mihi serviat, etiamsi dominium in eo non habui, potest dici torqueri eum in caput meum non debere. Idem est et in libero homine, qui bona fide servit. Sed nec libertum torqueri in patroni caput constitutum est. Nec fratrem quidem in fratris imperator noster cum divo patre suo rescripsit, addita ratione, quod in eum, in quem quis invitus testimonium dicere non cogitur, in eum nec torqueri debet. Servum mariti in caput uxoris posse torqueri divus Traianus Sernio Quarto rescripsit. Idem Mummio Lolliano rescripsit damnati servos, quia desierunt esse ipsius, posse in eum torqueri. Si servus ad hoc erit manumissus, ne torqueatur, dummodo in caput domini non torqueatur, posse eum torqueri divus Pius rescripsit. Sed

111 *Dig.* 48.18.1.pr.-20; cf. *Bas* 60.50.1.

[Of interrogations].
2209. Torture is customarily applied to uncover crimes. But let us consider when and to what extent this should be done. The deified Augustus decreed that torture should not be the starting point, nor should undue trust be placed in it, and this is also stated in an epistle of the deified Hadrian to Sennius Sabinus. The words of the rescript are as follows: 'Resort to the torture of slaves should only occur when the defendant is suspected and other evidence has brought the case to such a point that it appears only a confession of the slaves is lacking.' The deified Hadrian made a similar ruling in a rescript to Claudius Quartinus: this rescript expressed that the most suspected individual should be the starting point, and the judge should believe that he can most easily extract the truth from him. Those whom the accuser has brought from his own home should not be subjected to torture, nor should it easily be believed that the beloved daughter of both parents has been substituted, as stated in a rescript by the deified brothers to Lucius Tiberianus. They also wrote similarly in a rescript to Cornelius Proculus, that the credibility of a case should not be based solely on the torture of one slave, but the case should be examined by arguments. The deified Antoninus and Hadrian wrote in a rescript to Sennius Sabinus that if slaves are accused of having carried off gold and silver with their master, they should not be interrogated about their master; even if they voluntarily say something, it should not harm the master. The deified brothers wrote in a rescript to Lelianus Longinus that a slave of heirs should not be subjected to torture in matters concerning the inheritance, even if there is suspicion that the heirs sought ownership through a fictitious sale. It has often been stated in a rescript that a municipal slave can be tortured in capital cases involving citizens, because he is not their slave, but a slave of the city. Similarly, for other slaves of corporations, the slave is seen not as belonging to many individuals, but to the corporation itself. If a slave serves me in good faith, even if I do not have ownership, he should not be tortured in a case against me. The same applies to a free person serving in good faith. It is also established that a freedman cannot be tortured against his patron. Our emperor, along with his deified father, wrote in a rescript that a brother cannot be tortured against a brother, with the reasoning that one should not be forced to testify unwillingly against someone, and thus should not be tortured. The deified Trajan wrote in a rescript to Servius Quartus that a husband's slave can be tortured against the wife. He wrote similarly to Mummius Lollianus that the slaves of a condemned person can be tortured against him because they have ceased to be his. If a slave is manumitted to avoid torture, the deified Pius wrote that he can be tortured, as long as he is not tortured against his former owner. The deified brothers

et eum, qui cognitionis susceptae tempore alienus fuit, licet postea rei sit effectus, torqueri in caput posse divi fratres rescripserunt. Si quis dicatur nullo iure emptus, non prius torqueri poterit, quam si constiterit venditionem non valuisse: et ita imperator noster cum divo patre suo rescripsit. Item Severus Spicio Antigono ita rescripsit: 'Cum quaestio de servis contra dominos neque haberi debeat neque, si facta sit, dicturi sententiam consilium instruat: multo minus indicia servorum contra dominos admittenda sunt.' Divus Severus rescripsit confessiones reorum pro exploratis facinoribus haberi non oportere, si nulla probatio religionem cognoscentis instruat. Cum quidam deponere pretium servi paratus esset, ut servus torqueretur contra dominum, imperator noster cum divo patre suo id non admiserunt. Si servi quasi sceleris participes in se torqueantur deque domino aliquid fuerint confessi apud iudicem: prout causa exegerit, ita pronuntiare eum debere divus Traianus rescripsit. Quo rescripto ostenditur gravari dominos confessione servorum. Sed ab hoc rescripto recessum constitutiones posteriores ostendunt. In causa tributorum, in quibus esse rei publicae nervos nemini dubium est, periculi quoque ratio, quod servo fraudis conscio capitalem poenam denuntiat, eiusdem professionem exstruat.[112]

2210.[113] Qui quaestionem habiturus est, non debet specialiter interrogare, an Lucius Titius homicidium fecerit, sed generaliter, quis id fecerit: alterum enim magis suggerentis quam requirentis videtur. Et ita divus Traianus rescripsit. Divus Hadrianus Calpurnio Celeriano in haec verba rescripsit: 'Agricola Pompei Ualentis servus de se potest interrogari. Si, dum quaestio habetur, amplius dixerit, rei fuerit indicium, non interrogationis culpa.'

2211.[114] Quaestioni fidem non semper nec tamen numquam habendam constitutionibus declaratur: etenim res est fragilis et periculosa et quae veritatem fallat. Nam plerique patientia sive duritia tormentorum ita tormenta contemnunt, ut exprimi eis veritas nullo modo possit: alii tanta sunt impatientia, ut quodvis mentiri quam pati tormenta velint: ita fit, ut etiam vario modo fateantur, ut non tantum se, verum etiam alios criminentur. Praeterea inimicorum quaestioni fides haberi non debet, quia facile mentiuntur. Nec tamen sub praetextu

---

112 Mommsen proposed the reading *confirmat*, which indeed clarifies the sentence, but is unsupported by the manuscript tradition.

113 *Dig.* 48.18.1.21–2; cf. *Bas* 60.50.1.

114 *Dig.* 48.18.1.23–6; cf. *Bas* 60.50.1.

wrote in a rescript that a slave who was another's at the time of the inquiry, but became the defendant's afterward, can be tortured against him. If someone is said to have been purchased unlawfully, they cannot be tortured before it is determined that the sale was void, as our emperor and his deified father wrote in a rescript. Similarly, Severus wrote in a rescript to Spicius Antigonus: 'The interrogation of slaves against their owners should not occur, nor, if it has happened, should it shape the judge's sentence: much less should slave evidence against owners be admitted.' The deified Severus wrote in a rescript that confessions of the accused should not be considered conclusive if no investigation supports the inquiry. If someone is willing to pay the price of a slave to have him tortured against his owner, our emperor and his deified father did not permit it. If slaves are tortured as participants in a crime and confess something against their master before a judge, the deified Trajan wrote in a rescript that the judge should pronounce based on the circumstances. This rescript indicates that masters are burdened by the confessions of slaves. However, later constitutions show a departure from this rescript. In a case about tributes, which no one denies are the sinews of the commonwealth, a consideration of the risk by which a death penalty will be inflicted upon a slave conscious of a fraud magnifies his public acknowledgment.

2210. He who is about to conduct an interrogation (under torture) should not specifically ask whether Lucius Titius committed murder, but rather generally ask who did it: for the former seems more like suggesting than inquiring. And thus the deified Trajan wrote in a rescript. The deified Hadrian wrote in a rescript to Calpurnius Celerianus in these words: 'Agricola, the slave of Pompeius Valens, can be interrogated about himself. If, while the interrogation is being conducted, he says more, it will be evidence against him, not the fault of the interrogation.'

2211. It is declared by imperial constitutions that trust should not always or never be placed in interrogation (under torture): for it is a fragile and hazardous matter that could deceive the truth. Many defy torture with either endurance or insensitivity to pain, to the extent that the truth cannot be extracted from them in any way. Others are so impatient that they prefer to lie rather than endure torture. Thus, it happens that they confess in various ways, incriminating not only themselves but also others. Furthermore, one should not put faith in the torture of enemies, because they lie easily. However, trust in torture should not be entirely dismissed under the pretext of enmity; rather, after the case is properly investigated, trust should be given or not. Regarding a person who inimicitiarum detrahenda erit fides quaestioni,[115] causaque cognita habenda fides aut non habenda. Cum quis latrones tradidit, quibusdam rescriptis continetur non debere fidem haberi eis in eos, qui eos tradiderunt: quibusdam vero, quae sunt pleniora, hoc cavetur, ut neque destricte non habeatur, ut in ceterorum persona solet, sed causa cognita aestimetur, habenda fides sit nec ne. Plerique enim, dum metuunt, ne forte adpprehensi eos nominent, prodere eos solent, scilicet impunitatem sibi captantes, quia non facile eis indicantibus proditores suos creditur. Sed neque passim impunitas eis per huiusmodi proditiones concedenda est, neque transmittenda allegatio dicentium idcirco se oneratos, quod eos ipsi tradidissent: neque enim invalidum argumentum haberi debet mendacii sive calumniae in se instructae.

2212.[116] Si quis ultro de maleficio fateatur, non semper ei fides habenda est: nonnumquam enim aut metu aut qua alia de causa in se confitentur. Et extat epistula divorum fratrum ad Voconium Saxam, qua continetur liberandum eum, qui in se fuerat confessus, cuius post damnationem de innocentia constitisset. Cuius verba haec sunt: 'Prudenter et egregia ratione humanitatis, Saxa carissime, Primitivum servum, qui homicidium in se confingere metu ad dominum revertendi suspectus esset, perseverantem falsa demonstratione damnasti quaesiturus de consciis, quos aeque habere se commentitus fuerat, ut ad certiorem ipsius de se confessionem pervenires. Nec frustra fuit tam prudens consilium tuum, cum in tormentis constiterit neque illos ei conscios fuisse et ipsum de se temere commentum. Potes itaque decreti gratiam facere et eum per officium distrahi iubere, condicione addita, ne umquam in potestatem domini revertatur, quem pretio recepto certum habemus libenter tali servo cariturum.' Hac epistula significatur, quasi servus damnatus, si fuisset restitutus, ad eum pertinebit, cuius fuisset, antequam damnetur. Sed praeses provinciae eum quem damnavit restituere non potest, cum nec pecuniariam sententiam suam revocare possit. Quid igitur? Principi eum scribere oportet, si quando ei, qui nocens videbatur, postea ratio innocentiae constitit.

---

115 *F*[1] has *quaestionis*, but Mommsen *ad loc.* suggested *quaesitioni*, which agrees with *fides*.

116 *Dig.* 48.18.1.27; cf. *Bas* 60.50.1.

betrays bandits, some rescripts state that trust should not be placed in those who betray them: others, more comprehensive, caution that while trust should not be dismissed outright as with others, it should be judged based on the case whether trust should be given or not. Many betray others out of fear that those apprehended will name them, seeking impunity for themselves, which is why it is not easy to trust those who betray bandits. Broad impunity should not be granted to traitors of this kind, nor should the allegations of those who claim they were accused because they betrayed others be admitted as proof. An argument of falsehood or calumny against them should not be considered invalid.

2212. If someone confesses to a crime voluntarily, trust should not always be granted: sometimes people confess out of fear or for some other reason. An epistle of the deified brothers to Voconius Saxa states that a person who confessed to a crime should be released if their innocence is established after their conviction. The words of the epistle are as follows: 'Prudently and with a great sense of humanity, my dear Saxa, you condemned the slave Primitivus, who had confessed to homicide out of fear of returning to his master and who persisted in a false confession about his accomplices, whom he had also invented, so that you could be more certain about his confession. Your wise decision was not in vain, as it has been established under torture that he had no accomplices and that his confession was baseless. Therefore, you can act on this decree and order that he be sold by official order, with the condition that he shall never return to his former master's power, who, having received the price, will certainly be content to be rid of such a slave.' This epistle indicates that a condemned slave, if restored, will belong to the person to whom he belonged before being condemned. However, a provincial governor cannot restore a person he has condemned to his previous condition, as he cannot revoke his own financial sentence. What then? He should write to the emperor if, after conviction, evidence of the person's innocence emerges.

De dominorum saevitia.

2213.[117] Si dominus in servos saevierit vel ad inpudicitiam turpemque violationem conpellat, quae sint partes praesidis, ex rescripto divi Pii ad Aurelium Marcianum proconsulem Baeticae manifestatur. Cuius rescripti verba haec sunt: 'Dominorum quidem potestatem in suos servos inlibatam esse oportet nec cuiquam hominum ius suum detrahi: sed dominorum interest, ne auxilium contra saevitiam vel famem vel intolerabilem iniuriam denegetur his, qui iuste deprecantur. Ideoque cognosce de querellis eorum,[118] qui ex familia Iuli Sabini ad statuam confugerunt, et si vel durius habitos, quam aequum est vel infami iniuria adfectos cognoveris, venire iube, ita ut in potestatem Sabini non revertantur. Quod si meae constitutioni fraudem fecerit, sciet me admissum severius executurum.' Divus etiam Hadrianus Umbram quandam matronam in quinquennium relegavit, quod ex levissimis causis ancillas atrocissime tractaret.

2214.[119] Item divus Pius ad libellum Alfi Iuli rescripsit in haec verba: 'Servorum obsequium non solum imperio, sed et moderatione et sufficientibus praebitis et iustis operibus contineri oportet. Itaque et ipse curare debes iuste ac temperate tuos tractare, ut ex facili requirere eos possis, ne, si apparuerit vel inparem te inpediis esse vel atrociore dominationem saevitia exercere, necesse habeat proconsul u. c., ne quid tumultuosius contra accidat, praevenire et ex mea iam auctoritate te ad alienandos eos conpellere. Glabrione et Homullo cons.'

De naufragiis et *[incendiariis].*

2215.[120] Licere unicuique naufragium suum impune colligere constat: idque imperator Antoninus cum divo patre suo rescripsit.

2216.[121] Incendiariis lex quidem Cornelia aqua et igni interdici iussit, sed re varie sunt puniti. Nam qui data opera in civitate incendium fecerunt, si humillimo loco sunt, bestiis subici solent, si in aliquo gradu et Romae id

---

117 *Dig.* 1.6.2; cf. *Coll.* 3.3.1–4; *Inst.* 1.8.2; *Bas* 31.1.2; *Bas* 19.7.11.

118 I follow Mommsen, who prints '*eorum*' following the W manuscript and *Dig.* 1.6.2. Frakes preferred '*illorum*', following Schultz.

119 *Coll.* 3.3.5–6.

120 *Dig.* 47.9.12.pr; cf. *Bas* 60.20.4.

121 *Coll.* 12.5.

On cruelty of slave owners.
2213. If a master behaves cruelly towards his slaves or compels them to shameful and dishonourable acts, the duties of the provincial governor are clarified by a rescript of the deified Pius to Aurelius Marcianus, proconsul of Baetica. The words of the rescript are as follows: 'Indeed, the power of masters over their own slaves should be inviolate, and no one's right should be usurped. However, it is in the interest of masters that assistance against cruelty, hunger, or intolerable injustice should not be denied to those who rightly seek relief. Therefore, investigate the complaints of those who have fled from the household of Julius Sabinus to the statue [of the emperor], and if you find that they have been treated more harshly than is just or subjected to dishonourable mistreatment, order that they do not return under the power of Sabinus. If he acts contrary to my decree, he shall know that I will enforce this transgression more severely.' The deified Hadrian also relegated a certain matron named Umbra for five years because she had treated her handmaids atrociously for the slightest reasons.

2214. Similarly, the deified Pius replied in a rescript to Alfius Iulius in these words: 'The obedience of slaves should be maintained not only by authority but also by moderation, adequate provisions, and fair treatment. Therefore, you yourself must ensure to manage them justly and temperately, so that you can easily require their service, lest it should appear that you are unfit for your responsibilities or exercise harsh domination through cruelty. The honourable (*vir clarissimus*) proconsul may find it necessary to intervene preemptively to prevent any serious unrest and to compel you to sell them under my authority.' Given during the consulship of Glabrius and Omullus.

On shipwreck and arsonists
2215. It is established that anyone is permitted to gather their own shipwreck's remains without penalty; and Emperor Antoninus wrote this in a rescript together with his deified father.

2216. The Cornelian law indeed orders that incendiaries are banned from water and fire, but they are punished in various ways. For those who intentionally set fire in a city, if they are of lowly status, they are usually thrown to wild beasts in the arena; if they hold some position and committed the act in Rome, they fecerunt, capite puniuntur: aut certe [deportationis poena][122] adficiendi sunt qui haec committunt. Sed eis qui non data opera incendium fecerint plerumque ignoscitur, nisi in lata et incauta neglegentia vel lascivia fuit.

[De dardanariis etc.]

2217.[123] Annonam adtemptare et vexare vel maxime dardanarii solent: quorum avaritiae obviam itum est tam mandatis quam constitutionibus. mandatis denique ita cavetur: 'Praeterea debebis custodire, ne dardanarii ullius mercis sint, ne aut ab his, qui coemptas merces supprimunt, aut a locupletioribus, qui fructus suos aequis pretiis vendere nollent, dum minus uberes proventus exspectant, annona oneretur.' Poena autem in hos varie statuitur: nam plerumque, si negotiantes sunt, negotiatione eis tantum interdicitur, interdum et relegari solent, humiliores ad opus publicum dari. Onerant annonam etiam staterae adulterinae, de quibus divus Traianus edictum proposuit, quo edicto poenam legis Corneliae in eos statuit, perinde ac si lege testamentaria, quod testamentum falsum scripsisset signasset recitasset, damnatus esset. Sed et divus Hadrianus eum, qui falsas mensuras habuit, in insulam relegavit.

De abigeis.

2218.[124] De abigeis puniendis ita divus Hadrianus rescripsit concilio[125] Baeticae: 'Abigei cum durissime puniuntur, ad gladium damnari solent. Puniuntur autem durissime non ubique, sed ubi frequentius est hoc[126] genus maleficii: alioquin et in opus et nonnumquam temporarium damnantur.[127] Ideoque puto apud vos quoque sufficere genus poenae, quod maximum huic maleficio inrogari solet, ut ad gladium abigei dentur: aut si quis tam notus et tam gravis in abigendo fuit, ut prius ex hoc crimine aliqua poena affectus sit, hunc in metallum dari oportere.' Rescriptum divi Hadriani sic loquitur, quasi gravior poena sit metalli: nisi forte hoc sensit divus Hadrianus gladii poenam dicendo ludi damnationem. Est autem differentia inter eos qui ad gladium et eos qui ad ludum damnantur; nam ad gladium damnati confestim consumuntur vel

---

122 I follow the suggestion of Lenel, based on *Dig.* 47.9.12.1: ... *aut certe in insulam deportantur.*

123 *Dig.* 47.11.6; cf. *Bas* 60.22.6.

124 *Coll.* 11.7; cf. *Dig.* 47.14.1.pr.

125 consilio, *Dig.*

126 id, *Dig.*

127 Dantur, *Dig.* = *Dig.* 47.14.1.pr.

are punished by death, or at the very least they are sentenced to deportation. However, those who cause fire unintentionally are often pardoned, unless their actions were due to gross and reckless negligence or frivolity.

[On speculators etc.]
2217. Speculators are in the habit of interfering with or significantly disrupting the *annonae*. Their avarice is countered by both mandates and constitutions. The mandates specifically state: 'Furthermore, you [i.e., the provincial governor] must ensure that there are no speculators of any commodity, nor that the grain supply is burdened by those who hoard purchased goods or by the wealthy who refuse to sell their produce at fair prices while awaiting less abundant harvests.' The penalties imposed on these individuals vary. For the most part, if they are merchants, they are banned from trading, and at times they may be relegated. If they are of humble origin, they will be assigned to public works. Counterfeit scales, which also burden the grain supply, are addressed in an edict by the deified Trajan, who stated that the punishment of the Cornelian law would be inflicted on those individuals, just as if they had been convicted under the testamentary law for having written, signed, or read out a false will. The deified Hadrian also relegated to an island anyone found to possess false measures.

On cattle-thieves.
2218. On how cattle thieves should be punished, the deified Hadrian wrote thus in a rescript to the council of Baetica: 'Cattle thieves, when punished most severely, are usually sentenced to the sword. They are not, however, punished most severely everywhere, but only where this type of crime is more frequent; otherwise, they are condemned to hard labour, and sometimes only for a limited period. Therefore, I think that for you, this type of punishment suffices, which is the maximum that is habitually inflicted for this offence, that they be sentenced to the sword. And if someone is so notorious and serious in cattle theft that he has previously received a punishment for this crime, he should be sent to the mines.' The rescript of the deified Hadrian speaks as if relegation to the mines is a graver punishment, unless perhaps the deified Hadrian meant condemnation to the arena when he spoke of the death penalty. There is, however, a difference between those condemned to the sword and those condemned to the arena. Those condemned to the sword are executed immediately, or certainly must be dead within a year; this is stipulated in the mandates. Indeed, those condemned to the arena are not necessarily killed, but they can be manumitted

certe intra annum debent consumi; hoc enim mandatis continetur. Enimvero qui in ludum damnantur, non utique consumuntur, sed etiam pilleari et rudem accipere possunt post intervallum, siquidem post quinquennium pilleari, post triennium autem rudem induere eis permittitur. Eodem rescripto divi Hadriani diligentissime expressum est non ubique parem esse poenam abigeorum.

2219.[128] Abigei autem proprie hi habentur, qui pecora ex pastu et ex armentis subtrahunt et quodammodo depraedantur et abigei studium quasi artem exercent equos de gregibus vel boves de armentis abducentes. Ceterum si quis bovem aberrantem vel equum in solitudine[129] abduxerit non est abigeus, sed fur potius. Sed et qui porcum[130] vel capram vel verbecem abducunt, non tam graviter ut hi[131] qui maiora animalia abigunt plecti debent.

2220.[132] Quamquam autem Hadrianus metalli poenam, item operis[133] vel etiam gladii praestituerit, at tamen qui honestiore loco nati sunt, non debent ad hanc poenam pertinere, sed aut relegandi erunt aut removendi[134] ordine. Romae tamen etiam bestiis subici abigeos videmus: et sane qui cum gladio abigunt, non inique hac poena adficiuntur.

2221.[135] Qui pecora, de quorum proprietate faciebat controversiam, abegit, ut Saturninus quidem scribit, ad examinationem civilem remittendus est. Sed hoc ita demum probandum est, si non color abigeatus quaesitus est, sed vere putavit sua iustis rationibus ductus.

De furibus.

2222.[136] Fures ad forum remittendi sunt diurni, nocturnique extra ordinem audiendi et causa cognita puniendi, dummodo in poena eorum sciamus operis

128 *Coll.* 11.8.1–2 = *Dig.* 47.14.1.2.
129 The *Digest* has the more sensible *solitodine relictos.*
130 porcam *Dig.*
131 Quam *Dig.*
132 *Coll.* 11.8.3–4 = *Dig.* 47.1.3.
133 Following Frakes. Mommsen has *temporari.*
134 movendi *Dig.*
135 *Dig.* 47.14.1.4.
136 *Coll.* 7.4 = *Dig.* 47.17.1.

and receive the wooden sword after an interval. Specifically, they are allowed to receive the cap of liberty after five years and the wooden sword after three years. In the same rescript of the deified Hadrian, it is very carefully stated that the punishment for cattle theft is not the same everywhere.

2219. Cattle thieves are those specifically considered to be those who steal cattle from pasture and herds, and in a certain way, plunder. Cattle thieves practise their craft by abducting horses from flocks or oxen from herds. However, if someone abducts a stray bull or horse in the wilderness, he is not a cattle thief but rather a common thief. Furthermore, those who steal a pig, a she-goat, or a castrated ram should not be punished as severely as those who steal larger animals.

2220. Although Hadrian established the punishment of relegation to the mines, hard labour, or even the death penalty, those of noble birth should not be subjected to this punishment but should either be exiled or removed from their rank. In Rome, however, we see cattle thieves subjected to fighting wild beasts in the arena: and certainly, those who drive off cattle by the threat of a sword are not unjustly subjected to this punishment.

2221. If anyone has driven off cattle, over whose ownership he was making a contention, as indeed Saturninus writes, he should be remitted to civil examination. However, this is only to be proven if it is not a pretext for cattle theft, but if he truly believed, based on just reasons, that the cattle were his.

On thieves.
2222. Thieves who operate by day should be brought back to the forum [to be tried], while thieves who operate at night should be heard outside the order, and, after the case has been thoroughly investigated, punished by the governor,

publici temporarium[137] modum non egrediendum. Idem et in balneariis furibus. Sed si se telo fures defendunt vel effractores vel ceteri his similes nec quemquam percusserunt, metalli poena humiliores, honestiores vero relegatione adficiendi erunt.

[De effractoribus et expilatoribus].
2223.[138] De his, qui carcere effracto evaserunt, sumendum supplicium divi fratres Aemilio Tironi rescripserunt. Saturninus etiam probat in eos, qui de carcere eruperunt sive effractis foribus sive conspiratione cum ceteris, qui in eadem custodia erant, capite puniendos: quod si per neglegentiam custodum evaserunt, levius puniendos.[139] Expilatores, qui sunt atrociores fures (hoc enim est expilatores), in opus publicum vel perpetuum vel temporarium dari solent, honestiores autem ordine ad tempus moveri vel fines patriae iuberi excedere. Quibus nulla specialis poena rescriptis principalibus imposita est: idcirco causa cognita liberum erit arbitrium statuendi ei qui cognoscit. Simili modo et saccularī et derectarii erunt puniendi, item effractores. Sed enim divus Marcus effractorem equitem romanum, qui effracto perforatoque pariete pecuniam abstulerat, quinquennio abstinere iussit provincia Africa, unde erat, et urbe et Italia. Oportebit autem aeque et in effractores et in ceteros supra scriptos causa cognita statui, prout admissum suggerit, dummodo ne quis in plebeio operis publici poenam vel in honestiore relegationis excedat.

[De stellionatu].
2224.[140] Stellionatus accusatio ad praesidis cognitionem spectat. Stellionatum autem obici posse his, qui dolo quid fecerunt, sciendum est, scilicet si aliud crimen non sit quod obiciatur: quod enim in privatis iudiciis est de dolo actio, hoc in criminibus stellionatus persecutio. Ubicumque igitur titulus criminis deficit, illic stellionatus obiciemus. Maxime autem in his locum habet: si quis forte rem alii obligatam dissimulata obligatione per calliditatem alii distraxerit vel permutaverit vel in solutum dederit: nam hae omnes species stellionatum continent. Sed et si quis merces supposuerit vel obligatas averterit vel si corruperit, aeque stellionatus reus erit. Item si quis imposturam fecerit vel

---

137 Mommsen has *temporari*, following *Dig.* 47.17.1. Frakes reasonably prefers *temporarium*, with an explanation *ad loc.*

138 *Dig.* 47.18.1; cf. *Bas* 60.35.11.

139 = *Bas* 60.28.1.

140 *Dig.* 47.20.3; cf. *Bas* 60.30.2; *Bas* 11.2.47.

provided that in punishing them we ensure that the duration of hard labour does not exceed due measure. The same applies to thieves operating in public baths. However, if the thieves, burglars, or others like them defend themselves with a weapon but have not injured anyone, those of humble origin should be punished by relegation to the mines, while those of higher status should be punished by exile.

On prison breakers and plunderers.
2223. The deified brothers wrote in a rescript to Aemilius Tiro concerning those who escape from prison that they should be subjected to punishment. Saturninus also approves that those who break out of prison, either by breaking the gates or by conspiring with others who were in the same custody, should be punished by death: but if they escape through the negligence of the guards, they should be punished more leniently. Plunderers, who are more ferocious thieves (for this is what plunderers are), should be sentenced to hard labour either indefinitely or for a set period, while those of noble birth should be temporarily removed from their rank or ordered to leave the borders of their country. For these, no specific punishment is imposed by imperial rescripts. Therefore, after the case has been examined, the judge will have the discretion to decide. Similarly, swindlers and con artists should be punished like plunderers. The deified Marcus ordered that a Roman knight who was a burglar and stole money by breaking and piercing a wall should be kept away from Africa, where he was from, and from Rome and Italy for five years. It should equally be decided in the case of burglars and of others mentioned above based on an examination of the case, according to the offence committed, as long as no one exceeds the punishment of hard labour for a person of humble birth or relegation for a nobleman.

[On trickery].
2224. An accusation of trickery pertains to the jurisdiction of the provincial governor. It should be known that an accusation of trickery can be brought against those who have done something deceitfully, specifically if no other crime can be charged. For what is an action for deceit in private law is an accusation of trickery in criminal law. Therefore, wherever a crime's title is missing, we apply the charge of trickery. It particularly applies in cases such as: if someone deceitfully alienates an object that is under obligation by concealing the obligation, sells it, exchanges it, or gives it to a creditor instead of fulfilling a debt. All these actions fall under the category of trickery. Similarly, if someone

collusionem in necem alterius, stellionatus poterit postulari. Et ut generaliter dixerim, deficiente titulo criminis hoc crimen locum habet, nec est opus species enumerare. Poena autem stellionatus nulla legitima est, cum nec legitimum crimen sit. Solent autem ex hoc extra ordinem plecti, dummodo non debeat opus metalli haec poena in plebeis egredi. In his autem, qui sunt in aliquo honore positi, ad tempus relegatio vel ab ordine motio remittenda est. Qui merces suppressit, specialiter hoc crimine postulari potest.[141]

LIBER IX.

[De libertis coercendis].
2225.[142] Patronorum querellas adversus libertos praesides audire et non translaticie exsequi debent, cum, si ingratus libertus sit, non impune ferre eum oporteat. Sed si quidem inofficiosus patrono patronae liberisve eorum sit, tantummodo castigari eum sub comminatione aliqua severitatis non defuturae, si rursum causam[143] querellae praebuerit, et dimitti oportet. Enimvero si contumeliam fecit aut convicium eis dixit, etiam in exilium temporale dari debebit: quod si manus intulit, in metallum dandus erit: idem et si calumniam aliquam eis instruxit vel delatorem subornavit vel quam causam adversus eos temptavit.

[De saccularis].
2226.[144] Saccularii, qui vetitas in sacculos artes exercentes partem subducunt, partem subtrahunt, item qui derectarii appellantur, hoc est hi, qui in aliena cenacula se dirigunt furandi animo, plus quam fures puniendi sunt: idcircoque aut ad tempus in opus dantur publicum, aut fustibus castigantur et dimittuntur, aut ad tempus relegantur.

141 = *Bas* 60.30.3.
142 *Dig.* 37.14.1; cf. *Bas* 49.1.1.
143 causa F^{1}.
144 *Dig.* 47.11.7; cf. *Bas* 60.22.7.

substitutes obligated goods, diverts, or destroys them, he will be guilty of trickery. Likewise, if someone commits fraud or conspires to kill another, he could be accused of trickery. Generally speaking, as I mentioned, in the absence of a specific crime title, this charge applies, and it is not necessary to list all instances. There is no legitimate punishment for trickery because it is not a crime defined by law. However, those convicted of this are customarily punished outside the realm of the formulaic system, provided that the punishment does not extend to condemning people of humble origin to the mines. For those of higher status, temporary relegation or removal from their order is appropriate. Those who substitute commodities can be specifically prosecuted under this charge.

Book 9.

[On controlling freedmen]
2225. Governors must hear the complaints of patrons against their freedmen and must not handle them perfunctorily, for if a freedman is ungrateful, it is proper that he does not go unpunished. If a freedman is undutiful to his patron (whether male or female) or their children, he should be chastised under the threat of future severe punishment if he provides cause for complaint again, and then he should be dismissed. However, if he has insulted or verbally abused them, he should be sentenced to temporary exile. If he has committed physical violence, he should be condemned to the mines. The same applies if he has fabricated a slanderous accusation against them, suborned an accuser, or attempted any other charge against them.

[On swindlers].
2226. Swindlers (*saccularii*), who engage in prohibited and skilful practices, partly for the purpose of embezzling, partly for stealing, and those who are called *derectarii* – that is, those who direct themselves to the upper rooms of others with the intention of theft – should be punished more severely than thieves. They are therefore either given to hard labour for a set period, flogged and then released, or relegated for a set period.

[De praevaricatoribus].
2227.[145] Sciendum, quod hodie is, qui[146] praevaricati sunt,[147] poena iniungitur extraordinaria.

[De expilata hereditate].
2228.[148] Si expilatae hereditatis crimen intendatur, praeses provinciae cognitionem suam accommodare debet: cum enim furti agi non potest, solum superest auxilium praesidis. Apparet autem expilatae hereditatis crimen eo casu intendi posse, quo casu furti agi non potest, scilicet ante aditam hereditatem, vel post aditam antequam res ab herede possessae sunt. Nam in hunc casum furti actionem non competere palam est: quamvis ad exhibendum agi posse, si qui vindicaturus exhiberi desideret, palam sit.

De termino moto.
2229.[149] Eos qui terminos moverunt non inpune id facere debere divus Hadrianus Terentio Gentiano XVII k. Sept. se III consule rescripsit, quo rescripto poenam variam statuit. Verba rescripti ita se habent: '[Quin][150] Pessimum factum eorum [sit],[151] qui terminos finium causa positos abstulerunt, dubitari non potest. Poenae tamen modus ex condicione personae et mente facientis magis statui potest: nam si splendidiores sunt personae, quae convincuntur, non dubito quin occupandorum aliorum finium causa id admiserint: et possunt in tempus, ut cuiusque patitur aetas, relegari; [id est si iuvenior in longius, si senior recisius: si vero alii negotium gesserunt et ministerio functi sunt],[152] castigari et sic in biennium aut triennium ad opus publicum dari. Quod si per ignorantiam aut fortuito lapides usus causa furati sunt, sufficit eos verberibus coerceri.'

---

145 *Dig.* 47.15.2.
146 Omitted in F^1.
147 The syntactical ambiguity, where the main sentence is in the singular and the clause in plural is attested in all MSS and modern editions (cf. Lenel and Mommsen *ad loc.*).
148 *Dig.* 47.19.2; cf. *Bas* 60.29.2.
149 *Coll.* 13.3.
150 Unattested in MSS, but suggested by Lenel *ad loc.*
151 Unattested in MSS, but suggested by Lenel *ad loc.*
152 Frakes, following Mommsen, assumed that this note was a later gloss.

[On unfaithful advocates].
2227. It should be understood that, today, those who have engaged in collusion are subject to an extraordinary form of punishment.

[On spoliation of an inheritance].
2228. If a charge of spoliation of an inheritance is brought forward, the provincial governor should conduct the judicial inquiry, as an *actio furti* cannot be pursued, leaving only the governor's support. It is evident that a charge of spoliation of inheritance can be pursued in cases where an *actio furti* cannot be brought, namely before the inheritance is entered upon, or after, but before the goods has been taken into possession by the heir. For in this case, an *actio furti* is not applicable. It should be clear, though, that an action to display (*ad exhibendum*) can be pursued if the claimant needs the inheritance to be displayed.

On boundary lines removed.
2229. The deified Hadrian wrote in a rescript to Terentius Gentianus, on the 16th of August of his third consulate, that those who move boundary markers should not go unpunished, and in this rescript, he set a variable punishment. The words of this rescript are thus: 'It cannot be doubted that it is a most deplorable act for those who removed the stones set to mark boundaries. The mode of punishment, however, should be predominantly set according to the social status of the culprit and his state of mind. For if they are distinguished persons who are convicted, there is no doubt that they have done so to occupy the lands of others, and they can be relegated for a set period, as the age of each person permits [that is, longer for a younger person, shorter for an older one: if indeed others committed the deed and performed a duty, they should be castigated] and thus should be given two or three years of hard labour. But if they had stolen the stones to use them, unaware that they were boundary markers, it suffices that they are restrained by scourging.'

[De annona].
2230.[153] Lege Iulia de annona poena statuitur adversus eum, qui contra annonam fecerit societatemve coierit, quo annona carior fiat. Eadem lege continetur, ne quis navem nautamve retineat[154] aut dolo malo faciat, quo magis detineatur: Et poena viginti aureorum statuitur.

Ad legem Fabiam.
2231.[155] Frequens est etiam legis Fabiae cognitio in tribunalibus praesidum, quamquam [eam][156] quidam procuratores Caesaris usurpaverint tam in provinciis quam Romae. Sed enim iam eo perventum est constitutionibus, ut Romae quidem praefectus urbis solus super ea re cognoscat, si intra miliarium centesimum sit iniuria commissa: enimvero si ultra centesimum, praefectorum praetorio erit cognitio. In provincia est praesidum provinciarum, nec aliter procuratori Caesaris haec cognitio iniungitur, quam si praesidis partibus in provincia fungatur. Plane post sententiam de Fabia latam procuratoris partes succedunt huiusce rei. Attamen procurator qui nullam provinciam regit licet de capitalibus causis cognoscere nec soleat, tamen ut de lege Fabia possit cognoscere, imp. Antoninus constituit. Idem legis Iuliae de adulteris coercendis constitutione imperatoris Antonini quaestionem accepit. Lege autem Fabia tenetur, qui civem Romanum eumve, qui in Italia liberatus sit, celaverit vinxerit vinctumve habuerit, vendiderit emerit, quive in eam rem socius fuerit: cui capite primo eiusdem legis poena iniungitur. Si servus quis sciente domino fecerit, dominus eius sestertiis quinquaginta milibus eodem capite punitur. Eiusdem legis capite secundo tenetur, qui alieno servo persuaserit, ut dominum fugiat quive alienum servum invito domino celaverit vendiderit emerit dolo malo, quive in ea re socius fuerit: iubeturque populo sestertia quinquaginta milia dare. Et reliqua.

2232.[157] Sciendum est[158] legem Fabiam ad eos non pertinere, qui, cum absentes servos haberent, eos vendiderunt: aliud est enim abesse, aliud in fuga esse. Item non pertinere ad eum, qui mandavit servum fugitivum persequendum et distrahendum: nec enim fugam vendidit. Amplius dicendum est et si quis

153 *Dig.* 48.12.2; cf. *Bas* 60.44.2.
154 Mommsen suggested (in margins) *detineat*, based on the end of the sentence.
155 *Coll.* 14.3.
156 Lenel added *eam*, although unsupported by MSS.
157 *Dig.* 48.15.2; cf. *Bas* 60.48.1; *Ep.* 16.37.
158 Mommsen *ad loc.* assumed that the antecedent of this phrase is missing.

[On the grain supply].
2230. By the Julian Law concerning the grain supply, a punishment is set against anyone who acts against the grain supply or forms a society to make the grain supply more expensive. The same law stipulates that no one shall retain a ship or a sailor, or act with malicious intent to cause further delay. A penalty of twenty gold coins is set.

Concerning the Fabian law.
2231. The judicial inquiry of the Fabian Law often falls within the jurisdiction of the provincial governors' courts, although some imperial procurators have taken it upon themselves, both in the provinces and in Rome. However, it is established by imperial constitutions that in Rome, only the urban prefect has jurisdiction over this matter, if the crime is committed within one hundred miles. If it is beyond one hundred miles, the jurisdiction will belong to the praetorian prefect. In the provinces, the provincial governors have jurisdiction, and it is only assigned to the imperial procurator if he is acting in the capacity of a governor in the province. Clearly, after a judgement regarding the Fabian Law has been issued, the duties of the procurator follow. However, even a procurator who does not govern a province may preside over capital cases, although he generally refrains from doing so, and he may preside over cases under the Fabian Law according to a constitution of Emperor Antoninus. Similarly, regarding the Julian Law on the Suppression of Adultery, the procurator can hold an inquiry due to a constitution of Emperor Antoninus. Under the Fabian Law, a person is liable if he conceals, subdues, or has in subjugation a Roman citizen or someone who has been manumitted in Italy; if he buys or sells such a person, or if he is associated with such an act: the punishment for this is specified in the first chapter of the law. If a slave does this with the knowledge of his master, the master is punished by the same chapter with a fine of 50,000 sestertii. Under the second chapter of the law, a person is liable if he persuades another's slave to flee from his master, or if he conceals another's slave against the master's will, buys or sells another person's slave fraudulently, or if he is involved in such acts: he is ordered to pay 50,000 sestertii to the public. And so forth.

2232. It should be known that the Fabian Law does not pertain to those who, while having absent slaves, sold them. For it is one thing for a slave to be absent and another to be a fugitive. Likewise, this law does not pertain to a person who instructed that a runaway slave be pursued and sold, for they did not sell a fugitive. Furthermore, it should be stated that if someone ordered

Titio mandaverit servum fugitivum adprehendendum, ut, si adprehendisset, eum emptum haberet, cessare senatus consultum. Hoc autem senatus consulto domini quoque continentur, qui fugam servorum suorum vendiderunt.

[De variis delictis].
2233.[159] Sunt praeterea crimina, quae ad executionem praesidis pertinent: ut puta si quis instrumenta sua prodita esse dicat: nam huius rei executio praefecto urbis a divis fratribus data est.

2234.[160] Sunt quaedam, quae more prouinciarum coercitionem solent admittere: ut puta in prouincia Arabia σκοπελισμὸν crimen appellant, cuius rei admissum tale est: plerique inimicorum solent praedium inimici[161] σκοπελίζειν, id est lapides ponere indicio futuros, quod, si quis eum agrum coluisset, malo leto periturus esset insidiis eorum, qui scopulos posuissent: quae res tantum timorem habet, ut nemo ad eum agrum accedere audeat crudelitatem timens eorum qui scopelismon fecerunt. hanc rem praesides exequi solent grauiter usque ad poenam capitis, quia et ipsa res mortem comminatur.

2235.[162] In Aegypto qui chomata rumpit vel dissolvit (hi sunt aggeres, qui quidem[163] solent aquam niloticam continere), aeque plectitur extra ordinem: et pro condicione sua et pro admissi mensura quidam opere publico, alii autem metallo plectuntur, et metallo quidem secundum suam dignitatem. Si quis arborem sycaminonem exciderit, nam et haec res vindicatur extra ordinem non levi poena, idcirco quod hae arbores colligunt aggeres niloticos, per quos incrementa nili dispensantur et coercentur. Et deminutiones aeque coercentur: chomata etiam et diacopi, qui in aggeribus fiunt, plecti efficiunt eos, qui id admiserint.

[De exhibitione reorum].
2236.[164] Si quis reum criminis, pro quo satisdedit, non exhibuerit, poena pecuniaria plectitur. Puto tamen, si dolo non exhibeat, etiam extra ordinem esse damnandum. Sed si neque in cautione neque in decreto praesidis certa

159 *Dig.* 47.11.8; cf. *Bas* 60.22.8.
160 *Dig.* 47.11.9; cf. *Bas* 60.22.9.
161 Lenel assumed that this word is a gloss.
162 *Dig.* 47.11.10; cf. *BS.* 60.51.15 sch. 11.
163 quidem] ibidem? Mommsen 1870 *ad loc.*
164 *Dig.* 48.3.4; cf. *Bas* 60.35.4.

Titius to apprehend a fugitive slave so that, once apprehended, he would be considered purchased, the senatus consultum is irrelevant. By this senatus consultum, slave owners who sold their runaway slaves are also included.

[On various delicts].
2233. There are also crimes that pertain to the jurisdiction of the provincial governor: for example, if someone claims that his documents have been disclosed. The jurisdiction for this matter has been given to the urban prefect by the deified brothers.

2234. There are certain crimes for which the customs of the provinces are accustomed to permit coercion. For example, in the province of Arabia they call by the name of 'skopelismos', a crime whose nature is as follows: Often, enemies tend to 'skopelise' the estate of their enemies – that is, they place stones as a warning, indicating that if anyone were to cultivate that land they would meet a cruel death by the ambushes of those who placed these rocks. This matter instils so much fear that no one dares to approach that land, fearing the cruelty of those who have committed skopelismos. Governors are accustomed to enforcing this matter severely, even to the extent of capital punishment, because the act itself threatens death.

2235. In Egypt, anyone who breaks or dismantles embankments (which indeed contain Nile water) is equally punished by the governor: some, depending on their status and the severity of the offence, are assigned public works, while others are sentenced to the mines, the severity of their punishment corresponding to their rank. If someone cuts down a sycamore tree, such an act is also punished severely, as these trees reinforce Nile embankments, crucial for regulating and restraining the Nile's floods. Similarly, offences involving the breaking or cutting of embankments and sluices are punished.

[On producing accused persons].
2236. If anyone fails to produce the defendant accused of a crime for whom he provided security, he is punished with a fine. However, if he fails to deliver him intentionally, he should be prosecuted by the governor. But if neither a specific

quantitas comprehensa est, ac nec consuetudo ostenditur, quae certam formam habet, praeses de modo pecuniae, quae inferri oporteat, statuet.

[De poenis 1.]
2237.[165] Si quis forte, ne supplicio adficiatur, dicat se habere quod principi referat salutis ipsius causa, an remittendum[166] sit ad eum, videndum est. Et sunt plerique praesidum tam timidi, ut etiam post sententiam de eo dictam poenam sustineant nec quicquam audiant: alii omnino non patiuntur quicquam tale allegantes: nonnulli neque semper neque numquam remittunt, sed inquirunt, quid sit, quod allegare principi velint quidque quod pro salute ipsius habeant dicere, post quae aut sustinent poenam aut non sustinent. Quod videtur habere mediam rationem. Ceterum, ut mea fert opinio, prorsus eos non debuisse, posteaquam semel damnati sunt, audiri, quidquid allegent. Quis enim dubitat eludendae poenae causa ad haec eos decurrere magisque esse puniendos, qui tamdiu conticuerunt, quod pro salute principis habere se dicere iactant? Nec enim debebant tam magnam rem tam diu reticere.

2238.[167] Si quos comitum vel legati sui reos proconsul invenerit, utrum punire eos debeat an successori servare, quaeri potest. Sed multa exstant exempla, quae non tantum officialium suorum nec sub se agentium, verum suos quoque servos poena adfecerunt: quod quidem faciendum est, ut exemplo deterriti minus delinquant.

2239.[168] Nunc genera poenarum nobis enumeranda sunt, quibus praesides adficere quemque possint. Et sunt poenae, quae aut vitam adimant aut servitutem iniungant aut civitatem auferant aut exilium aut coercitionem corporis contineant.[169] Aut damnum cum infamia aut dignitatis aliquam depositionem aut alicuius actus prohibitionem.

2240.[170] Vita adimitur, ut puta si damnatur aliquis, ut gladio in eum animadvertatur. Sed animadverti gladio oportet, non securi vel telo vel fusti vel laqueo

---

165 *Dig.* 48.19.6.pr; cf. *Bas* 60.51.6.
166 MSS has *remittendum*. Mommsen suggested (in margins) *remittendus* on the basis of *BS. ad loc.*
167 *Dig.* 48.19.6.1; cf. *Bas* 60.51.6.
168 *Dig.* 48.19.6.2 and 48.19.8.pr; cf. *Bas* 60.51.6, 8.
169 = *Dig.* 48.19.6.8.
170 *Dig.* 48.19.8.1–3; cf. *Bas* 60.51.8.

amount is specified in the security nor in the governor's decree, and if there is no established custom with a clear form, the governor shall determine the amount of pecuniary penalty that should be imposed.

[On punishments 1].
2237. If someone, to avoid punishment, claims to have something to report to the emperor for his own safety, whether it should be referred to the emperor must be considered. Many governors are so timid that even after a verdict has been passed on the accused, they delay the execution of the sentence and do not hear anything. Others completely refuse to allow any such allegation. Some neither always nor never allow it, but inquire what they wish to report to the princeps and what they have to say for his safety; thereafter, they either delay the punishment or do not delay it. This seems to strike a middle ground. However, in my opinion, once they are convicted, they should not be heard regarding whatever they claim to report. Who doubts that they rush to report it to evade punishment and that those who have remained silent for so long should be punished more severely for boasting about what they claim to have for the safety of the princeps? They should not have kept silent about such an important matter for so long.

2238. If the proconsul finds any of his attendants or his legate's associates guilty, it can be questioned whether he should punish them or leave them for his successor. Indeed, there are many examples where they have subjected not only their officials and subordinates but also their own slaves to punishment. This should be done so that others, deterred by the example, commit fewer offences.

2239. Now we must enumerate the kinds of punishment by which governors can affect anyone. There are penalties that either take life, impose slavery, revoke citizenship, or include exile or corporal punishment. Or [punishments that involve] loss with infamy, deposition from a position of dignity, or prohibition from certain actions.

2240. Life is taken away, for example, if someone is condemned to be executed by the sword. But it is necessary that the punishment be carried out by the sword, not by an axe, or a spear, or a club, or a noose, or in any other way.

vel quo alio modo. Proinde nec liberam mortis facultatem concedendi ius praesides habent. Multo enim vel veneno necandi. Divi tamen fratres rescripserunt permittentes liberam mortis facultatem. Hostes autem, item transfugae ea poena adficiuntur, ut vivi exurantur. Nec ea quidem poena damnari quem oportet, ut verberibus necetur vel virgis interematur, nec tormentis: quamvis plerique dum torquentur deficere solent.

[171] Corpora eorum qui capite damnantur cognatis ipsorum neganda non sunt: et id se observasse etiam divus Augustus libro decimo de vita sua scribit. Hodie autem eorum, in quos animadvertitur, corpora non aliter sepeliuntur, quam si fuerit petitum et permissum, et nonnumquam non permittitur, maxime maiestatis causa damnatorum. Eorum quoque corpora, qui exurendi damnantur, peti possunt, scilicet ut ossa et cineres collecta sepulturae tradi possint.[172]

2241.[173] Est poena, quae adimat libertatem: huiusmodi ut puta, si quis in metallum vel in opus metalli damnetur. Metalla autem multa numero sunt et quaedam quidem provinciae habent, quaedam non habent: sed quae non habent, in eas provincias mittunt, quae metalla habent. Praefecto plane urbi specialiter competere ius in metallum damnandi ex epistula divi Severi ad Fabium Cilonem exprimitur. Inter eos autem, qui in metallum et eos, qui in opus metalli damnantur, differentia in vinculis tantum est, quod qui in metallum damnantur, gravioribus vinculis premuntur, qui in opus metalli, levioribus, quodque refugae ex opere metalli in metallum dantur, ex metallo gravius coercentur. Quisquis autem in opus publicum damnatus refugit, duplicato tempore damnari solet: sed duplicare eum id temporis oportet, quod ei cum superesset fugit, scilicet ne illud duplicetur, quo adprehensus in carcere fuit. Plane si decennio damnatus fuit et initio statim fugit, videndum est, utrum duplicari ei tempora debeant, an vero perpetuari vel transferri in opus metalli: et magis est, ut transferatur aut perpetuetur. Generaliter enim dicitur, quotiens decennium excessura est duplicatio, non esse tempore poenam artandam. In ministerium metallicorum feminae in perpetuum vel ad tempus damnari solent. Simili modo et in salinas. Et si quidem in perpetuum fuerint damnatae, quasi servae poenae constituuntur: si vero ad tempus damnantur, retinent civitatem. Solent praesides in carcere continendos damnare aut ut in vinculis contineantur: sed id eos facere non oportet. Nam huiusmodi poenae interdictae

---

171 *Dig.* 48.24.1.

172 Cf. *Bas* 60.69.1.

173 *Dig.* 48.19.8.4–13; cf. *Bas* 60.51.8.

Thus, the governors do not have the right to grant permission for a voluntary death. Indeed, not even by poison. However, the divine brothers (the emperors) issued a rescript permitting the freedom to choose death. Enemies, as well as deserters, are punished by being burned alive. Nor is it appropriate that anyone be condemned to a punishment whereby they are killed by beatings or scourging, or by torture, although many tend to die while being tortured.

The bodies of those condemned to death should not be denied to their relatives, as even the deified Augustus writes in the tenth book of his life. However, today the bodies of those punished are not buried unless it has been requested and permitted, and sometimes permission is not granted, especially in the case of those condemned for offences of treason. Also, the bodies of those condemned to be burned can be requested, namely so that their bones and ashes may be handed over for burial after being collected.

2241. There is a punishment that deprives of liberty. An example of such punishment: if someone is condemned to the mines or to labour in a mine. There are many mines, some provinces have them, others do not. However, those that do not have them send [the accused] to those that do. It is clearly stated in a letter from the deified Severus to Fabius Cilo that the power to condemn to the mines specifically belongs to the urban prefect. The difference in fetters between those condemned to the mines and those sentenced to labour in a mine is as follows: those condemned to the mines endure heavier chains, while those sentenced to labour in a mine have lighter ones. Fugitives among those sentenced to labour in a mine are condemned to the mines, and fugitives among those condemned to the mines are subjected to even harsher punishment. Anyone who escapes after being sentenced to public works is usually sentenced to double the time, but this doubling should only apply to the time that was remaining when the escape occurred. It is clear that the time spent in prison should not be included in this calculation. If someone has been sentenced to ten years and escapes right at the beginning, it must be determined whether the sentence should be doubled, extended indefinitely, or if they should be transferred to labour in a mine, but it is preferable for them to be transferred or for the sentence to become perpetual. It is generally understood that once the doubling exceeds ten years, the punishment cannot be limited by time. Women are also often condemned to the mines, either permanently or for a specified period, and similarly to salt mines. If they are condemned permanently, they become quasi-slave women due to this punishment. Governors are accustomed to sentencing those who should be held in custody or even those who should be put in chains, but they should refrain from doing so. Such punishments are sunt: carcer enim ad continendos homines, non ad puniendos haberi debet. In calcariam quoque vel sulpurariam damnari solent: sed hae poenae metalli magis sunt. Quicumque in ludum venatorium fuerint damnati, videndum est, an servi poenae efficiantur: solent enim iuniores hac poena adfici. Utrum ergo servi poenae isti efficiantur an retineant libertatem, videndum est. Et magis est, ut hi quoque servi efficiantur: hoc enim distant a ceteris, quod instituuntur venatores aut pyrricharii aut aliam quam voluptatem, gesticulandi, vel aliter se movendi gratia. Servos in metallum vel in opus metalli, item in ludum venatorium dari solere nulla dubitatio est: et si fuerint dati, servi poenae efficiuntur nec ad eum pertinebunt, cuius fuerint antequam damnarentur. Denique cum quidam servus in metallum damnatus beneficio principis esset iam poena liberatus, imperator Antoninus rectissime rescripsit, quia semel domini esse desierat servus poenae factus, non esse eum in potestatem domini postea reddendum. Sed sive in perpetua vincula fuerit damnatus servus sive in temporalia, eius remanet, cuius fuit, antequam damnaretur.

2242.[174] Inter poenas est etiam insulae deportatio, quae poena adimit civitatem Romanam. Deportandi autem in insulam ius praesidibus provinciae non est datum, licet praefecto urbi detur: hoc enim epistula divi Severi ad Fabium Cilonem praefectum urbi expressum est. Praesides itaque provinciae quotiens aliquem in insulam deportandum putent, hoc ipsum adnotare debeant, nomen vero eius[175] scribendum principi, ut in insulam deportetur: sic deinde principi scribere missa plena opinione, ut princeps aestimet, an sequenda sit eius sententia deportarique in insulam debeat. Medio [modo] autem tempore, dum scribitur, iubere eum debet in carcere esse. Decuriones civitatium propter capitalia crimina deportandos vel relegandos divi fratres rescripserunt. Denique Priscum in homicidio et incendio nominatim ante quaestionem confessum in insulam deportari iusserunt.

174 *Dig.* 48.22.6; cf. *Bas* 60.54.6.

175 The obscure syntax led Mommsen to add this comment: *adnotare debent nomine eius*?

prohibited: prison should be used for containment, not punishment. Governors also often sentence to limestone quarries or sulphur quarries, but these punishments essentially equate to condemnation to the mines. Those sentenced to hunting games must be examined to determine whether they are treated as punishment slaves: usually, young individuals are subjected to this punishment. It should be investigated whether they become punishment slaves or retain their freedom. In most cases, they are indeed made punishment slaves, as this differs from others who choose to be hunters or professional dancers, or pursue other forms of pleasure through gestures or movements. There is no doubt that slaves can be sentenced to the mines, labour in a mine, or assigned to hunting games, and if they are assigned, they do not revert to their former owner once condemned. Finally, if a slave who had been sentenced to the mines is granted clemency by the emperor, Emperor Antoninus recently wrote in a rescript that because the slave ceased to belong to his master after being sentenced, he should not be returned to the power of his master afterward, whether sentenced indefinitely or for a set period.

2242. Amongst the punishments, there is also deportation to an island, which deprives [the individual] of Roman citizenship. However, the right of deporting to an island was not granted to provincial governors, although it was granted to the urban prefect, as explicitly stated in an epistle of the deified Severus to the urban prefect Fabius Cilo. Therefore, whenever provincial governors consider deporting someone to an island, they must make note of this decision; the individual's name should be sent in writing to the emperor for approval to be deported to an island. Subsequently, once the full case has been written and sent to the emperor, he will evaluate whether the sentence should be followed and whether deportation to an island is warranted. In the meantime, during the writing process, the governor should order that the individual remains in jail. The deified brothers wrote in a rescript that municipal decurions must be deported or relegated for capital crimes. Finally, in the case of Priscus, who had confessed to murder and arson before the inquiry, they ordered his deportation to an island.

LIBER X.

[De poenis 2.]
2243.[176] Relegatorum duo genera: sunt quidam, qui in insulam relegantur, sunt, qui simpliciter, ut provinciis eis interdicatur, non etiam insula adsignetur. In insulam relegare praesides provinciae possunt, sic tamen, ut, si quidem insulam sub se habeant (id est ad eius provinciae formam pertinentem, quam administrant), et eam specialiter insulam adsignare possint inque eam relegare, sin vero non habeant, pronuntient quidem in insulam se relegare, scribant autem imperatori, ut ipse insulam adsignet. Ceterum non possunt damnare in eam insulam, quam in ea provincia cui praesunt non habeant. Interim quoad imperator insulam adsignet, militi tradendus est relegatus. Haec est differentia inter deportatos et relegatos, quod in insulam relegari et ad tempus et in perpetuum quis potest. Sive ad tempus sive in perpetuum quis fuerit relegatus, et civitatem Romanam retinet et testamenti factionem non amittit. Ad tempus relegatis neque tota bona neque partem adimi debere rescriptis quibusdam manifestatur, reprehensaeque sunt sententiae eorum, qui ad tempus relegatis ademerunt partem bonorum vel bona, sic tamen, ut non infirmarentur sententiae quae ita sunt prolatae. Est quoddam genus quasi in insulam relegationis in provincia Aegypto in Oasin relegare. Sicut autem relegare in insulam quisquam, quae non est sub se, non potest, ita ne in provinciam quidem relegandi ius habet, quae non est sub se: forte praeses Syriae in Macedoniam non relegabit. Sed extra provinciam suam potest relegare. Item in parte certa provinciae moraturum relegare potest, ut forte non excedat civitatem aliquam vel regionem aliquam non egrediatur. Sed et in eas partes provinciae, quae sunt desertiores, scio praesides solitos relegare. Interdicere autem quis ea provincia potest quam regit, alia non potest: et ita divi fratres rescripserunt. Unde eveniebat, ut, qui relegatus esset ab ea provincia, in qua domicilium[177] habuit, morari apud orginem suam posset. Sed imperator noster cum divo patre suo huic rei providerunt. Maecio enim Probo praesidi provinciae Hispaniae rescripserunt etiam ea provincia interdici, unde quis oriundus est, ab eo qui regit eam provinciam, ubi quis domicilium habet. Sed et eos, qui, cum incolae non essent, in ea provincia quid admiserint, aequum est ad rescripti auctoritatem pertinere. Dubitatum est, an interdicere quis alicui possit provincia, in qua oriundus est, cum ipse ei provinciae praesit, quam incolit, dum sua non interdicit, ut solent Italia interdicere, qui

176 *Dig.* 48.22.7.pr.-19; cf. *Bas* 60.54.7.

177 Although MSS has *domilium*, that must be a corruption of the original *domicilium*.

Book 10.

2243. There are two types of those who are relegated: some are relegated to an island, while others are simply banned from the provinces without being assigned to any specific island. The governors of provinces can relegate someone to an island, provided that if they have an island under their jurisdiction (that is, one that belongs to the territory of the province they govern), they can specifically assign that island and relegate the person to it. If they do not have an island, they should pronounce that they are relegating the person to an island, but then write to the emperor, so that he may assign an island. However, they cannot condemn someone to an island that is not within the province they govern. Meanwhile, until the emperor assigns an island, the relegated person is to be handed over to the soldiers.

This is the difference between those who are deported and those who are relegated: persons can be relegated to an island either for a certain period of time or permanently. Whether someone is relegated temporarily or permanently, they retain their Roman citizenship and do not lose the right to make a will. It is made clear in some rescripts that those who are temporarily relegated should not have all or part of their property taken away, and the judgements of those who have deprived temporarily relegated persons of part or all of their property have been criticised, though the judgements that have already been issued are not invalidated. There is a type of relegation similar to relegation to an island in the province of Egypt, which is relegation to the Oasis. Just as one cannot relegate someone to an island that is not under their jurisdiction, so too does one not have the right to relegate someone to a province that is not under their control. For instance, a governor of Syria cannot relegate someone to Macedonia. However, they can relegate someone outside their province. Similarly, they can relegate someone to a specific part of a province, so they do not exceed a certain city or region. I know that governors have also been accustomed to relegating people to the more deserted parts of a province. A person can only ban from the province he governs, not from another province, as the divine brothers have decreed in their rescripts. Therefore, it has occurred that someone who was relegated from the province where he had his residence could stay in his place of origin. But our emperor, together with his divine father, has provided for this matter. For they have decreed to Maecius Probus, governor of the province of Hispania, that it is also permissible to ban someone from the province of their origin by the authority of the governor of the province where they have their residence. It is also fair that those who, though not residents, have committed an offence in a certain province, should fall under the authority of the rescript.

patria non interdicunt: vel an per consequentias videatur etiam provinciae interdixisse, cui praeest. Quod magis erit probandum. Per contrarium autem is, qui originis provinciae praeest, non est nanctus ius interdicendi ea provincia, quam incolit is qui relegatur. Si quis eam sententiam admiserit, ut is, qui in alia provincia commisit, possit relegari ab eo qui ei provinciae praeest: eveniet, ut relegatus iste tribus provinciis praeter Italiam debeat abstinere, et in qua deliquit et quam incolit et originis. Et si ex diversis provinciis oriri videatur propter condicionem vel suam vel parentis patronorum: vel pluribus provinciis consequenter interdictum ei dicemus. Quibusdam tamen praesidibus, ut multis provinciis interdicere possint, indultum est: ut praesidibus Syriarum, sed et Daciarum. Constitutum eum, cui patria interdictum est, etiam urbe abstinere debere: contra autem si cui urbe fuerit interdictum, patria sua interdictum non videtur. Et ita multis constitutionibus cavetur. Si cui plane non patria sua, sed aliqua civitate interdictum sit, videndum est, an etiam patria sua itemque urbe interdictum dicamus: quod magis est. His, qui relegantur, dies excedendi a praesidibus dari et potest et solet: etenim moris est ita pronuntiari 'illum provincia illa insulisque eis relego excedereque debebit intra illum diem'. Relegatum plane libellum dare principi posse divi fratres rescripserunt. Solet praeterea interdici sententia quibusdam, ne intra patriae territorium vel muros morentur: ne excedant patriam vel in vicis quibusdam morentur.

2244.[178] Solet decurionibus ordine interdici vel ad tempus vel in perpetuum. Item potest alicui poena iniungi, ne honores adipiscatur: nec ea res facit, ut decurio esse desinat, cum fieri possit, ut quis decurio quidem sit, ad honores autem non admittatur. nam et senator quis esse potest et tamen honores non repetere. Potest alicui et unus honor interdici, sic tamen, ut, si cui honore uno interdictum sit, non tantum eum honorem petere non possit, verum ne eos quoque, qui eo honore maiores sunt: est enim perquam ridiculum eum, qui minoribus poenae causa prohibitus sit, ad maiores adspirare. Maioribus tamen prohibitus minores petere non prohibetur. Sed muneribus si quis poenae

178 *Dig.* 48.22.7.20–22; cf. *Bas* 60.54.7.

There was doubt as to whether someone could be banned from the province of their origin if they are the governor of the province they inhabit, as long as they do not ban themselves, as those who ban people from Italy without banning them from their homeland usually do: or whether, by implication, it seems that they have also banned them from the province they govern. The latter view is more acceptable. On the other hand, the governor of the province of origin does not have the right to ban someone from the province they inhabit. If someone accepts this opinion, that the one who committed an offence in another province can be relegated by the governor of that province, it will result in the relegated person being required to stay away from three provinces, excluding Italy: the one in which they committed the offence, the one they inhabit, and the one of their origin. And if they seem to originate from different provinces due to their own or their parents' or patrons' circumstances, we will say that multiple provinces are consequently interdicted to them. However, some governors, such as those of Syria and Dacia, have been granted the right to ban someone from multiple provinces. It is established that someone who has been banned from their homeland must also abstain from the city: conversely, if someone has been banned from the city, it does not seem that they are also banned from their homeland. This is provided for in many constitutions. If someone is banned not from their homeland but from a certain city, it must be considered whether they are also banned from their homeland and the city as well: this is more likely. The governors can and usually do set a date by which the relegated person must leave. For it is customary to pronounce, 'I banish that person from that province and its islands, and they must leave by this date.' The divine brothers have decreed that a relegated person can certainly submit a petition to the emperor. Moreover, it is common to include in the judgement that certain individuals are prohibited from residing within the territory or walls of their homeland: they are not to exceed their homeland or reside in certain villages.

2244. It is customary for decurions to be banned from their rank either for a set period or in perpetuity. Similarly, punishment can be inflicted upon someone to prevent him from aspiring to honours. But this does not mean he ceases to be a decurion, as it is possible for someone to be a decurion but not to be admitted to honours. Indeed, one can be a senator and yet not hold honours. A particular honour can be interdicted from someone in such a way that, if he is forbidden from one honour, he cannot seek that honour, nor any honours greater than it. It is highly illogical that someone prohibited from minor honours due to punishment should aspire to greater ones. However, being prohibited from greater honours does not prevent someone from seeking minor ones. If someone causa fuerit prohibitus, nihil valebit sententia: neque enim immunitatem poena tribuere debet. Ergo et si honoribus quis in poenam fuerit prohibitus, poterit dici, si honores isti habuerunt mixtam muneris gravem impensam, infamiam illi ad hoc non profuturam.

2245.[179] Potest praeses quendam damnare, ne domo sua procedat.

2246.[180] Moris est advocationibus quoque praesides interdicere. Et nonnumquam in perpetuum interdicunt, nonnumquam ad tempus vel annis metiuntur vel etiam tempore quo provinciam regunt. Nec non ita quoque interdici potest alicui, ne certis personis adsit. Potest et ita interdici cui, ne apud tribunal praesidis postulet, et tamen apud legatum vel procuratorem non prohibetur agere. Si tamen apud legatum prohibitus fuerit postulare, credo per consequentias ne quidem apud praesidem relictam illi postulandi facultatem. Nonnumquam non advocationibus cui interdicitur, sed foro. Plus est autem foro quam advocationibus interdicere, si quidem huic omnino forensibus negotiis accommodare se non permittatur. Solet autem ita vel iuris studiosis interdici vel advocatis vel tabellionibus sive pragmaticis. Solet et ita interdici, ne instrumenta omnino forment neve libellos concipiant vel testationes consignent. Solet et sic, ne eo loci sedeant, quo in publico instrumenta deponuntur, archio [archivo] forte vel grammatophylacio. Solet et sic, ut testamenta ne ordinent vel scribant vel signent. Erit et illa poena, ne quis negotiis publicis interveniat: hic enim privatis quidem interesse poterit, publicis prohibebitur, ut solent quibus sententia praecipitur δημοσίων ἀπέχεσθαι.

2247.[181] Sunt autem et aliae poenae: si negotiatione quis abstinere iubeatur vel ad conductionem eorum quae publice locantur accedere, ut ad vectigalia publica. Interdici autem negotiatione plerumque vel negotiationibus solet: sed damnare, ut quis negotietur, an possit videamus. Et sunt quidem hae poenae, si quis generaliter tractare velit, inciviles invitum hominem iubere facere quod facere non potest: sed si quis specialiter tractaverit, potest esse iusta causa compellendi cuius ad negotiationem: quod si fuerit, sequenda erit sententia.

---

179 *Dig.* 48.22.9; cf. *Bas* 60.54.9.

180 *Dig.* 48.19.9.pr.-8; cf. *Bas* 60.51.9.

181 *Dig.* 48.19.9.9–10.

is prohibited from *munera* due to punishment, the sentence will be void, as punishment should not grant immunity. Therefore, if someone is prohibited from honours due to punishment, it can be said that, if these honours entail significant public service, infamy will not benefit him in this instance.

2245. The governor can order a person not to leave his/her home.

2246. Provincial governors also have the authority to forbid someone from practising advocacy. This prohibition can be in perpetuity or for a set period, measured either in years or for the duration of their governance of the province. Additionally, someone can be forbidden from assisting certain persons. Thus, a person may be prohibited from pleading before the governor's tribunal but still allowed to pursue matters before a legate or a procurator. However, if one is banned from pleading before a legate, I believe that, by extension, they would also be prohibited from pleading before the governor. Sometimes, a person is banned not just from advocacy but from the forum itself. Being excluded from the forum is more severe than being excluded from advocacy, as it means the person is entirely barred from participating in any public affairs. It is also customary to ban law students, advocates, notaries, and those skilled in business. They are often prohibited from forming public records, drafting petitions, or attesting to witnesses. Furthermore, they are barred from residing in places where public records are kept, such as archives or record offices. They are also prohibited from organising, writing, or signing wills. There is also a punishment that forbids someone from intervening in public matters. Such individuals can attend to private matters but are barred from public matters, like those who are ordered by a verdict to refrain from public affairs.

2247. There are also other punishments: for instance, someone might be ordered to abstain from commercial activities or from participating in the leasing of public properties, such as public revenues. It is customary to be banned from commerce altogether or only from certain branches of commerce. However, let us examine whether it is possible to condemn someone to engage in commercial activity. Generally speaking, these punishments are uncivil, as it is unreasonable to force someone to do what they cannot do against their will. However, if considered in detail, there can be a just cause for compelling someone to engage in commercial activity. If such a specific case arises, the judgement should be followed.

2248.[182] Interdum pecuniaria poena irrogatur iis qui relegatos suscipiunt: interdum etiam ipsi relegantur, si quidem illi ob magnum crimen relegati sunt.

2249.[183] Istae fere sunt poenae quae iniungi solent. Sed enim sciendum est discrimina esse poenarum neque omnes eadem poena adfici posse. Nam in primis decuriones in metallum damnari non possunt nec in opus metalli, nec furcae subici vel vivi exuri. Et si forte huiusmodi sententia fuerint affecti, liberandi erunt: sed hoc non potest efficere qui sententiam dixit, verum referre ad principem debet, ut ex auctoritate eius poena aut permutetur aut liberaretur. Parentes quoque et liberi decurionum in eadem causa sunt. Liberos non tantum filios accipere debemus, verum omnes liberos. Sed utrum hi soli, qui post decurionatum suscepti sunt, his poenis non adficiantur, an vero omnes omnino liberi, etiam in plebeia familia suscepti, videndum est: et magis puto omnibus prodesse debere. Plane si parens decurio esse desierit, si quidem iam decurione fuerit editus, proderit ei, ne adficiatur: enimvero si posteaquam plebeius factus est tunc suscipiat filium, quasi plebeio editus ita erit plectendus. Statuliberum quasi liberum iam puniendum divus Pius Salvio Marciano rescripsit.

2250.[184] Divus Hadrianus Aquilio Braduae ita rescripsit: 'Panniculariae causa quemadmodum intellegi debeat, ex ipso nomine apparet. Non enim bona damnatorum pannicularia significari quis probe dixerit, nec, si zonam circa se habuerit, protinus aliquis sibi vindicare debebit: sed vestem qua is fuerit indutus, aut nummulos in ventralem, quos victus sui causa in promptu habuerit, aut leves anulos, id est quae rem non excedit <HSV>.[185] alioquin si quis damnatus digito habuerit aut sardonychica aut aliam gemmam magni pretii vel si quod chirographum magnae pecuniae in sinu habuerit, nullo iure illud in pannicularia ratione retinebitur.' Pannicularia sunt ea, quae in custodiam receptus secum attulit: spolia, quibus indutus est, cum quis ad supplicium ducitur, ut et ipsa appellatio ostendit. Ita neque speculatores ultro sibi vindicent neque optiones ea desiderent, quibus spoliatur, quo momento quis punitus est.[186] hanc[187] rationem non compendio suo debent praesides vertere, sed nec

---

182 *Dig.* 48.22.11. As noted by Lenel, this text is absent from *F.* and is supplemented by *Bas* 60.54.11.
183 *Dig.* 48.19.9.11–16.
184 *Dig.* 48.20.6; cf. *Bas* 60.52.6.
185 Lenel suggested emending to HSV.
186 Lenel questioned whether this phrase is a gloss.
187 Mommsen and Lenel have a comma after *est*, not a full stop.

2248. At times, a pecuniary punishment is inflicted upon those who receive the relegated; at other times, they themselves are relegated, if indeed those they received were relegated for a major crime.

2249. These are approximately the punishments that are usually applied. However, it should be known that there are different kinds of punishment and not everyone can be subjected to the same punishment. For instance, decurions cannot be condemned to the mines or to hard labour in a mine; they cannot be subjected to the fork or burned alive. If, by chance, they have been subjected to such a sentence, they must be released; but this cannot be done by the person who passed the sentence. Instead, he must refer the matter to the emperor so that the punishment can be either changed or annulled by the emperor's authority. Parents and children of decurions are treated similarly. We should understand 'children' to mean not only sons but all offspring. Whether this protection applies only to those born after the parent became a decurion or to all children, including those born into a plebeian family, should be considered. I believe it should benefit all children. Clearly, if a parent ceases to be a decurion, if the child was born while the parent was still a decurion, the protection remains; but if the child was born after the parent became a plebeian, the child will be treated as a plebeian. The deified Pius wrote in a rescript to Salvius Marcianus that a statuliber (a slave conditionally freed) should be punished as if he were already free.

2250. The deified Hadrian wrote in a rescript to Aquilius Bradua: 'What should be understood by the term "pannicularia" is apparent from the name itself. For one could not properly say that the assets of the condemned mean "pannicularia"', nor, if someone wears a belt, should anyone immediately claim it for himself. Rather, it refers to the clothes in which he is dressed, the coins in his belt used for his sustenance, or small rings, which is an object of value no greater than five aurei. Otherwise, if a condemned person has on his finger a sardonyx or another gem of great value or a promissory note for a large sum of money in his pocket, it cannot be rightfully considered "pannicularia". "Pannicularia" are the items that the prisoner carries with him into custody: the clothes he is wearing when led to execution, as the name itself suggests. Thus, neither should the agents claim anything more for themselves, nor should the officers desire what is taken at the moment the person is punished. Governors should not convert these resources for their own benefit or allow the officers or pati optiones sive commentarienses ea pecunia abuti, sed debent ad ea servari, quae iure praesidum solent erogari, ut puta chartiaticum quibusdam officialibus inde subscribere, vel si qui fortiter fecerint milites, inde eis donare: barbaros etiam inde munerari venientes ad se vel legationis vel alterius rei causa. plerumque etiam inde conrasas pecunias praesides ad fiscum transmiserunt: quod perquam nimiae diligentiae est, cum sufficiat, si quis non in usus proprios verterit, sed ad utilitatem officii patiatur deservire.

[De discessu].
2251.[188] Meminisse oportebit usque ad adventum successoris omnia debere proconsulem agere, cum sit unus proconsulatus et utilitas provinciae exigat esse aliquem, per quem negotia sua provinciales explicent: ergo in adventum successoris debebit ius dicere. Legatum suum ne ante se de provincia dimittat, et lege Iulia repetundarum et rescripto divi Hadriani ad Calpurnium Rufum proconsulem Achaiae admonetur.

188 *Dig.* 1.16.10; cf. *Bas* 6.2.12.

prison staff to misuse these funds. Instead, these funds should be preserved for legitimate purposes, as governors customarily distribute them, for example, for supplies like paper for clerks, or to reward soldiers for their bravery, or to give gifts to barbarians coming as envoys or for other purposes. Often, governors also send the collected money to the treasury, which is an excessive diligence, as it is sufficient if they do not use it for personal purposes but allow it to serve the needs of their office.

[On parting].
2251. It must be remembered that the proconsul must conduct all affairs until the arrival of his successor, since there is only one proconsulship and the well-being of the province requires that there be someone through whom the provincials can manage their affairs. Therefore, until the arrival of his successor, he must continue to dispense justice. He is also reminded by both the Lex Julia on extortion and the rescript of the deified Hadrian to Calpurnius Rufus, proconsul of Achaia, that he should not dismiss his legate from the province before himself.

COMMENTARY

Book 1

§ 2142

The proconsul must ensure: *observare ... oportet*: For the notion of and criteria for a good provincial governor, see Mantovani 1993–4; Ando 2006.

... not to burden the province: Roman emperors and jurists were attentive to not overburdening the inhabitants of the Roman provinces with taxation (fiscally or in kind), both before and after the *Constitutio Antoniniana*. One common form of taxation in the provinces was billeting (*hospitium*). By billeting, Roman authorities referred to the duty of provincials to house Roman soldiers and other officials during their stay in the province. However, a series of imperial pronouncements acknowledged the burden billeting imposed on provincials and aimed to curtail its abuse, including its prohibition among the privileges bestowed on those deemed fit. Hence, Modestinus quoted a letter of Commodus, which granted immunities from certain liturgies for rhetoricians, grammarians, philosophers, and physicians. This letter, reiterating a previous constitution of Antoninus Pius, included exemption from billeting, alongside other liturgies (Modestinus, *libro secundo excusationum*, *Dig.* 27.1.6.8). Later constitutions continued to regulate the duty of billeting and to curtail its abuse, cf. *C.Th.* 7.8.1 (the prohibition of billeting in Jewish synagogues); *C.Th.* 7.8.3 (no person shall be immune from billeting in their private home, except a small group of elected magistrates); *C.Th.* 7.8.5 (the billeting of the emperor and his entourage); *C.Th.* 7.8.8 (an exemption from billeting for armorers); *C.Th.* 7.8.9 (billeting on landed properties); *C.Th.* 8.8.15 (a prohibition of property owners billeting at another person's home under the pretence of the oath of military service). Furthermore, *C.Th.* 7.9 and 12.41 limited billeting to housing alone, excluding other goods such as oil, wood, or nutriments (all included under *salgamum*).

Aufidius Servianus: Nothing else is known of Aufidius Severianus, except that he lived under Septimius Severus and his son Caracalla. The context suggests that he served as a proconsul during this time. Cf. *PIR*[2] A 392.

... wrote in a rescript: The so-called replied letters (*rescripta*) were a seminal source of law under the Roman Empire. Gaius (1.5), who did not use the technical term '*rescriptum*' but used '*epistula*', classified these replies under the rubric of imperial constitutions. These letters ('*rescripta*') were formal responses to official queries, both from individuals and magistrates. The emperor responded to these letters in the chancellery known as *ab epistulis*, with the support of a group of advisers who had the authority to respond in the name of the emperor ('*ius respondendi*'). These *rescripta* gradually replaced the *responsa* of jurists, which became obsolete by the time of Hadrian. Classical jurists habitually quoted these *rescripta*, which held the force of law upon publication and were disseminated throughout the Roman Empire; cf. Nörr 1981 and Sirks 2001. On the *ius respondendi*, see Tuori 2004.

No proconsul may have personal attendants: At the time Ulpian composed his *de officio proconsulis* (more than half a century before Gallienus' military reforms), the *stratores* were not grooms, as their name might suggest, but part of the governor's guard. This role is confirmed by inscriptions such as *CIL* xiii, 8203 = *ILS* 2418 and Nesselhauf n. 11, which placed the *stratores* under the command of the *pedites singulares* within the governor's guard. Similarly, Arrian (*Ektaxis* 22) mentioned having a guard of 200 men while governor of Cappadocia, under their own centurions (for these men being *stratores*, see Speidel 1974: 544). Inscriptions like *AE* 1900, 160 suggest that *stratores* were entrusted with crucial tasks such as city defence (Pflaum 1952: 307–30; Speidel 1974: 543). They enjoyed elevated social status and were organised as an autonomous unit with their own commanders – centurions or even higher-ranking officers – and their own headquarters (*tabularium*); see *CIL* xiii, 8150, *AE* 1929, 125; *tabularium*: *CIL* xiii, 6746. The *stratores* formed an elite force that would later evolve into the new *equites promoti* and *stablesiani*. In proconsular provinces the governor had to recruit and train *stratores* from the cohorts stationed there (cf. *AE* 1959, 12). However, there was no absolute prohibition against the governor having *stratores* altogether, as noted by Speidel 1974: 545, who cited the dissenting view of Mommsen 1887/8: 263: n. 4.

... soldiers serve in that capacity: Huschke proposed the following emendation: *inter ministerio – in excidisse 'eo'*; SZ 9, 340.

The senate decided during the consulship of Cotta and Messala: Marcus Aurelius Cotta Maximus Messallinus, who promulgated this *senatus consultum*, was the son of Marcus Valerius Messalla Corvinus (consul 31 BCE). Cotta belonged to the patrician *gens Valerii*. Several sources mention the consulate of Aurelius Cotta and his nephew Marcus Valerius Messalla in the year 20 CE, cf. *CIL* vi, 32270; Tac. *Ann.* 3.2.3, and *Dig.* 1.16.4.2 = Ulp. *de officio proconsulis*. Another *senatus consultum* from their consular year is mentioned in *Dig.* 48.2.12.3, in an excerpt from Venuleius Saturninus' treatise on criminal proceedings: *Si servus reus postulabitur, eadem observanda sunt quae si liber esset, ex senatus consulto Cotta et Messala consulibus* ('if a slave is mentioned as an accused, the same procedures must be followed as if he were free, according to the *senatus consultum* of Cotta and Messala during their consulship'). However, Tacitus asserts that Cotta proposed a bill in the senate in 24 CE – four years after his consulship – which made magistrates liable for their wives' misconduct in the provinces: *at Messalinus Cotta haud minus claris maioribus sed animo diversus censuit cavendum senatus consulto, ut quamquam insontes magistratus et culpae alienae nescii provincialibus uxorum criminibus proinde quam suis plecterentur* ('On the other hand, Messalinus Cotta, from an equally illustrious family but of different character, pressed for a senatorial decree stating that even though innocent and unaware of their wives' guilt, magistrates should be penalised for their wives' offences in the provinces as if they were their own', Tac. *Ann.* 4.20.4). This bill may have been prompted by the prosecution of Sosia Galla, wife of Gaius Silius, a legate in Germania Superior. Sosia was a close friend of Agrippina, widow of Germanicus, and both were exiled on charges of treason (Tac. *Ann.* 4.18–19). Ronald Syme suggested that Cotta may have aimed to curry favour with Tiberius by attacking the popular Germanicus (Syme 1978: 130). This bill suggests that Ulpian may have erred in dating this *senatus consultum* to Cotta's consular year. However, Ulpian was correct in attributing this law to Cotta, who promulgated it during the consulship of Cethegus and Varro (Cyrielle 2011: 571, following Fanizza 1977: 208–9). Cotta's bill aligned with – and perhaps was influenced by – Aulus Caecina's famous speech in 21 CE advocating the prohibition of provincial governors' wives from accompanying them to their provinces (Tac. *Ann.* 3.33). In fact, during the reign of Tiberius, wives were only allowed to accompany their husbands – who held imperium – to their assigned provinces, a right revoked by Augustus (Suet. *Aug.* 24.1; Tac. *Ann.* 1.80). For the general Roman attitude towards Roman women in the provinces during the early principate see Marshall 1975. While the original prohibition mainly concerned the military duties of provincial governors, its inclusion in Ulpian's *de officio proconsulis* suggests its application extended equally to senatorial provinces.

… any misconduct by the wives of magistrates: The term *officium*, which Cicero perceived as a moral duty, is used by classical jurists to denote magisterial jurisdiction. Unlike Cicero's *officia*, the magistrate's duties are enumerated by law.

Cross into the province: In theory, the provinces were divided into two categories. The first category, where an army was stationed, was governed by a representative of the emperor (*legatus Augusti*). The second category, where there were no legions, was governed by a proconsul chosen from the Senate. In practice, this division was not as rigid regarding the operational methods of provincial governors or any perceived division between the Senate and the emperor. Furthermore, for the provincials themselves and their institutions, there was no practical distinction between these two categories of governors; see Ando 2000: 152–74; Millar 2002: 271–320.

Before entering his assigned province: The extent of the provincial governor's jurisdiction en route to his province was already addressed in the late Republican era by the *lex de provinciis praetoris* (RS § 12, Cic. *Fam.* 1.9.25). This law affirmed that the governor holds imperium, which grants jurisdiction as soon as he leaves Rome, but this authority is limited until he enters his designated province. For the full reception of jurisdiction upon entering his province, refer to Fanizza 1994.

Edict: The term '*edictum*' here, as well as in the following sentence ('*edictum decessori suo miserit …* '), simply refers to an official letter. It should not be confused with the so-called 'edictum provinciale'. Provincial governors issued an edict upon arriving in their assigned province from the late Republic until the reign of Hadrian, excluding the principate of Augustus (Buckland 1934: 81). Cicero mentioned his own edict as governor of Cilicia (*ad Att.* 6.1), which followed the pattern of Scaevola's provincial edict (*ibid.*). He recommended his brother to follow this model of provincial edicts as governor of Attica (*ad Att.* 6.8.5; *ad Fam.* 2.10.321) and referenced Bibulus' edict as governor of Syria (*ad Att.* 6.1.15). Cicero also discussed Verres' provincial edict from Sicily (*in Verr.* 2.2.13.32; 2.2.37.90). Two centuries later Gaius composed a commentary on the provincial edict (*ad edictum provinciale*) in thirty-two books, of which 335 fragments have survived (Lenel *EP* 1: § 189–237). However, the extent and purpose of the so-called 'edictum provinciale' are still debated (cf. Ando 2006: 178; Marshall 1964; Galsterer 1986: 16–17). According to the *lex Irnitana* § 85, the edict of the provincial governor was habitually displayed in a prominent place, providing the framework for all legal proceedings under his jurisdiction (cf. Galsterer 1986; 1988; Crawford 1988; Ando 2000: 73–80; Gonzales and Crawford 1986: 148–50). However, since a Roman province was an administrative unit, not a judicial one, and Roman law focused on civic status (e.g., *cives Romani*, *civitates*, *incolae*, *adventae*, etc.) rather than the location of the court, it is evident that the 'edictum provinciale' pertained only to non-Romans. It became obsolete after the *Constitutio Antoniniana*, when Ulpian composed his *de officio proconsulis*.

Administrative matters: The term *actus* often denotes public employment or state business, especially judicial matters: *actus rerum* (Suet. *Aug.* 32; *Claud.* 15, 23). Also used absolutely as *actus* (*Dig.* 39, 4, 16; 40, 5, 41; L&S s.v. 'actus' B1).

... uncertainties and unforeseen events disturb the provincials: Throughout this treatise, Ulpian emphasises the exclusive nature of proconsular jurisdiction, stressing that both incoming governors and their predecessors must ensure the clarity of the governor's identity.

ἐπιδημία: The meaning of *ἐπιδημία* (*epidemia*) as an entry point is attested in *IG*[3] 1023.

Greatly [Latin: *magni*]: The term *magni* serves adverbially to denote a quality of the greatest value; cf. *L&S* s.v. *magnus*.

Customs and privileges: See *SIG* 849; Robert 1977; Ando 2000: 131–74.

[Latin *usque adeo*]: *Usque adeo* means 'as far as'; cf. *L&S* s.v. B1c.

Our Emperor Antoninus Augustus [Caracalla] wrote in a rescript responding to the desires of the Asians that the proconsul must approach Asia by sea and first dock at Ephesus of the metropoleis: Discord and feuds between Greek cities were commonplace (Sartre 1991: 190–8). The cities often contested honours and titles (cf. Robert 1977, regarding the dispute between Nicomedia and Nicea over supremacy in Bithynia). Dio of Prusa noted that Roman governors were inclined to exploit these rivalries for their own gain (D.Chr. *Or.* 38.36–8). Therefore, it was crucial for the governor to be aware of these disputes and to carefully manage the hierarchy among the cities in his province.

§ 2143

the proconsul should delegate jurisdiction: The meaning of *iurisdictio* is discussed in *Dig.* 2.1. The three points relevant to the duty of the proconsul are: (i) that jurisdiction entails adjudication on all matters pertaining to property rights, including the imposition of guardians and the appointment of judges: *Ius dicentis officium latissimum est: nam et bonorum possessionem dare potest et in possessionem mittere, pupillis non habentibus tutores constituere, iudices litigantibus dare* ('the duty to administer the law is extensive: for he can give *bonorum possessio* and to order a *missio in possessionem*, he can constitute tutors to wards who lack them and to assign judges to litigants', *Dig.* 2.1.1); (ii) that the grant of *iurisdictio* also means the grant of all powers without which this jurisdiction is inapplicable: *Cui iurisdictio data est, ea quoque concessa esse videntur, sine quibus iurisdictio explicari non potuit* ('to whom *iurisdictio* is given, these things are seen to be given, without which *iurisdictio* could not be uncoiled', *Dig.* 2.1.2); (iii), which is imperative for the extent to which a provincial governor can delegate his jurisdiction to members of his staff, that *imperium* (and, with it, *iurisdictio*) could be unadulterated (*merum*) or mixed (*mixtum*). Unadulterated *iurisdictio* includes the so-called *ius gladii* (see below). Mixed *iurisdictio* is the one delegated by the holder of a full *iurisdictio.* It encompasses *bonorum possessio*, but not capital punishment: *Imperium aut merum aut mixtum est. Merum est imperium habere gladii potestatem ad animadvertendum facinorosos homines, quod etiam potestas appellatur. Mixtum est imperium, cui etiam iurisdictio inest, quod in danda bonorum possessione consistit. Iurisdictio est etiam iudicis dandi licentia* ('*imperium* can be unadulterated or mixed. Unadulterated *imperium* is to have the power to enforce a capital punishment to criminals, and it is also called *potestas.* Mixed *imperium*, to whom who has *iurisdictio*, is consisted of giving *bonorum possessio. Iurisdictio* is the right of appointing judges', *Dig.* 2.1.3).

to his legate: Mandare ... legato suo: the habit of delegating judicial authority to a designated subordinate was well established in Roman administration, going back at least to the late Republican era; cf. the advice of Cicero to his brother when governor of Asia in the years 61–59 BCE (Cic. *Q. Fr.* I 1, 20). Cicero himself did so in Cilicia *Att.* V 21, 6. More importantly, the *lex de provinciis praetoriis* marked the proconsul's quaestor and legates as key legal aids, upon which jurisdiction should be delegated: *Roman Statutes*, 1. 12.

For it is indeed very absurd to delegate jurisdiction to another before he himself has acquired it (since it does not belong to him until he has entered that province): Krüger, in his edition of the *corpus iuris civilis*, assumed that this explanatory phrase was not written by Ulpian himself and was added either by Tribonian or by an anonymous hand anytime between the publication of Ulpian's work and the composition of the *Digest*.

§ 2144
Prisoners: The term 'custodia' is used here to denote prisoners (cf. *L&S* s.v. B2). However, the context suggests a more confined meaning of 'detainees awaiting trial'. In fact, the unique term *praeauditas custodias* emphasises even more the preliminary stage of these detainees' judicial process. The duty of the legate must have been to conduct an inquiry into these cases. Their findings would therefore allow the new proconsul to set free those who deserve it: *ad se remittant, ut innocentem ipse liberet* ('be returned to him, for [the proconsul] himself to liberate the innocent'), thereby augmenting his image as a just ruler and that of the emperor, whose authority the governor embodied.

Cognitio: The term 'cognitio' is understood by some modern jurists to denote a new legal procedure – both criminal and civil – which emerged at the time of Augustus. This new procedure no longer included a division of the legal process into a preliminary stage (*in iure*) in front of a Republican magistrate or a provincial governor and a second (*apud indicem*) in front of a *iudex* (cf. Rüfner 2016). Proceedings in this new form were heard by an official who fulfilled both the role of the magistrate and that of the *iudex*. As the name itself suggests, this process originated from the duty of the official to inquire into cases brought before him (Turpin 1999). However, it is uncertain whether the term *cognitio* was used in a technical sense by contemporaries. Similarly, the words *extra ordinem* or *extraordinarius* were at times associated with *cognitio*. Here, too, a technical meaning is debated.

The single-phased procedure emerged for three reasons. First, there was no clear remedy within the formulary system, which led the emperors to introduce a remedy from outside (Rüfner 2016: 258). Furthermore, from Augustus onwards, the Roman emperors positioned themselves as a judicial authority (Buti 1982: 35; Kaser and Hackl 1996: 446–7). Thirdly, provincial governors found the constraints of the formulary system and the requirement to appoint a *iudex* inapplicable (Rüfner 2016: 258). The term *cognitiones* itself alluded to an official inquisition by a Roman magistrate, which would have had the same effect as proceedings *in iure* (Plin. *Ep.* 6.31.2; 6.31.8; *Dig.* 28.5.93). Pliny assumed that holding *cognitio*, which means an official inquiry with legal ramifications, was part of the governor's duties, as his correspondence with Trajan on the matter of the Christians suggests (Plin. *Ep.* 10.96.1; 10.96.8; for *cognoscere* as an investigation of a magistrate under the *ius honorarium* see *Dig.* 29.2.99; 21.2.39.pr). Furthermore, the Roman emperor had a designated *a cognitionibus* on his staff (Dio 75.15.5; Philostr. *VS.* 2.32; Hirschfeld 1877: 329ff; Millar 2005: 19). While there is no direct evidence disclosing the range of their duties, it is assumed that they assisted the governor in executing these inquiries, rather than exercising judicial duties themselves. While Kunkel assumed that 'all civil and criminal proceedings came under the official *cognitio*, a procedural system which, in the unitary course which it took as well as in the official character of its judges, displays a much closer similarity to a modern system of justice than do the procedural forms of the later Republic or the early Empire', Turpin pointed out that this is incongruent with the use of the term *cognitiones* (and its cognates) in the Roman sources themselves (Kunkel 1973: 143; Turpin 1999: 532).

Release the innocent: Previous editors of the *Digest* have noted the discrepancy between the plural 'solent' and the singular 'ipse liberet'. Mommsen included the following lemma *ad loc*: *ipse liberet* firmant B: fuitne *ipsi liberent* (Schulting)? Huschke (1888: 340) suggested *aut innocentes ipsi liberent.*

This type of delegation is extraordinary: The meaning of *extra ordinem* here is not technical. Rather, it alludes to the problematic time sequence of the governor delegating authority he still does not have. In fact, the text of the *Basilika* is particularly helpful here, as it explains that the meaning of *extraordinaria* is beyond the scope of law, but not against it: *Τοῦτο δὲ τὸ πρόσταγμα ἔξω τῶν ὡρισμένων ἐστὶ καὶ οὐ παρὰ τὴν κρατήσασαν παρὰ τοῖς νόμοις ἀκρίβειαν* ('this matter is outside of that which is settled, not beyond the power [i.e., of the proconsul] but beyond the exactness of the laws').

The power of the sword: = *Dig.* 50.17.70. Mommsen assumed that the *ius gladii*, which means the right to sentence Roman citizens to death, was part of the governor's authority by the time of Ulpian (Mommsen 1889: 229 ff; 1887/8: 262 ff), relying *inter alia* on Ulpian *Dig.* 1.18.6.8. Garnsey, however, convincingly demonstrated that the *ius gladii* has never been bestowed and has always been an integral aspect of the governor's jurisdiction (Garnsey 1968; and cf. Jones 1968 and Pflaum 1950: 117–25). The meaning of the term *ius gladii* itself requires clarification, as it could shed light on the extraordinary aspect of its delegation by the proconsul to a legate. Cassius Dio explained that the right of a governor to wear a military cloth and a sword is reserved for those who could try and discipline soldiers, which were only the *legati Augusti pro praetore* (Dio 55.13.6–7; Garnsey 1968: 52). Furthermore, Dio emphasised that this right is personal and cannot be delegated to a quaestor or an assessor (Dio 55.14.5–6). Garnsey suggested that what Dio had in mind was, in fact, the *ius gladii* (Garnsey 1968: 52). Hence, the proclamation of Ulpian that this type (*genus*) of bestowal of power is extraordinary (*extraordinarium est*) addressed not the jurisdiction of the proconsul but its delegation to his legate. This understanding of the extraordinary aspect of this *cognitio* is corroborated by a statement of Venuleius Saturninus in his treatise on the duty of the proconsul: *Si quid erit quod maiorem animadversionem exigat, reicere legatus apud proconsulem debet: neque enim animadvertendi coercendi vel atrociter verberandi ius habet* ('if anything would surpass a major crime, the legate must go back to the proconsul: he does not have the power to punish by death or severely scourge', *Dig.* 1.16.11).

Legates should not consult the emperor but their proconsul, and the proconsul must respond to the inquiries of his legates: The hierarchy hereby depicted not only offers a glimpse into the mechanism of the provincial imperial government but also allows an educated guess pertaining to the titular of the many names mentioned in the *Digest* as recipients of imperial correspondence of this sort.

§ 2146
Long-established custom is usually observed as if it were a right and a law in matters that are not derived from written sources: Perozzi

(1906: 31, n. 2) argued that the phrase '*in his quae non ex scripto descendunt*' ('descend not from writing') is an interpolation, probably by Tribonian (or a member of his committee). He further argued that the division between written laws and those which are not written is of Greek origin and that it was alien to classical Roman jurists.

It is tempting to read '*quae non ex scripto descendunt*' as an allusion to Cicero's comment in his letter to his brother on the third part of the *edictum provinciale*, which rested on the edicts of the urban praetor: *Tertium, de reliquo jure dicundo ἄγραφον reliqui, Dixi me de eo genere mea decreta ad edicta urbana accommodaturum* ('The third category, containing all else to do with the administration of justice, I left unwritten, stating that my rulings under this head would conform to the edicts published in Rome; and so I manage, and so far everyone is satisfied', Cic. *Ad Att.* 6.1.15). However, it is more plausible that Ulpian referred here to local and long-established judicial habits. This is in tune with the status of custom in Roman law more generally (cf. Schiller 1938; Thomas 1963: 47–8, and *passim*; Humfress 2012).

Book 2

§ 2147

The most celebrated: Despite what the phrase '*provinciae caput*' might suggest, it is highly debated whether Roman provinces had capitals. In fact, Rudolf Haensch concluded that the Roman provincial system did not include official provincial capitals. Likewise, the term *provinciae caput* – which is rarely used, especially in official documents – referred to the governor's main place of residence and activities (Haensch 1997b: 37–64). Furthermore, Ulpian says here '*celebrem civitatem vel provinciae caput*' ('the most celebrated, or the capital of the province'), which means either the most celebrated city or the head/capital of the province, as these notions appear synonymous to him and reflect repute, not official status. Similarly, the title of *provinciae caput* was not a synonym for 'metropolis', which designated an important city where the governor resided and held assizes.

He should grant holidays according to the customs and traditions: Festivals were pivotal to civic life, culture, and self-representation. In the Hellenistic world they consisted of processions, sacrifices, feasts, and games, and were organised by the cities themselves. For the connection between civic life, local identity, and festivals, see Price 1984: 101–32. Furthermore, the Greek cities habitually competed with one another over reputation and honours (cf. Merkelbach 1978; Jones 1978: 83–94; Price 1984: 126–32). In turn, Greek authors habitually promulgated the need for and importance of concord. This comment of Ulpian must have addressed that issue, guiding the provincial governor not to incite such inter-city rivalry.

... whether they need repairs or any other maintenance: Cf. *Sarta tecta tua praecepta usque habui mea modestia* (Plaut. *Trin.* 2, 2, 36).

§ 2148

Jurisdiction: The literal meaning of *iurisdictio* is 'speaking the law'. It denoted the conferred sovereign powers to hold court and exercise justice. Initially the term applied only to private law, but from the second century CE onwards it was also applied to criminal law, where the *cognitio* process was used. In this context, the term *iurisdictio* equates to the complete process of instigating a legal inquiry, conducting the legal process, and passing judgement. The main facet of *iurisdictio* was to appoint judges, either through the grant of a formula or otherwise. However, particularly relevant to the provincial governor bearing *imperium*, his *iurisdictio* also allowed him to perform certain acts on his own authority, like recognising and giving rights of legal ownership, collection of objects, appointing guardians, appointing judges (§ 2143), and restoring to a former state (*restitutio ad integrum*, cf. *Dig.* 2.14.58; *Dig.* 4.4.16.5). It is particularly relevant to the provincial governor that *iurisdictio* included all authorities without which it would have been devoid (§ 2143). This clarification also accounts for the mechanism of *cognitio*. In his treatise on the duty of the proconsul Ulpian emphasised that the *iurisdictio* of the governor is full (*plenissimam autem iurisdictionem*). In fact, Ulpian noted elsewhere that *iurisdictio* should not be confused with *imperium*, as the former is limited while the latter is complete. More specifically, *imperium* also included the right to inflict capital punishment, but *iurisdictio* was limited to bestowing possession and appointing judges (§ 2143). Another important attribute of *iurisdictio* is that its bearer can bestow it upon another. In fact, as we have seen above (§ 2143), the provincial governor habitually bestowed *iurisdictio* on his legate(s). However, Ulpian confirmed in his *Digest* that this right was preserved only to those who held *iurisdictio* by law, not to persons who held it on account of being entrusted with it by another: *More maiorum ita comparatum est, ut is demum iurisdictionem mandare possit, qui eam suo iure, non alieno beneficio habet* ('It has been provided by ancestral custom that he who can give *iurisdictio* is the one who has it by law, not through the *beneficium* of another', *Dig.* 2.1.5). The person to whom *iurisdictio* has been delegated exercised it not in his own name, but in the name of its bearer by law: *Dig.* 2.1.16; cf. Kaser and Hackl 1996: 185 ff.

Special procedure: The meaning of the term *ius extra ordinem* or *extraordinarius*, and its association with the notion of *cognitio(nes)*, has long been at the heart of scholarly disputes (cf. Turpin 1999). To elucidate this phrase of Ulpian it is noteworthy that traditional Republican procedures have been, in time, replaced by procedures known as *cognitio(nes)*. A legal procedure could have followed regular or special (*extra ordinem*) rules when special sorts of crime had been committed and when the rules of the *quaestio* were not followed (Bawman 1996: 50), or in civil cases, when the distinction between procedures *in iure* and procedures *apud iudicem* was put to the side (Kaser and Hackl 1996: 436). However, the *cognitio* procedure was one thing, and procedures *extra ordinem* (or *extraordinarius*) were another (Turpin 1999: 506; Millar 1968; Orestano 1980).

There is nothing in the province which is not settled by him: This statement of Ulpian has been obliquely challenged by Alan Rodgers in his examination of the eighty-fourth chapter of the *Lex Irnitana*, which concerns the limits of the jurisdiction of the *duoviri* and poses an obligatory *vadimonium* for a hearing before the praetor in Rome. Rodger interpreted the duty of *vadimonium* as a limitation *de facto* of the provincial governor's jurisdiction; cf. Rodger 1990, *contra* (most convincingly) Burton 1996.

Certainly, if it involves a fiscal pecuniary case that falls under the responsibility of the imperial procurator, it would have been better if he refrained: This limitation of the proconsul's jurisdiction and the admonition/prohibition of Ulpian to the proconsul to abstain from cases pertaining to *fiscalis pecuniaria* touch upon the delicate relations between the emperor's private property and that of the state, and, more generally, upon the provincial taxation mechanism. As part of his administrative reforms, Augustus separated the fiscal and judicial duties of the provincial governor in order to diminish corruption and extortion of provincials by their Roman governors, as well as to eliminate all potential political opposition from local governors who could until then muster power and resources in their allocated provinces (Hirschfeld 1877: 8; Brunt 1990: 53–95, 487–506). At the same time, Augustus and future emperors maintained considerable assets in the provinces and used their private resources for the common good. However, the nature and the extent of the separation between the emperor's private assets and those of the state are unclear, with some scholars contending that the term *fiscus* denoted both the emperor's private resources as well as public funds (cf. Jones 1950; Brunt 1990: 134–62; Ando 2006: 180), and others maintaining that the term *fiscus* referred exclusively to imperial property: *Caesar omnia habet, fiscus eius privata tantum ac sua: et universa in imperio eius sunt, in patrimonio propria* ('Everything belongs to Caesar, yet the only private and personal property he has is the imperial treasury; all things are his by right of his authority, but his personal property is acquired by right of inheritance', Seneca, *de beneficiis* 7.6.3. Cf. Millar 1963; 1964; 1965; 1977: 175–201). Furthermore, the emperor managed his property not through the provincial governors but through imperium-bearing procurators, which explains why Ulpian advised his proconsul to refrain from exercising his jurisdiction in cases pertaining to the *fiscus* (Millar 1964, 1965; Brunt 1990: 163–87). In fact, Claudius had already affirmed that his procurators represented himself and that their jurisdiction had as much validity as if it came from the emperor himself: *Eodem anno saepius audita vox principis, parem vim rerum habendam a procuratoribus suis iudicatarum, ac si ipse statuisset* ('The emperor was often heard during that year to state that judgements given by his procurators ought to have as much validity as if the ruling had come from himself', Tac. *Ann.* 11.60 with Millar 1964). Furthermore, although imperial procurators would, in theory, hold no jurisdiction in senatorial provinces since the reign of Augustus onwards, reality was quite different (Millar 1964: 184 sqq.). During the early principate we find procurators, or *praefecti*, exercising criminal and civil jurisdiction like that of the governors of the senatorial provinces, perhaps with a more limited *ius gladii* (Pflaum 1950: 110 sqq.). Procurators in the senatorial provinces are well attested from Augustus onwards. Their responsibilities pertained to the management of imperial property in these provinces. A document from Crete attests to the involvement of a provincial procurator in restoring public plots (*praedia publica*) on the direct authority of Nero, as well as an explicit resolution of the senate (Abbot and Johnson 1921 no. 55). It is possible that Ulpian assumed that the proconsul might defer cases pertaining to *fiscalis pecuniaria* to the provincial procurator. Documents alluding to their jurisdiction revolving around similar cases might support that. Hadrian instructed the procurator to participate in a dispute revolving around the lease of public land (*vectigal*) where a temple of Zeus had stood since the Hellenistic era (*CIL* iii, 355, 14191; *OGIS* 502; *IGR* 4, 571). On the role of the procurators in these instances see Hurlet

2006: 242–4. A letter of the proconsul of Asia, for example, recorded his request from the provincial procurator to preside over a boundary dispute with the assistance of a *mensor* (land surveyor) (*OGIS* 502 = *IGR* iv, 571 = Abbot and Johnson 1921 no. 82; cf. a similar letter of Hadrian *Syll*^{3} 837 = *IGR* 1156a = Abbot and Johnson 1921 no. 83 = *FIRA* 2 I. 80; and a letter of Pius *Syll*^{3} 849 = Abbot and Johnson 1921 no. 100). Particularly relevant here are various excerpts from legal sources confirming that disputes over *bona caduca*, aiming to decide whether it would go to the *fiscus*, were settled by procurators (*Dig.* 11.1.22; 8.40.3; 6.35.3; 3.28.10; 7.45.5; 9.49.5; 9.51.8; *Dig.* 2.15.8.19; Millar 1964: 365). More generally, the *fiscus* was often a party in a legal dispute (Millar 1963: 31 sqq.). In fact, Hadrian established the magistrature of *advocatus fisci* who represented the *fiscus* in such disputes (SHA, *Vit. Hadr.* 20.6). On this office see Hirschfeld 1905: 48–52; Magie 1950: 626–8, 1489. It is therefore understandable why the authority of the proconsul – if exercised – could have been seen as interfering with that of the emperor. In fact, some emperors tried cases to which the *fiscus* was a party themselves (cf. Plin. *Pan.* 58). However, a century before Ulpian composed his *de officio proconsulis*, Pliny hinted that procurators presided over disputes between the *fiscus* and *privati* (Plin. *Pan.* 36; Millar 1964: 364). Thus, Ulpian's admonition that the proconsul should abstain from presiding over disputes pertaining to *fiscalis pecuniaria* was meant to prevent a provincial governor from being forced to obstruct imperial interests.

§ 2149

All cases that require investigation: The term *cognitio(nes)* refers to a legal procedure in which a magistrate (originally an imperium-bearing provincial magistrate) initiated an inquiry that would lead to a judicial process. Hence, the *cognition* process combined procedures *in iure* (i.e., in front of a magistrate) and procedures *apud iudicem* (i.e., in front of a judge), and it was instigated not by a private person but by a Roman magistrate. The empirical aspect of the *cognitio* process is understood both from its *modus operandi* and from its name itself, which is derived from the verb *cognoscere*; cf. Kaser and Hackl 1996: 189. Under the Principate, the judicial function of the emperor has habitually been described as conducting *cognitiones*; cf. Plin. *Ep.* 6.31.6; 6.31.8; *Dig.* 28.5.93. In fact, a junior magistrature of an assistant to the emperor in holding these procedures, known as *a cognitionibus*, is well documented from the second century CE onwards (Hirschfeld 1877: 329ff). Pliny, writing to Trajan from

Bithynia and asking how to approach the Christians, used the term *cognitio* to denote such an inquiry: *Cognitionibus de Christianis interfui numquam* ('I have never been part of *cognitio* procedures concerning Christians', Plin. *Ep.* 10.96.1.9).

Decree ... letter: *Omnia ... expediri* = *Dig.* 50.17.71. Ulpian highlighted here a hierarchy between *decreta* and *libelli*, and then prohibited cases demanding *cognitiones* from being resolved by *libelli*. The term *decretum* (from the verb *decernere*) denoted a ruling or an official decision of a Roman official. This term is used to qualify decisions of the Roman praetor, provincial governor, the emperor, the senate, priestly colleges, and, later in the Christian era, the councils. Gaius *Inst.* 4.140 associated *decreta* with the praetors (in Rome) and provincial governors in their allocated provinces. Furthermore, Gaius associated *decreta* with positive decisions and *interdicta* with negative ones (i.e., prohibitions). It was the praetorian office or the provincial governor which issued these rulings (*Dig.* 37.1.3.8). Examples of *decreta* revolve around cases of protection of minors, appointment of tutors or guardians, *restitutio ad integrum*, inheritance rights of wards, *bonorum possessio*, and others (see below). While this term could have referred to any imperial decision, it usually means a decision the emperor made in his capacity as a judge.

§ 2150

Those who prepare or buy cases [Latin]: While *L&S* list under *concinnator causarum* an advocate (s.v. *concinnator* II, with reference to this text), the context clearly distinguishes the *concinnator* from the *advocatus*. The first term bears a negative tone, in contrast with the positive one of the latter; cf. Arn. 4, 149: *criminum*, Sid. *Ep.* 3, 13.

... his edict: This could not refer to the so-called 'provincial edict', which would have been obsolete after the *Constitutio Antoniniana*.

To whom it is permitted to prosecute: A formal taxonomy of Roman jurists during the Republic and High Empire never existed. Attempts to distinguish the *advocatus* from the *patronus*, the *cognitor*, or the *orator* predominantly reflect social and cultural themes. The *procurator*, however, is different, as he pleaded in the name of parties who were absent. In fact, Tacitus highlighted the decline in the status of Republican orators by saying that those who practised oratory were then called *orator(es)* and now; Tac.

Dial. 1. The interlocutors in the *Dialogue* perceive the *advocatus* as a person who pleads on behalf of one of the parties in legal disputes; cf. *Dial.* 3–4. However, epigraphic evidence suggests that provincial jurists, at least in the Greek East, assisted their cities and provinces to conduct their legal affairs; cf. Jones 2007.

§ 2151

He can correct a disobedient freedman either with words or with the punishment of the rod: Anna Dolganov has pointed out in a discussion of P. *Oxy.* 2.237 col. VII ll. 19–29 = *Sel. Pap.* 2.258 that such cases fell under the governor's *ex officio* authority. She draws parallels with *SB* 12.10929 col. III, ll. 14–16, and to this excerpt of Ulpian; Dolganov 2023: 89; 2019: 39–41; 2022: 681.

The proconsul should promptly hear and adjudicate: As has already been mentioned, the proconsul enjoyed full jurisdiction: *Cum plenissimam autem iurisdictionem proconsul habeat* ('as the proconsul has full *iurisdictio*', § 2148), and as the procedure of appointing judges has already been in place by the Republican *lex de provinciis praetoriis*, of the turn of the second century BCE [*RS* § 1, 12, in particular Cnidus IV, 1.31–9, with Ferrary 2008], which speaks of εξουσία πάντων πραγμάτων (power of all affairs). This entry must imply that in these cases the proconsul could have presided on his own, without needing to appoint judges (in a two-phase judicial process) or rely on members of his *consilium* (in a *cognitio* process).

§ 2152

He must ensure … certain order: Beseler 1911: 91 argued that the phrase *scilicet … prospexerunt* is a later interpolation, possibly by Tribonian. More generally, Peter Garnsey has convincingly demonstrated the hypothesis that the legal system in Rome favoured the interests of the higher orders in Roman society (Garnsey 1970: 275). Roman culture never associated equality with equity, as already noted by Cicero: *ipsa aequabilitas est iniqua, cum habeat nullos gradus dignitatis* ('equality itself is unjust, as it allows no ranks of dignity', *Rep.* 1.27). However, although Roman law and court procedure differentiated the *honestiores* from the *humiliores*, Ulpian emphasised that the court's modus operandi must follow the official guidelines, and, more importantly, that no one should be above the law. For the legal implications of social status see Garnsey 1970.

He should generally grant advocates: Mitteis 1912: 234 argued that the word *plerumque* and the following phrase *feminis ... debebit* are not Ulpian's, on account of style. Mitteis further speculated that these words were probably introduced by Tribonian (or another member of his committee).

... vulnerable individuals: Ulpian touches upon three important issues that are not mutually exclusive: not having an advocate in a legal dispute essentially deprived that party of their ability to procure justice through the courts; the provincial governor was to appoint an advocate to a deprived party in circumstances similar to those in which he would appoint them a guardian; and finally, by providing and appointing an advocate to a deprived party, the provincial government relied on an institutional mechanism – not dissimilar to the public physician – which in later societies bears the title of a public defender. On public physicians in the Greek, Hellenistic, and Roman worlds see Pohl 1905; Cohn-Haft 1956; Nutton 1977. In the forensic application of these doctors see Amundsen and Ferngern 1978; Israelowich 2014.

§ 2153
restore a minor to their original status: The term *restitutio in integrum* means reinstatement to the former state. In a legal context it signifies an extraordinary praetorian (in Rome, or of a pro magistrate in a province) remedy aimed at rectifying an unjust loss. This remedy followed an investigation (*causae cognitio*), allowing the praetor to overturn a previous decision through a decree (*decretum*). A magistrate could grant *restitutio in integrum* as an exercise of imperium, not jurisdiction (cf. *Dig.* 4.1; *CJ* 2.21–41; 43; 46; 47; 49; 52–3).

§ 2155
... that arises from a crime: The term *maleficium* lacks a precise technical meaning and could denote either a *crimen* or a *delictum.*

sign: The phrase *in crimen subscribere* means to sign at the bottom of the charge.

Punishment: Classical jurists composed treatises on penalties (*de poeniis*), with excerpts from such works by Venuleius Saturninus, Modestinus, and Paul preserved in books 47–9 of Justinian's *Digest.* These works primarily offer anecdotal accounts rather than a systematic theory of penal systems or general guidelines. Additionally, under Roman law, there was no clear distinction between criminal and civil law in terms of procedures, the identity of the prosecutor, or the nature of compensation (*remuneration*) to the injured party or the state, or as a penalty. The distinction between a pecuniary compensation and a *poena* requires clarification. Here, *poena* could signify compensation exceeding the actual damage caused or a penalty in the form of imprisonment, confiscation of property to the treasury, or corporal punishment.

Charge [Latin]: The term *crimen* in this context refers to the actual document of the charge.

§ 2156

The accused: The term *reus* can denote a defendant in a civil case (cf. *Dig.* 50.17.125; 50.17.41 pr.) or an accused in a criminal case. In this context, Ulpian probably refers to the defendant. As noted previously (§ 2144), defendants could be detained before trial. Moreover, the term *custodia* is associated with the responsibility of the debtor in specific contracts. It often appears in conjunction with *culpa* and *negligentia* in a negative sense, and *diligentia* positively. *Custodia* is positioned between the less severe *culpa* and the absolute *vis maior*. It is not surprising to find Ulpian's hierarchy where some detainees are held in *carcer*, while others are entrusted to the care of the army, a *fideicommissarius*, or themselves. The *carcer* served as a place of detention for those awaiting or undergoing trial, and for convicts awaiting execution, not as a place of long-term incarceration: *carcer enim ad continendos homines, non ad puniendos haberi debet* ('a prison should be used to confine people, not to punish them', *Dig.* 48.19.8.7 = § 2241, below).

Fideicommissarius: sponsoribus Ulp. (?). *Sponsor*, *fideiussor*, and *fidepromissor* represent different forms of surety through *stipulatio*. They fall under the general category of *adpromissio* and vary in their extent of liability when assuming surety.

Book 3

§ 2158

Concerning those who are in their own right: Roman law stipulated the appointment of a guardian in four instances for persons *sui iuris*. A guardian holding the title of *tutor* was mandated for minors and women *sui iuris* (cf. Gai. 1.196; *CJ* 1.22 pr.). Similarly, lunatics (*furiosi*) and spendthrifts (*prodigi*) also required a guardian but, in these cases, the guardian was known as a *curator* (Gai. 3.106; *Dig.* 27.10.1). The role of the guardian was to assist the persons under their care in managing their property. Hence, individuals *in potestate*, *in manu*, or *in mancipio* did not require a guardian as they did not have any property to manage (Jolowicz and Nicholas 1972: 121).

During the time of the XII Tables a *paterfamilias* could appoint a *tutor* to any person in his household who would become *sui iuris* after his death (cf. Jolowicz and Nicholas 1972: 121; Frier and McGinn 2004: 424). In the absence of a will, the *tutela* passed to the person who would, according to the rules of intestacy, succeed to the property of the ward (*pupillus*) upon their death. This meant the nearest agnate or the nearest agnates jointly. Failing agnates, it would go to the gentiles. The *cura* of lunatics was first assigned to the agnates and, in their absence, to the gentiles. The XII Tables were equally attentive to the need for a *prodigus* (spendthrift) of a guardian. If a person wasted property received by succession on intestacy as *suus heres*, they could be prohibited by magisterial interdiction from dealing with the property, and the management would then pass to the agnates (Epit. Ulp. 12.2).

By the classical period guardianship became an institution aimed at protecting incapable individuals in managing property. However, during the period of the XII Tables guardianship was assigned to successors on intestacy and was designed to protect the interests of future *heredes*. By the time of Gaius it was often the case that the care of a lunatic or a spendthrift belonged to one person under the law of the XII Tables. However, the *praetor* often assigned the administration to someone else because the *legitimus heres* was unfit: *Saepe ad alium e lege duodecim tabularum curatio furiosi aut prodigi pertinet, alii praetor administrationem dat, scilicet cum ille legitimus inhabilis ad eam rem videatur* ('often the care of a lunatic or a spendthrift pertains to one person according to the *XII Tables*, and the praetor gives the administration to another, especially when the rightful one seems inept for that matter', *Dig.* 27.10.13).

Epit. Ulp. 12.1 marked the following distinction between curators: *curatores aut legitimi sunt, id est qui lege duodecim tabularum dantur, aut honoratii, id est a praetore constituuntur* ('curators are either legitimate, that is given by the law of the XII Tables, or distinguished, that is constituted by the praetor') (cf. Watson 1967: 113). Thus, under the Principate, the diagnosis of a lunatic and the subsequent appointment of a curator was no longer restricted to the family. This development is particularly significant because the main driving force behind Roman legal development during this period was remedy based. Therefore, if someone believed that an individual with whom they were legally involved was insane, it was their responsibility to approach the *praetor* (if in Rome) or the governor (if in the provinces). The ability of the *praetor* or the governor to appoint a curator had to be taken as an affirmation of the diagnosis.

Celsus: Publius Juventius Celsus (*Dig.* 50.3.20.6) was a praetor in 106 or 107 CE and a member of Hadrian's *consilium*. He later served as governor of Thrace, twice as consul, and governor of Asia. Cassius Dio reports that Celsus was involved in the conspiracy against Domitian but managed to escape unharmed (Dio 67.13). Celsus was a student of his father, who was also a prominent jurist. He was a prominent member of the Proculian school, alongside Neratius Priscus. Celsus was a prolific legal author, and many of his works are quoted in the *Digest*. For a catalogue of his known works see Schiller 1978: § 121. For the hierarchy of authority (provincial and municipal) see Fournier 2010: 295–396; Hackl 1997.

Indecorous: The adjective *indecorus, a, um* appears twice in the *Theodosian Code* as moral grounds for prohibition of assuming a formal position (cf. *CTh* 12.1.112 for a position of an *archieros*, which means a teacher of distorted Christian doctrine, *CTh* 15.6.2.0).

Insteius Celer: Lenel gives Instio, but Mommsen's lemma of Insteio (?) *ad loc* is probably accurate. Q. Insteius Celer was consul in 128(?) CE (cf. *AE* 1973, 36 from the city of Rome), with Halfmann 1979: no. 58, Syme 1982: 195. See also Syme 1984: 183, n. 73.

It is not new that those, even if they seem to be sound of mind by their utterances: Composure of speech was seen as a seminal indicator of lucidity, and its absence as a symptom of mental disorder. In fact, the first appearance of a physician in Latin literature – in Plautus' *Manaechmi* – is requested to diagnose a patient's mental state (Plaut. *Men.* 890). To produce such a diagnosis, the doctor interviews the patient (Plaut. *Men.* 892–4). Indeed, anamnesis was how Greek physicians advocated an examination of a patient's mental state should be conducted, and Plautus must have followed this Greek medical tradition in his portrayal of the doctor (Baumbach 1983: 100). However, as Ulpian clearly noticed, one's actions should also be considered when diagnosing *prodigi* and in appointing them a guardian.

For it is reasonable: The use of *aequius* (fairness), much like that of *utilius* (usefulness) and *benignius* (liberality), was common in disputes among jurists (cf. Frier 2023: 179).

§ 2159
Having held an inquiry into the case: The phrase *causa cognita* in the ablative absolute is ubiquitous in Roman legal writings. It means 'after having examined the case' and often alludes to a factual inquiry. The imposition of a magisterial inquiry into the details of a case that would have formally been resolved by a *paterfamilias* resonates well with similar quasi-infringements into the *patria potestas* in Ulpian's age and the growing involvement of official institutions. Parallels include the involvement of physicians and midwives in the decision of which newborns should be reared (cf. Israelowich 2017) and the curtailment of unjustified violence towards one's slave (cf. Israelowich 2023).

§ 2161
Consulere alicui or alicui rei: To be mindful of something.

The senatorial order: The first attestation of the term '*decurio*' is found in the municipal *Lex Tarentina*. From the Augustan era onwards the *ordo decurionum* referred to a municipal upper tier, the members of which acted as benefactors to their city. Later, during the High Empire, it is possible to see the equivalence between the terms 'senate', 'ordo', and 'decuriones'. An *ordo* refers to a group of the members of the *curia*, classed by order and rank. The names included in the *ordo decurionum* are inscribed on an official album, alongside all names of the *conscripti* (*Dig.* 50.3). The municipal *curia* is modelled after the Roman Republican senate. The existence of an *ordo decurionum*, much like the title itself, is derived from and indicative of municipal law (cf. *AE* 2002, 1293 = 2004, 1331). An epigraphic survey suggests that the *decuriones* and the *ordo decurionum* authorised and executed decrees of public works, surveys, public ornaments, and the commemoration of local benefactors (*ob merita*). For an epigraphic survey see Le Roux 2022.

For a limited set of time: Comparing the text of Ulpian with *CJ* 10.61.59.1 and P. *Giss.* 40, Mayer was able to demonstrate that Ulpian merely paraphrased the original wording of Caracalla's edict (i.e., the so-called *Constitutio Antoniniana*). Thus, for example, τὰς πολ[ιτι]κ̣ὰ̣ς [τ]ι̣μ̣ὰς corresponds to the *ordo* of the decurions. Mayer further assumed that, as the *advocationes* are unmentioned in the original edict, in the composition of which Ulpian might have been involved, it must be a later interpolation (Mayer 1910: 34–6).

The whole body of legal aids: I translate *advocatio* here as the whole body of legal aids. While the *advocatus* (i.e., the person practising as an advocate on behalf of a client) was commonplace since the Middle Republic, the commercial aspect of this profession was probably not the primary concern of this clause. While at first they were forbidden from receiving wages (*merces*) for their service, a series of enactments during the early Principate allowed advocates to receive a payment known as *palmarium* after having secured a positive result. Two *senatusconsulta*, one *senatusconsultum claudianum* (47 CE), and another, the *senatusconsultum de advocatione* (55 CE), eased the prohibition on advocates practising for a fee. However, in reality, the lower tier of advocates must have practised with nearly no regulation, and therefore could not have been 'removed from the bar'. A series of enactments, collated under the title *de advocatis diversorum iudiciorum* (*C.* 12.7.4), clearly show that an upper tier of advocates assumed quasi-official positions, the highest of which was the *advocatus fisci* (first appointed by Hadrian), who was in charge of the interests of the fisc (*C.* 2.9). It is also plausible that the advocates who were to be provided by the governor for those who confronted a much more powerful adversary in court, mentioned in § 2151, were also referred to in this pronouncement.

Or any other office: Cf. *CJ* 10, 61, 1.

Having completed the period of relegation: This edict of Caracalla was probably included in the so-called *Constitutio Antoniniana*, which bestowed Roman citizenship on (almost) all inhabitants of the Roman world. The *Constitutio Antoniniana* itself is known from P. *Giss.* 40. The edict Ulpian cited in his treatise on the duty of the proconsul is also cited in *CJ* 10.61.1 and in P. *Giss.* 40 col. 2, lines 3–6. This phrase also appears at P. *Oxy.* 2755. In essence, the edict hereby quoted is a reiteration and an extension of an amnesty decree, which Caracalla issued after the murder of Geta. The second one (lines 6–11 of the second column of P. *Giss.* 40 and P. *Oxy.* 2755) also granted citizenship to those who did not have it then, and those who lost it (lines 3–6 of the second column of P. *Giss.* 40 = *CJ* 10.61.1 and paraphrased here by Ulpian). P. *Giss.* 40 can be dated to 215/16 CE, based on Caracalla's visit to Alexandria mentioned in the second column. For the text itself, its edition, and the question of whether it contained one or more constitutions see now van Minnen 2020.

Bastards: An illegitimate child (*spurius*) is a child whose father is unknown or a child whose father cannot legally be the father: *Volgo concepti dicuntur qui patrem demonstrare non possunt, vel qui possunt quidem, sed eum habent, quem habere non licet. qui et spurii appellantur παρὰ τὴν σποράν* ('those known to be conceived by a multitude are those who cannot identify their father, or that they can, but have him (as a father) which they are not allowed to have. They are called spurii, because (of the Greek term) *spora* (i.e., seed, or offspring)', *Dig.* 1.5.23). Cf. Gai. 1.64; Epit. Gai. 1.4.8; Epit. Ulp. 4.2, 5.7; *Coll.* 6, 2, 4; *CTh* 3, 12, 2. Const. et Constans AA. et Iulianus C. ad Volusianum vic. urbis; *Brev. Alar.* 3, 12, 1. Interpr; *Brev. Alar.* 3, 12, 2. Constantinus et Constans AA. et Iulianus C. ad Volusianum vicarium urbis.

Lollianus Avitus: L. Hedius Rufus L. Avidius (*PIR*^{2} H 40) was *cos. ord.* in 144 CE, *curator operum publicorum* in 146 (*CIL* VI 1008), and proconsul of Africa in 157–8 (*IRT* 533, 534), before becoming consular legate of Pontus-Bithynia, where his presence was recorded in 159 and 165 (*IGR* III 84); Alföldy 1977: 323.

It will certainly not be in the interest of the senatorial order ...: The importance of maintaining a steady number of decurions is made in *lex Irnitana* § 31. Ulpian was equally aware of it, both here and in *Dig.* 50.2.2.pr. For the scholarly debate on the size of the *ordo decurionibus* (before and after the discovery of the *lex Irnitana*) see Nicols 1988. It is also noteworthy that Beseler 1926: 275 assumed (perhaps too harshly) that the words *nulla – oportet* and later *cessantibus – habere* are interpolated, both based on syntax and because the word competitor is unmentioned elsewhere in legal texts (cf. VIR s.v.).

The deified Severus ... their beliefs: It is tempting to assume that the last sentence of the paragraph included in *Dig.* 50.2.3 is an interpolation. The term *superstitio* itself appears rarely in judicial writings and in only four other instances in the *Digest*. The first, by Ulpian, in the context of voluntary, compulsory, and judicial oaths (*De iureiurando sive voluntario sive necessario sive iudiciali*), records a rescript of Antoninus Pius that affirmed the validity of a superstitious oath, although not if this belief is publicly disapproved: *Divus Pius iureiurando, quod propria superstitione iuratum est, standum rescripsit* ('the deified Pius wrote in a rescript concerning oaths, that an oath by a superstitious individual should stand', *Dig.* 12.2.5.1.1).

The second, also by Ulpian, in the context of the Aedilian Edict, excludes *superstitio* as grounds for an *actio redhibitoria* under the Aedilian Edict: *alioquin, inquit, futurum, ut in infinito hac ratione multos sanos esse negaremus ut puta levem superstitiosum iracundum contumacem et si qua similia sunt animi vitia* ('otherwise, he said, it will occur that we will deny indefinitely that many are healthy, following this rational, if you acknowledge light *superstitio*, lightheadedness, obstinances, or similar things as faults of the mind', *Dig.* 21.1.1.9).

The third occurrence of *superstitio* is in *Dig.* 28.7.8.pr., in the context of conditions on institutions (*De condicionibus institutionum*), once again by Ulpian, excludes the validity of a superstitious oath: *...cum enim faciles sint nonnulli hominum ad iurandum contemptu religionis, alii perquam timidi metu divini numinis usque ad superstitionem, ne vel hi vel illi aut consequerentur aut perderent quod relictum est, praetor consultissime intervenit* ('for there are no few men who are easy to take an oath through contempt of religion, others who are extremely fearful of the divine to the extent of *superstitio*, the praetor most wisely intervened so that neither former nor later will lose themselves').

Here, the original meaning of *superstitio*, denoting inexplicable and exaggerated fear of the gods, is most visible. The fourth occurrence of the term *superstitio* in the *Digest*, and the only one not by Ulpian (48.19.30. pr.2), is in a discussion of penalties (*de poenis*). It prohibits anyone from inciting fears in the superstitious mind, assuming, of course, they are prone to such anxieties: *Si quis aliquid fecerit, quo leves hominum animi superstitione numinis terrentur, divus Marcus huiusmodi homines in insulam relegari rescripsit* ('if someone would have done something by which men's feeble souls are terrorised by *superstitio* of divine will, the deified Marcus wrote in a rescript that they are relegated to an island').

This is attributed to Modestinus, a near contemporary of Ulpian, who must have understood the meaning of *superstitio* in the same way as Ulpian, and before it became so closely associated with Christians and their persecution.

The positive, or at least neutral, tone of the term *superstitio* in the third book of the treatise on the duty of the proconsul is perplexing. Honoré, in a discussion of Ulpian's view of the relationship between law and religion, referred to this passage in passing but did not raise doubts concerning its authenticity. Mommsen pointed out that it appears both in the *Codex Florentininus* and in the *Collectio const. eccl.* p. 1310.

Grodzynski's diachronic study of the notion of *superstitio* indicates a consistent shift from the original Mid-Republican sense of excessive fear of the gods and an equivalent of the Greek *δεισιδαιμονία* to the meaning of superstition from the third century CE onwards. However, by that stage, the term *superstitio* had come to be closely associated with Christianity as a *religio illicita* and its persecution. Scholarship on Christian persecution under the Roman Empire is vast; however, see de Ste Croix 1963 and Barnes 1968. For the association between Christianity and *superstitio* see Janssen 1979 and Nagy 2002. For the use of Codex Theodosianus see Salzman 1987. For a study of Jewish *superstitio* during the High Empire see Ovadiah and Mucznik 2014, who do not discuss this passage.

§ 2162

... a list: The description by Ulpian of documenting the names on the album is corroborated by the album from Canusium (*ERCanosa* I, no 35.) and § 31 of the *lex Irnitana*. However, only the *lex Irnitana* mentions a quorum of decuriones.

Regarding the listing of names: see *Dig.* 50.3 *de albo scribendo.*

The municipal law: By the time of Ulpian, the phrase '*lex municipalis*' alluded to a municipal law that regulated the function of the municipium and followed a general scheme. The term initially appears in an inscription from Patavium in honour of an otherwise unattested Marcus Iunius Sabinus as *quattuorvir aediliciae potestatis* in accordance with the *lex Iulia municipalis* (*CIL* V 2864 = *ILS* 5406). Modern scholars assign the law to Julius Caesar and assume that the *lex municipalis* regulated municipal administration. Perhaps the most significant piece of evidence here is the so-called *Tabulae Heraclenses*, dated to 45 BCE and recording a detailed set of municipal regulations (probably a collection of several statutes) by which the city of Heraclea, which received Roman citizenship at 89 BCE, was controlled. It is impossible to assert a geographical scope for the original *lex Iulia municipalis* (possibly the whole of Italy). However, epigraphic evidence from the Flavian era onwards suggests that a municipal law (or constitution) became ubiquitous (at least in the Latin municipia) during this period. The so-called *lex Irnitana*, *lex Malacitana* (*CIL* II 1964 = *ILS* 6089), and *lex*

Salpensana (*CIL* II 1963 = *ILS* 6088) followed an identical structure (though varying in details, such as the number of decuriones in each city's *ordo*).

Book 4

§ 2163

Rutilius Lupus: The name Rutilius Lupus appears only once in the *Digest* (or in any other legal text). The identity of Rutilius Lupus mentioned here is hard to determine. It could not have been the same M. Rutilius Lupus who was praefectus of Egypt under Trajan (113–17 CE, Brunt 1975: 144) and praefectus annonae from 107 to 112 CE (*CIL* IX, 1435; cf. Veyne 1958: 212–13; D'Escurac 1976: 45, 52–3, 80, 84, 88).

A constitution: The terms *constitutio* or *constitutiones principum* are general expressions denoting imperial enactments. Gaius's often-quoted phrase enumerates six elements: laws, plebiscites, *senatus consulta*, imperial constitutions, official responses of those authorised to respond in the name of the emperor, and responses of legal experts: *Constant autem iura populi Romani ex legibus, plebiscitis, senatus consultis, constitutionibus principum, edictis eorum, qui ius edicendi habent, responsis prudentium. Lex est, quod populus iubet atque constituit. Plebiscitum est, quod plebs iubet atque constituit. Plebs autem a populo eo distat, quod populi appellatione universi cives significantur, connumeratis et patriciis; plebis autem appellatione sine patriciis ceteri cives significantur; unde olim patricii dicebant plebiscitis se non teneri, quia sine auctoritate eorum facta essent; sed postea lex Hortensia lata est, qua cautum est, ut plebiscita universum populum tenerent: Itaque eo modo legibus exaequata sunt* ('Roman law consists of statutes, plebiscites, senatus consulta, constitutions of the emperors, edicts of magistrates authorised to issue them, and opinions of jurists. A statute is a command and ordinance of the people; a plebiscite is a command and ordinance of the commonalty. The commonalty and the people are thus distinguished: the people are all the citizens, including the patricians; the commonalty are all the citizens, except the patricians. Whence in former times the patricians maintained that they were not bound by the plebiscites, as passed without their authority; but afterwards a statute called the *lex Hortensia* was enacted, which provided that the plebiscites should bind the people, and thus plebiscites were made co-ordinate with statutes', Gai. 1.2–3). However, by the classical era, 'whatever the emperor wishes has the force of law' (*Quod principi placuit, legis habet vigorem*) (*Dig.* 1.4.1.pr. Cf. *CJ* 1.14).

A magistrature: The term *magistrature* is used here to refer to a public office or duty, known in Latin as *munus* and in Greek as *λειτουργία*. Unlike municipal posts, such as *duoviri*, aediles, or praetors, a liturgy was a public service performed by an individual at their own expense. Festus (125) quotes the grammarian Verrius, of the Augustan era, who associated *munus* with *officium*, which he perceived as an office held. This view was shared by Cicero, who explained *munus*, alongside *ius* and *officium*, as the elements of *civitas* (Cic. *Rep.* 2.57). The Severan jurists Paulus and Marcianus explained *munus* as deriving from a moral obligation (Paulus, *Dig.* 50.16.18; Marcianus, *Dig.* 50.16.214). Moreover, there seems to have been a ubiquitous understanding that *municeps* and *municipium* are inseparable from *munus* (cf. Fest. 117, 127, 155; Gell. *NA* 16.13.6; Ulpianus, *Dig.* 50.1.1; Paulus, *Dig.* 50.16.18). Epigraphic evidence shows that undertaking *munera* brought honour to its holder. Particular liturgies could have included the organisation of the gladiatorial games (*munus gladiatorium*), the organisation of a cult, or the organisation and execution of public works and services.

Scarcely support themselves [Latin]: It is tempting to emend '*suo*' to '*suis*' because the singular is inconsistent with the plural it qualifies. However, there are two strong arguments against such emendation. The first is that all manuscripts have '*suo*'. The second is the singular '*ei*' further on in the sentence.

The wealthy: The Roman provincial government relied on local elites to maintain order and collect taxes from the very beginning (cf. Derow 1989; Ando 2006: 181). In a letter to his brother, Cicero wrote approvingly that the best citizens govern local communities (Cic. *Q. fr.* 1.1.25). A more proactive approach is attributed by Pausanias to Lucius Mummius, who, in 146 BCE, ended democracies in peninsular Greece and established magistracies based on property qualifications (Paus. 7.16.9). The term *locupletes*, as it is hereby applied, should not be confused with the *dekaprotoi* (δεκάπρωτοι). This college of the ten wealthiest *decuriones* can be attested from the middle of the first century CE in the east, with the *decuriones* as their counterpart in the west (cf. Jones, *LRE* 730 sqq.). Rather, the term *locupletes* denotes an upper municipal tier of those who could have offered benefactions to their cities as elected magistrates. These magistrates, chosen from the well-to-do, provided their cities with baths and gymnasia (gymnasiarch), supervision of markets and food supply (*agoranomos*), festivals and cults, and a long list of other designated magistracies. The principal motive for these benefactions was a sense of audience (Gleason 2006: 237, following Veyne 1976).

Elected to the curia: The term *curia* denoted the assembly of a municipal council under Roman rule. It is used both in *coloniae* and *municipia*. The **curia** always designates a building set on public land, usually in the city's forum (cf. Vitr. *De arch.* 5.1–2; Eder, W. 'Curia'. *BNP*).

Those who are in debt to the city: The term *debitores rerum publicarum* (literally 'debtors of public matters', but meaning those in debt to the city) alludes to those who were in debt to the treasury, the emperor, the province, or a city – in other words, those who were in debt not to a private person. These debts could have been formed in one of two ways: sums due (e.g., unpaid taxes) or standing debts resulting from loans. A loan originated from a real contract, *stricti iuris*, or a *stipulatio*. I translate the phrase '*debitores rerum publicarum*' as 'those who are in debt to the city' to avoid confusion with 'public debt', which nowadays denotes the debt of the city/state rather than an individual's debt to the city/state. Note also the comment of Marcian that those who are in debt to the city cannot act as ambassadors: *Sciendum est debitorem rei publicae legatione fungi non posse* ('it should be known that he who is in debt to the city cannot become legate', *Dig.* 50.7.5.pr).

A debt: The term '*mutua peculia*' means a debt. In the classical era, the term '*mutuum*' denoted a consensual contract by which a person gave another person a sum of money as a loan and the recipient received the money with the same intention. Cf. Gai. 3.90: *Re contrahitur obligatio velut mutui datione; mutui autem datio proprie in his fere rebus contingit, quae res pondere, numero, mensura constant, qualis est pecunia numerata, vinum, oleum, frumentum, aes, argentum, aurum; quas res aut numerando aut metiendo aut pendendo in hoc damus, ut accipientium fiant et quandoque nobis non eaedem, sed aliae eiusdem naturae reddantur. unde etiam mutuum appellatum est, quia quod ita tibi a me datum est, ex meo tuum fit.* ('An obligation by the delivery of an object is contracted, for example, in the case of a loan for consumption. This generally takes place with reference to things which are susceptible of being weighed, counted, or measured, such as money, wine, oil, grain, bronze, silver, and gold. This kind of property we transfer either by counting, measuring, or weighing it with the understanding that it shall belong to him who receives it, and that, at some time or other, not the same article, but another of the same nature, shall be returned to us, and therefore an obligation of this kind is called mutuum, because what was given to you by me, from being mine becomes yours').

Pledges: *Pignus* (a pledge), alongside *depositum*, *mutuum*, and *commodatum*, are contracts that Justinian classifies as real contracts. *Creditor quoque qui pignus accepit re obligatur, qui et ipse de ea ipsa re quam accepit restituenda tenetur actione pigneraticia. sed quia pignus utriusque gratia datur, et debitoris, quo magis ei pecunia crederetur, et creditoris, quo magis ei in tuto sit creditum, placuit sufficere, quod ad eam rem custodiendam exactam diligentiam adhiberet: quam si praestiterit et aliquo fortuito casu rem amiserit, securum esse nec impediri creditum petere.* ('A creditor, also, who has accepted a pledge is also liable on account of the property, and may be forced by an action of pledge to make restitution of the article received. But because a pledge is given for the benefit of both, namely for the debtor, in order that the money may be credited to him, and for the creditor, so that what he lends may be the more secure, it has been held that it is sufficient if the latter uses exact diligence in the preservation of the property; and if he has done this and has lost the same by some accident, he is safe, and not barred from bringing suit for the loan', *Inst.* 3.14.4). Cf. Jolowicz and Nicholas 1972: 299–301.

Sureties: Cf. *Inst.* 3.20: *Pro eo qui promittit solent alii obligari, qui fideiussores appellantur, quos homines accipere solent dum curant ut diligentius sibi cautum sit.* ('For him who promised, others are in the habit of being obliged, who are called fideiussores. People are accustomed to accept them in order that sufficient security may be provided for them'). See also *Dig.* 27.7; 4.1; *CJ* 5.57.8, 41.

Aufidius Herennianus: It is probably the same Aufidius Herennianus who was *cos. ord.* alongside Septimius Severus in 171 CE; *RE* s.v. Aufidius § 22. *PIR*[2] I, n. 1394.

An undertaking [*pollicitatio*]: *Pollicitatio* usually means an undertaking for the common good. However, unlike a *munus*, it is a single undertaking, clearly defined upon taking. Cf. *Dig.* 50.12 *De pollicitationibus*. Ulpian mentioned elsewhere that a person who has pledged an undertaking in return for an office must fulfil his pledge: *Si quidem ob honorem promiserit decretum sibi vel decernendum vel ob aliam iustam causam, tenebitur ex* *pollicitatione.* ('If anyone promised anything in return for an honour decreed to him, or that should be decreed, or for any other just cause, he is held accountable on the basis of *pollicitatio*', *Dig.* 50.12.11). And elsewhere: *Si ob honorem pollicitatio fuerit facta, quasi debitum exigatur.* ('If a promise has been made for an honour, it should be measured like a debt', *Dig.* 50.12.3.pr.).

Levies: *Intributio* is a post-classical term meaning a levy. It is used five times in the *Digest*, four times by Ulpian himself and once by Paul. More specifically, it refers to a levy (or tax) imposed on property. Cf. *Viae sternendae immunitatem veteranos non habere Iulio Sossiano veterano rescriptum est. nam nec ab intributionibus, quae possessionibus fiunt, veteranos esse excusatos palam est.* ('It is stated in a rescript to the veteran Iulius Sossianus that veterans do not have immunity from paving roads. Indeed, it is clear that veterans are not exempt from levies which originate from their possessions', *Dig.* 49.18.4). Cf. *Dig.* 50.1.22.7. Paul. 1 sent. Ulpian offers a definition: *Stipendium a stipe appellatum est, quod per stipes, id est modica aera, colligatur. idem hoc etiam tributum appellari Pomponius ait. et sane appellatur ab intributione tributum vel ex eo quod militibus tribuatur.* ('"*Stipendium*" is named after "stips" (donations), for by stipes, that is modest coins, it is collected. Similarly, Pomponius said this is also called "*tributum*". And surely "*tributum*" is named after *intributio*, or because it is tributed to the soldiers', *Dig.* 50.16.27.1). It is also used in the *Sententiae*, traditionally attributed (erroneously) to Paul, 1.1a.9; 2.7.1.; 2.7.4; 2.7.5.

Possessors: I translate the Latin term '*possessor*' as possessor to avoid confusion between ownership rights and the right of use (*usus fructus*) or between property and possession. However, Ulpian must have used possessor in the sense of an owner here.

Municipes: The term *municeps* originally meant a citizen of a free town. However, as Ulpian is writing after the enactment of the so-called *Constitutio Antoniniana*, the division between free cities and all others has been rendered obsolete. By the third century it merely means a citizen of a given city. An *incola*, however, is a resident who lacks full citizenship.

Incolae: Roman jurists distinguished citizens of cities (*municipales*) from mere residents (*incolae*). Cf. *Dig.* 50.1 *Ad municipalem et de incolis*; *CJ* 10.40.

§ 2165
Modestinus: Herennius Modestinus was a distinguished and prolific jurist and a pupil of Ulpian (*Dig.* 47.2.52.20). He was probably *a libellis* to Alexander Severus from 223 to 225 CE and a *praefectus vigilium.*

Laelius Bassus: otherwise unattested.

§ 2166
Paving roads: For paving roads as a common type of *munera*, from which there is no immunity, see *Dig.* 50.5.11.0 Hermog. 1 *iuris epit.* Based on the evidence from *Tabula Heracleensis* 7, it appears that the management of road maintenance fell under the jurisdiction of the aediles.

Iulius Sossianus: Otherwise unattested.

Aelius Firmus et Antoninus Clarus: Both are otherwise unattested.

§ 2167
... they could not be compelled to accept such an office unwillingly: The assumption of *munera*, without a strict legal requirement to do so, has been persuasively explained by Paul Veyne as an expression of a moral imperative (Veyne 1976).

§ 2168
Impuberes: *Impubes, -eris,* means a person under the age of puberty. *Impuberes* lacked full legal capacity under Roman law. However, the law did not specify a particular age. The Romans had a more ad hominem approach to the distinction between youth and adulthood, acknowledging a certain level of individuality on the matter.

Venidius Rufus: A military commander and provincial governor. He governed Cilicia until 196 CE, when he was transferred to Syria Phoenice. Later, he was appointed consular governor of Lower Germany (Alföldy 1967, p. 48, n. 58).

§ 2169
A son: The father–son relationship is crucial here, as a father could give only his son as a substitute to act on an embassy (*Dig.* 50.7.5.4).

Ambassador: Serving on an embassy of the city or province to the emperor was one of the seminal duties of the members of the municipal élite. The emperor habitually received provincial and municipal embassies to learn their needs and resolve disputes (cf. Plin. *Pan.* 79.6–7; Millar 1977: 375–85). These embassies could have requested political emendations, as is well attested by the hearing Augustus held after the death of Herod in 4 BCE (Josephus, *BJ* 2.7.3; *Ant.* 13.2; Millar 1977: 376). The service on such embassies was burdensome. The grounds for immunity from this service are discussed by jurists (cf. *Dig.* 50.7 and Millar 1977: 382–3).

Immunity: *Vacatio, -onis* c. gen. obj. means an exemption from a duty.

Our imperator: I.e., Caracalla. As mentioned in the preface, Ulpian composed almost all his work between 213 and 217, under the reign of Caracalla.

Claudius Callistus: Otherwise unattested.

Rescript: This was probably a *subscriptio*, as the response of Severus and Caracalla was included at the bottom of the letter Claudius Callistus had dispatched (cf. Millar 1977: 382).

The intervals of offices: As the service on an embassy was burdensome, it was decreed that after such service the person who undertook it is immune for two years from such service.

Only requires service: Those elected to act on embassies were also granted travel expenses known as *viaticum* or *legativus* (cf. *IGR* iv, 1156, i = Syll^3 837 with the comments of Robert, *Hellenica* vi, 80–4, ll. 17–18; IG vii, 2870; *Dig.* 50.7.3: *His, qui non gratuitam legationem susceperunt, legativum ex forma restituatur* ('to those who did not undertake the role of ambassador without pay, an ambassador's expenses will be given back, according to their rank'); Millar 1977: 383).

§ 2170
If someone ... : The meaning of the term *consuetudo, -inis* has long intrigued jurists and legal historians (cf. Mitteis 1891; Alonso 2013; 2020; Humfress 2012; Kaser 1939: 76–81; Gaudemet 1956: 149–50; Schiller 1938). Alonso (2013; 2020), following Humfress (2012), Kaser (1939: 76–81), Gaudamet

(1956: 149–50), and Schiller (1938), argued convincingly that *consuetudo* habitually denoted local (municipal, regional, or provincial) customs and administrative practices, not necessarily written. On the possibility of 'handbooks' of local laws and provincial habits, composed by Roman governors for their use, see Yiftach-Finako (2009). This was not alien to Roman thinking, as much of Rome's archaic law had never been actively enacted (except for the *XII Tables*, of course). Furthermore, exegesis of these laws as the basis for legal development prevailed well into the classical era (cf. Kaser 1939). For the similarity between *consuetudo* and *aequitas* as a basis for legal argumentation, see Humfress (2012: 24, n. 6). Ulpian said elsewhere that including *mos* in the legislative process allowed the praetor to secure equity (*Dig.* 25.4.1.14; Ulp. *Ad edictum* 24). Kaser (1939: 76–81) and Alonso (2020: 55, n. 54) cite the following texts to demonstrate a consistent use of the term *consuetudo* in the sense of administrative practice since the late Republic onwards: Cicero, *In Verr.* II 3.6.15, 3.15.38, 3.57.131, 3.62.142, 3.98.227, where *consuetudo* (*superiorum, a maioribus tradita*) refers to the habit of Verres' predecessors in the government of Sicily of continuing to collect the *decuma* in line with the regulations of the *lex Hieronica*. See also *In Verrem* II 5.22.57 (number of *laudationes pro reo*), *pro Quinctio* 6.28 (*missio in possessionem*), *pro Balbo* 7.17 (concession of citizenship), *pro Caecina* 8.23 (interdict). This is also the case in the excerpts of the jurists collected in the *Digest*: Ulpian, *On the Duties of the Proconsul* 1 (D.1.16.4.5) (*ingressus in provinciam* of the governor); Paul, *On the Edict* 6 (D. 3.4.6 pr.) (local *honores*) and 52 (D. 39.4.4.2) (*vectigalia*); Callistratus, *Judicial Inquiries* 1 (D. 50.2.11) (*decurionate*) and 4 (D. 22.5.3.6) (witness summons). Pliny, *Epistulae* 10.114–15 also concerns a question of public law.

The willingness of the imperial government to allow the continuance of these local practices (often described as *mos regionis*) alongside Roman law is nowadays perceived as a conscious Roman policy, from the second century CE onwards, to associate provincial diversity – if it did not clash with Roman interests – with social stability in the provinces. Modern scholars have concluded that, from the second century CE onwards, this pattern was instrumental in governing the provinces, as the Roman government was disinclined to impose its law and culture on the provincials (Alonso 2013: 379–86; Nörr 1969: 359–60; Humfress 2012; Mélèze-Modrzejewski 1970: 353–7; Mélèze-Modrzejewski 2014: 235–40). In fact, this was the main theme of Ando (2000).

This view finds its origin in an excerpt of the second century CE jurist Julian (110–c. 170 CE), which means before the enactment of the *Constitutio*

Antoniniana, which explained why some unwritten practices should be treated as law: *De quibus causis scriptis legibus non utimur, id custodiri oportet, quod moribus et consuetudine inductum est* ('as to those cases in which we do not use written laws, this should be maintained, which is brought forward by habits and customs', *Dig.* 1.3.32). While some scholars have questioned the authenticity of this excerpt, suggesting it is a post-classical interpolation (cf. Schiller 1938: 281), it is generally assumed that it pertained to provincial customs (cf. Schiller 1978: 263, 564–6; Humfress 2012: 26; Thomas 1963: 43; Stein 1995: 339).

It is noteworthy that when Ulpian composed his treatise on the duty of the proconsul after the *Constitutio Antoniniana* had been enacted, the universal grant of citizenship did not impose one judicial system throughout the Roman world or revoke local practices. In fact, on the evidence of (Ps.-)Menander, writing in the late third century CE, local customs were still in use (Treatise 1.3.363, lines 7–14). These practices were only replaced through a positive act of the emperor and his advisers during the third century onwards.

Book 5

§ 2171

He will ensue the origin of all [his new] patrons: A manumitted slave took the name of the gens of his manumitter (i.e., previous owner), who now became his/her patron.

§ 2172

Tutelage: *Tutela* is a guardianship over persons who are *sui iuris* but who cannot manage their property. There were various sub-categories of tutela, depending on the reasons for the requirement of guardianship (age, gender, or mental state) and the mechanism of its institution (e.g., *tutela fiducaria, tutela legitima, tutela legitima parentis, tutela legitima patronis, tutela testamentaria*).

Personal: For the distinction between *munera aut personae aut patrimoniorum*, see § 2164.

§ 2174

A reduction: *Deminutio* means a reduction. This could refer to a reduction in the scale of a financial commitment (as in this context) or in civic status, as in the case of *deminutio capitis*.

A promise: *Pollicitatio* [to a res publica. I set aside the more complex matter of *pollicitatio* of one person to another] is a promise of a gift or an opus made by a person towards a municipality. This promise was considered binding and could be sued for (*Dig.* 50.12 *De pollicitationibus*). Originally, such promises were made by newly elected officials to celebrate their election; Garnsey 1971: 116. It is similarly prevalent in inscriptions, cf. *AE* 1957, n. 0077; 1899, n. 0113; *CIL* viii, 27374 = *AE* 1997, 1649; *AE* 1948, n. 0116; *AE* 1933, n. 0067; *AE* 1901, n. 0191; *AE* 2005, n. 1689 = *CIL* viii, 26458 = *ILAfr* 514; *AE* 2009, n. 1232; *AE* 1991, n. 1619. It is one of three contractual constructions (alongside votum and indicium) which would have been undertaken unilaterally and yet became binding; Villers 1939: 3, and *passim.*

Debt: The term *aes alienum*, which literally means '(the) money of another person', means a debt.

Money: *Non ins.* Mommsen suggested inserting non to negate the honorem (i.e., the promise had been made not on account of an office), which seems to agree with the context but has no support in the MSS. The reason is that this clarification was only necessary if the pledge was not made on account of an office. But see contra, Villers 1939: 26.

Has begun to pay: Ulpian gives elsewhere a definition of 'works begun': *Coepisse sic accipimus, si fundamenta iecit vel locum purgavit. Sed et si locus illi petenti destinatus est, magis est, ut coepisse videatur. Item si apparatum sive impensam in publico posuit* ('We understand "begun" thus: if the ground-works have been laid, or if the place has been cleaned. And if the place has been designated to the one asking for it, for the most part, it should be seen as begun. Similarly, if preparation or expenditure has been placed in public', *Dig.* 50.12.1.3).

A project: The term opus here must refer to an undertaking. One would assume that the erection of a public building was intended, as one had to complete such a work once begun.

But also women: This is relevant for women both because they could have undertaken public roles (cf. *CIL* xiv, 2804 = *ILS* 6218 and, more generally, Hemelrijk 2004; 2006; 2012) and because they could have undertaken *pollicitatio*, as shown by the example of *ILAlg* i, 286 = *CIL* viii, 5365 = *CIL* viii, 17495, and *ILAlg* I, 287 = *CIL* vii, 5366.

The obligation of setting up statues of the prince: Dedications of statues of the emperor (and members of the imperial household) were a common practice of the ruler cult. Its carrying out was a form of liturgy: Price 1984: 170–206, and *passim*.

§ 2175

On judicial assembly: The term *conventus* here means a judicial assembly, the court of justice, known as the assize system. The assizes were annual assemblies of the governor's court in various cities of his allocated province, for the purpose of holding court. On the Roman assizes system see Burton 1975; Habicht 1975; Haensch 1997b; and Bryen 2012.

Queries: For the present participle of consuleo to denote a lawyer, see *L&S* v.s., 1B.

However, provincial governors ... matters of fact: In Roman law, a division between law and fact existed only to the extent that these two categories have been juxtaposed, but not as abstractions. More specifically, Roman law addressed this dichotomy under four circumstances: 1. Ignorance (*ignorantia iuris/facti*), 2. Conditions (*condiciones iuris/facti*), 3. Actions (*actiones in ius/in factum*), and 4. Questions (*quaestiones facti/iuris*). On the distinction between matter of fact and matter of law in the context of Roman jurisprudence cf. Georgescu 1948; Cornu Ténard 2011.

Religio: Rabello 1974: 74 rightly pointed out that the reliance on religio 'carries, we might say, a certain Justinianean flavour'. In fact, this phrase has been considered an interpolation on these grounds by Beseler 1930: 33 and Dell'Oro 1960: 142. Of course, the question of whether this sentence was interpolated at any time between when Ulpian published his *de officio proconsulis* and the compilation of the *Digest* pertains directly to the meaning of the word 'religio'. If it is a Justinianean interpolation, it should be translated as 'religion', or even 'true religion', particularly considering that Ulpian ascribed to Jews *superstitio* which they must preserve, § 2161. If this phrase is genuine, it should be better understood (and translated) as 'moral obligation'.

§ 2176

Defaming his master: By the time of Ulpian, slaves were still considered as res, and were subjected to the theoretically unbounded potestas of their owner, hence to his vitae necisque potestas. However, under certain circumstances a slave could bring an accusation against his/her owner. One of these circumstances was a breach of the prohibition of sexual abuse and castration of slaves by their owners for commercial purposes. These prohibitions were included under the *Lex Cornelia de sicariis et veneficiis*. Another was granted by a rescript of Antoninus Pius which banned random and inexplicable acts of cruelty. This rescript is also mentioned by Ulpian in this treatise (§ 2213) and will be discussed *ad loc.* For seeking asylum at imperial sanctuaries see Gamauf 1999: 130–5.

Refuge at a statue of the emperor: Slaves taking refuge at the statue of the emperor is an example of an expression of the Roman notion of clemency. See, for example: 'Even slaves have the right of refuge at the statue of a god; and although the law allows anything in dealing with a slave, yet in dealing with a human being there is an extreme which the right common to all living creatures refuses to allow' (*Servis ad statuam licet confugere; cum in servum omnia liceant, est aliquid, quod in hominem licere commune ius animantium vetet*, Seneca, *De Clementia*, 18.2).

A severe punishment: The construction of animadverto with in aliquem often means to execute: Cic. *In Verr.* 2, 2, 23; Liv. 1, 26. However, I translate it as 'punish severely' as it is adjoined to another punishment here.

Book 6

§ 2177

an illicit association: *Collegium* is a generic term denoting to a group of people who associated for a common religious, professional, or commercial purpose. *Collegia* played an instrumental part in Rome's social, economic, and religious life. The laws under which *collegia* operated have been initially set out in the *XII Tables* 8.27 = *Dig.* 47.22.4. The *collegia* had officers, regulations, and a body of members. *Collegia* could have had assets independently of their members. Title 47.22 of the *Digest*, from which this excerpt is taken (*De collegiis et corporibus*) is concerned predominantly with the hazards *collegia* could have posed to the social order, in the form of violence, or social stability, in the form of subversive religious practices and beliefs. In fact, the *collegia* were banned by Caesar and again by Augustus, who later prescribed in a *lex Iulia* under which conditions they can operate (*CIL* vi, 2193 = *ILS* 4966). *Collegia* of professionals were commonplace.

Inscriptions and papyri allude to *collegia* of bakers, belt-makers, butchers, carpenters, donkey-drivers, dyers, weavers, ferrymen, fullers, glass-makers, goldsmiths, greengrocers, hieroglyph carvers, potters, river-pilots, salt merchants, shoemakers, silversmiths, undertakers, and a broad range of other occupations; cf. Gibbs 2012, with references.

Usurp: *L&S* cite this passage, alongside Suet. *Claud.* 25; Cod. *Just.* 8.10.8; Plin. *HN* 35, 10.36.71: Liv. 34.32.2 id. 33.40.5; Tac. *Ann.* 14, 26, to mean 'To assume or appropriate unlawfully, to usurp'. This meaning of the verb is exclusively post-Augustan.

found guilty … : Several late Republican laws have been enacted to tackle violent crimes, the first of which was the *lex Plautia de vi* of 89 BCE. Two later Augustan *leges Iuliae* addressed public and private acts of violence. In addition, a praetorian edict against violence through the application of armed men is mentioned twice in Cicero's speech in defence of his client Marcus Tullius, who filed a countersuit for assault and property loss due to a neighbour with armed slaves. In a later letter to Gaius Trebatius Testa, Cicero mentions an exception in the praetor's interdict concerning violence; Cic. *Pro Tull.* 29, 44; *Ad Fam.* 7.13.2. The praetorian edict Cicero referred to is: *Unde tu illum vi hominibus coactis armatisve deiecisti aut familia tua deiecit, eo illum quaeque ille tunc ibi habuit restituas* ('Whence you have ejected a person by violence, with men collected or armed, or your family have ejected, thither you shall restore the designated person and whatever the designated person then had there', Lenel, *EP* § 245).

§ 2178

Unborn child: Roman jurists used the term *venter* to denote the fetus from the moment of conception until birth. During this time, the fetus enjoyed all the rights of a person under Roman law. The second-century CE jurist Julian is excerpted by Justinian in *Dig. 1.5* (*de statu hominum*) to express just that: *Qui in utero sunt, in toto paene iure civili intelleguntur in rerum natura esse* ('those who are in the uterus are perceived by the *ius civile* to be almost in existence', *Dig.* 1.5.27). Ulpian explained elsewhere that the wife of a prisoner is placed in possession of his property to protect the rights of a potential child she might be carrying, and who might entertain a hope to be born (*spes nascendi*) before his father is freed and in case his yet alive grandfather might die: *Si filius ab hostibus captus sit, uxor eius praegnas in possessionem soceri bonorum mittenda est: nam aliquo casu* *spes est id quod nascitur inter suos heredes futurum, ut puta si pater eius apud hostes decedat* ('if a son is captured by enemies, his pregnant wife should be placed in possession of the property of her father-in-law; for there is a hope that under certain circumstances a child is born and will become among the natural heirs (*suus heres*), for example, if his father would die in captivity', *Dig.* 37.9.1.8). Hence, the legal status of a posthumous child is defined and discussed separately from the medical (and, as Yan Thomas et al. have noticed, theological) question of when life begins; cf. Thomas 1986: 211 and *passim*; Thomas 2007: 31.

Curator: A *curator ventris* was entrusted by a *paterfamilias* to secure the inheritance rights of his unborn child in the case of being born posthumously. He acted as a curator for the *venter*, which meant both the mother and the unborn child, for ten months after the father deceased. He was entrusted by the father to safeguard the pregnancy and then to act as a curator for both the child, who is a *suus heres*, and the mother. Cf. the title *De ventre in possessionem mittendo et curatore eius* in the *Digest.* 37.9 with Thomas 1986.

The Judgement of a Good Man: The phrase '*boni viri arbitratu*' was habitually used in legal sources (and elsewhere). However, it was not a technical term or one used only in a legal context. Cato (*Agr.* 148) used this expression in the context of wine sold for future delivery when explaining how the parties were to guarantee the quality of the wine conveyed, considering what was promised when the sale had been agreed upon. Cato explained that the wine will be tasted by a *vir bonus* who will confirm the wine's quality upon tasting (*viri boni arbitratu degustato*).

§ 2179

Curator: A *curator furiosi* was appointed to manage the property of a *furiosus/furiosa.* According to the second-century jurist Paul, this curatorship was necessary, as the *furiosus/-a* could not manage their property: *In negotiis contrahendis alia causa habita est furiosorum, alia eorum qui fari possunt, quamvis actum rei non intellegerent: nam furiosus nullum negotium contrahere potest, pupillus omnia tutore auctore agere potest* ('in contracting business transactions there is one case for lunatics, another for those who can speak but do not understand the meaning of a thing (i.e., the young): for the lunatic can contract no transaction, and a ward can do it with the authority of a tutor', *Dig.* 50.17.5). The term *furiosus* itself should be translated as 'lunatic', and it is a different category from the *prodigus/-a*, which is best translated as a spendthrift. The *cura furiosi* can be dated back to the *XII Tables*, but its origin is probably in an even earlier custom. During Rome's early days a *curator furiosi* was appointed by the father or by the extended family in the case of intestacy. The curator was liable for losses caused by malice and incompetence at the end of his curatorship via an *actio negotiorum gestorum*. Cf. Manthe 1989.

After taking possession of the property according to the will: The *bonorum possessio secundum tabulas* referred to the possession granted by the praetor, by the terms of the will, to the individuals named as *heredes* when there was no one entitled to contest the will or when no one wished to challenge it. This possession was also granted *secundum tabulas* in situations where all the necessary legal procedures had not been followed if there were seven valid witnesses to the will (Gaius, II.147).

§ 2180

A foster sibling: *Dig.* 40.2.11.13 = *Bas* 48.2.13. *Libri numerus in inscriptione om. F.* (Lenel). While Lenel sensibly collated *Dig.* 40.2.11.11and *Dig.* 40.2.11.13 into a single section (§ 2180), Tribonian, in *Dig.* 40.2, under the title *De manumissis vindicta*, included an excerpt from Ulpian's second book on the *lex Aelia Sentia* in between. It reads *Vel si sanguine eum contingit (habetur enim ratio cognationis)* ('or is connected to him by blood (this is the meaning of being connected by birth)') and it serves as an explanation to *Dig.* 40.2.11.13, following the initial guideline presented in *Dig.* 40.2.11.11. The *lex Aelia Sentia* was enacted in 4 CE and discussed in Gai. 1.13–19, 36–41; 80; 3.72–76.

Paedagogus: *Paedagogus* is a transliteration of the Greek *παιδαγωγός*, which means a slave who acts as a governor and is in charge of the children.

Capsarius: Both Mommsen and Lenel pointed out that the phrase *id est qui portat libros* is a later gloss and is not Ulpian's.

Book 7

§ 2181

It is befitting … : The maintenance of peace, law, and order in the province, which Ulpian portrays as an easily achieved goal (*Quod non difficile optinebit*), took considerable effort on a municipal, provincial, and imperial level. Bandits, organised in quasi-military forms, presented a continuous threat to social order and constituted a considerable challenge to the authorities; cf. Wolff 2003; Pottier 2004. Despite the image that emerges from this excerpt of Ulpian, the task of maintaining public order was primarily municipal. However, a systematic approach to the upkeep of law and order is unattested in the Hellenistic or Republican period and was, in all likelihood, inaugurated by Augustus. Designated magistracies such as the irenarch (*εἰρηνάρχης*) and the guard in charge of territorial supervision (*παραφύλαξ*) were established. A municipal police force (διωγμῖται) was ubiquitous. A wide array of lower-rank municipal magistracies was also active in securing the peace; cf. Brélaz 2005: 157–203. The irenarch was employed to tour the countryside to survey disturbances of peace. While it is unclear whether the irenarch was nominated by the provincial governor, as can be inferred from Aelius Aristides *Or.* 50.72, or whether he was nominated by the cities themselves, as convincingly argued by Brélaz 2005: 108–14, this office was either inaugurated by the imperial government or simply encouraged. Provincial military forces were also employed. The provincial governor, particularly in the senatorial provinces where no army was stationed, had limited means at his disposal for maintaining the peace. These included the *stationarii*, the *regionarii*, and the *officiales*. In extreme circumstances, legions were activated, as can be inferred from the speech of Marcus Aurelius in the senate on the subject of *latrones manifesti* (*Dig.* 28.3.6.9).

This he will achieve … : The Roman emperor, and by derivation the provincial governor, is often depicted as a reactive figure. However, this excerpt from Ulpian portrays an image of an active governor who seeks to enforce law and order proactively, rather than awaiting litigants at his court. A similar train of thought is encapsulated in the phrase *rei publicae interest, ne crimina remaneant impunita* ('it is of the interest of the general public that crimes do not remain unpunished'); cf. *Dig.* 9.2.51(52).4.

Sacrilegious: The original meaning of the term is a person who steals sacred objects; cf. Cic. *Leg.* 2, 16, 40; Liv. 29, 18; Cic. *In Verr.* 2, 1, 3,

§ 9; Quint. 5, 10, 36; cf. id. 3, 6, 38; 3, 6, 41; 4, 2, 68; Sen. *Ira* 2, 28, 8; Vulg. *Act.* 19, 37. However, I translate it here as 'profane', following Ter. *Eun.* 419; Ov. *Met.* 4, 23; Ter. *Ad.* 304; Cic. *In Verr.* 2, 3, 28, § 69; Tib. 3, 5, 11; Mart. 9, 70, 2, which allows a wider understanding of Ulpian's train of thought.

§ 2182
Letters: In this context, the meaning of *litterae* is not merely a letter, but an official document produced by a Roman magistrate.

An official: The *apparitores* were salaried assistants of Roman magistrates. Subcategories of such assistants include secretaries (*scribae*), messengers (*viatores*), heralds (*praecones*), and attendants (*lictores*). The *apparitores* served for long periods of time, hence becoming an invaluable aspect of the imperial government. They belonged to associations such as *collegia* and *decuriae apparitorum*. Cf. Purcell 1983.

Allowed to enter: Ulpian referred elsewhere to a resolution of the senate which stated that anyone who conceals a fugitive is a thief: *pr. Is qui fugitivum celavit fur est* (Ulpianus, *libro primo ad edictum*).

§ 2183
The insane: For the legal status of lunatics (*furiosi*), see § 2158 above.

Prison: The Latin term *carcer* is derived from the verb *coercere*, which suggests a strong link to the magisterial power of *coercitio*. According to Varro (*Ling.* 5.151), the *carcer* was a place of detention, thus a place for holding the accused before and during trial, not a prison where the convicted served a sentence. This becomes clear from Ulpian's ninth book of this treatise, where he emphasised that the provincial governor should maintain a *carcer* for the detention, not the punishment, of people: *Solent praesides in carcere continendos damnare aut ut in vinculis contineantur: sed id eos facere non oportet. Nam huiusmodi poenae interdictae sunt: carcer enim ad continendos homines, non ad puniendos haberi debet* ('Governors are accustomed to condemning those who should be held to jail or even to be put in fetters, but it is advisable that they do not do that. Punishments of this sort are forbidden. Jail should be used to hold people, not to punish them', *Dig.* 48.19.8.9). Imprisonment was an essential part of an *imperium* bearer magistrate (*Dig.* 2.4.2). However, during the Republic, it probably fell under the jurisdiction of the *tresviri capitales* (Plaut. *Amph.* 155). See Rivière 1994 and 2004.

Persona: The term *persona* has a dual meaning here. The more common use of this word is a mask, or a false face, with a strong theatrical connotation. Hence, Marcus Aurelius and Lucius Verus thought that whether the offender feigned madness to escape culpability should be examined.

Parricide: *Parricidium*, which could be easily translated as parricide, and with more difficulty as the assassination of a parent, was the quintessential heinous crime in Roman culture. It is the charge Cicero's client faced in his first appearance at the court while defending Sextus Roscius (*de parricidio causa dicitur*; Cic. *Pro Sext. Rosc.* § 61). While the etymology of *parricidium* is still obscure (cf. Dyck 2010: 13ff), by the end of the Republic *parricidium* encompassed the murder of not only family members but also patrons (*Dig.* 48.9.1). The person convicted of *parricidium* was to be placed in a sack alongside a snake, a dog, an ape, and a cock and then – while still alive – tossed into the Tiber (*Dig.* 48.9.9; *Inst.* 4.18.6). However, a late Republican *lex Pompeia* subsumed the murder of a family member under the general umbrella of murder. Culprits were now tried before the standing courts (*quaestiones*) and – if found guilty – exiled (*Dig.* 48.9.1).

Punished: The passive form of the verb *plecto, -ere* means to blame. However, it was not a commonly used term. It appears in only two other instances in judicial writings with a similar meaning: *Dig.* 3.1.1.3 (Ulp. 6 *ad ed.*) and *CTh* 10.10.13 (*edictum ad provinciales*).

§ 2184

An accusation: The term *crimen* could have denoted the accusation, the legal process of handling a crime, or the offence itself. Until the classical era, *crimen* referred exclusively to criminal matters, with the term *delictum* covering wrongdoing prosecuted through private actions. The two terms were later used interchangeably because public prosecutions now also included *delicta*.

Subscriptio: The term *subscriptio* means a signature. In a criminal procedure, an accusation – written or oral – had to be signed by the accuser (*CJ* 7.57: *Comminationes epistulas programmata subscriptiones auctoritatem rei iudicatae non habere*).

Salvius Valens: (*PIR*[1] S 116), who is mentioned here as the governor of Aquitania, is in all likelihood not one of Pius' esteemed jurists mentioned in his *SHA* biography 12.1. Cf. Syme 1989a.

Prejudice: The technical term *praeiudicare* means to impair, cause damage, or prejudice.

Not easily ... : This refers to an act of deception in the context of all types of legal dispute or formal transaction. Gaius defined *calumnia* as a conscious act of deception with the intention of securing a favourable verdict: *nam calumniae iudicio X. partis nemo damnatur nisi qui intellegit non recte se agere, sed uexandi aduersarii gratia actionem instituit potiusque ex iudicis errore uel iniquitate uictoriam sperat quam ex causa ueritatis* ('no one is condemned in a *iudicium* of calumnia in the tenth part unless he knows that he did not conduct himself rightfully, but for the purpose of vexing his adversary he instituted an accusation and he was hoping for a victory more out of a judicial error or inequity than out of a right cause', *Gai.* 4.178).

Iulius Candidus: Proconsul of Asia under Antoninus Pius, in the year 143/4 CE. As Syme has noted, 'there is a plethora of persons called *Iulius Candidus*' (1983: 274). The recipient of this rescript was probably the same Iulius Candidus who was praetor in 121 CE (*AE* 1965, 337).

§ 2185
Salvius Carus: (*PIR*[1] S 99) served as proconsul Crete and Cyrene in 134/5 CE, under Hadrian; cf. Syme 1989a: 182.

§ 2186
Sacrilegium: The theft of sacred objects (*furtum sacrorum*), i.e., of *res religiosae*. Such an act was a capital offence. It was only during late antiquity (380 CE) that the notion of *sacrilegium* became associated with a violation of divine law, presumably due to an error or negligence, and without *mens rea*; *CJ* 9.29.1.

Pontius Proculus: Otherwise unattested.

After he has investigated: I translate *cognoverit* as 'has investigated'. The verb *cognoscere*, and its cognate *cognitio*, habitually referred to a judicial process undertaken by the emperor or an imperium-bearing magistrate. In this procedure, the judicial process was not divided into two parts, the first in front of a magistrate (*in iure*) and the second in front of a judge/judges (*apud iudicem*). The person conducting the *cognitio* process was free to conduct all relevant inquiries, summon witnesses, and subpoena documents and other pieces of evidence.

On the detention of the accused: *Reus* is the accused in either civil or criminal legal disputes.

§ 2187

A rescript in Greek: Although Latin was the official language, Greek was habitually used in public addresses in the Greek East.

Cast in chains: Literally 'cast in chains' (or 'of the fetters of prisoners'), but the expression *in vincula* has an idiomatic meaning of prison; cf. Cic. *In Verr.* 2.3.24: *aliquem aeternis tenebris vinculisque mandare* ('place someone in eternal darkness or chains'), Cic. *Cat.* 4.5.10: *de convivio in vincla atque in tenebras abripi*, Cic. *In Verr.* 2.4.10: *in vincula conjectus*, Caes. *Bell. Gal.* 3.9; 4.27: *in vincula duci*, Liv. 3.13.4; 3.49.2; 3.56.4; 3.57.5; 5.9.4; 9.34.24; 38.56.9; Vell. 2.7.2 al.: *in vinculis et catenis*; *Dig.* 1.2.2.16; 4.6.23; 11.5.1.4; 47.10.38; 48.3.5.

Fideiussor: *fideiussores* < *sponsores*? Lenel *ad loc.* The *fideiussor* (alongside the *sponsor* and the *fideipromissor*) was a surety of a debt or appearance in court through a *stipulatio.* The division of sureties into three categories was based on the pledge of the guarantor. However, by the classical era all three fused into one, who was called *fideiussor*; cf. *Inst.* 3.20; *Dig.* 46.1; *CJ* 2.23; 8.40.

Punishment: The distinction between the *poena* and the *supplicium* is consistent with the understanding of the *carcer* as a place of detention, which was not punitive per se.

Detention: While *supplicium* could mean any type of punishment, it usually refers to capital punishment.

§ 2188

Lucius Minicius Natalis was a distinguished magistrate. An inscription records his *cursus honorum*, which culminated in him serving as a consul suffect in 106 CE (*CIL* ii, 4509 = *ILS* 1061). Amongst various magistracies, he served as a *legatus proconsulis* in the province of Africa, later a praetorian governor of Numidia in 103/4 CE and a governor of Pannonia Superior, before serving as the proconsul of the important province of Africa in 121/2 CE; cf. Syme 1989b: 247 ff; Eck 1983.

Holidays: *feriae*, or *dies festi* were days in which agricultural, commercial, and official work has been interdicted. Amongst the activities included under the interdiction was judicial activity (*vacatio a forensibus negotiis*) cf. Cic. *Div.* 1,102; cf. Isid. *Nat.* 1,4. A breach of the interdiction was a punishable offence: Harmon 1978.

prosecution of persons in custody: Ulpian used the same expression in § 2144: *Solent etiam custodiarum cognitionem mandare legatis* ... ('Governors are accustomed to give jurisdiction pertaining detainees to their legates ... ') The term *cognitio* cannot have a technical meaning here. Nor is it associated with what certain modern scholars refer to as *cognitio extra ordinem* procedure. Rather, it denoted simply an inquiry, which must have been an informal and preliminary stage of the *forense negotium*. As in the case of the inquiry undertaken by the legate, which Ulpian discussed above, the *cognitio* was not part of the legal process (otherwise it would have been interdicted, alongside all *forenses negotia*). For an overview see Turpin 1999.

§ 2189

Absentees ... : Koschaker 1919: 368, n. 1 assumed that this cannot be genuine, especially since it is immediately restricted to *poenae graviores*. Instead, he suggested reading it as an explanatory gloss on the imperial rescript, which in the present version has been transmitted only in abridged and distorted form.

Iulius Frontinus: In all likelihood, it is the same Sextus Julius Frontinus who wrote the treatise *De aquaeductu* and *Strategemata*. Although a *novus homo*, Frontinus ascended to the consulate three times, was an accomplished general, and was governor of Britain. On the career of Frontinus see Ward Perkins 1937.

Adsidius Severus: It is possible that Adsidius Severus is identical to the consular Annidius Severus, recorded in *ILS* 7378. Cf. Groag in *PIR*², A 107, and 625, and Syme 1958: 5 n. 51.

For it is better that a guilty ... : This principle seems out of place in a guidebook to a provincial governor, as it articulates a basic principle of the Roman penal system and, more generally, jurisprudence. In fact, Nogrady (2006), having studied Ulpian's outline of the Roman criminal law in books 7–9 of this work, has convincingly concluded that Ulpian attempted a general and systematic outline of contemporary criminal law, rather than focusing exclusively on provincial matters.

according to the custom of private judgements: The division between *iudicia publica* (criminal proceedings) and *iudicia privata* became manifest in the legislation of Augustus; *Inst.* 4.18.1; cf. *Dig.* 5.1.2.1. They are called public, because any member of the public is given an official authority to instigate such procedures: *Publica autem dicta sunt, quod cuivis ex populo exsecutio eorum plerumque datur* ('they are called public because their execution is habitually given to each member of the public', *Inst.* 4.18.1). However, only certain laws belonged in this category: *Non omnia iudicia, in quibus crimen vertitur, et publica sunt, sed ea tantum, quae ex legibus iudiciorum publicorum veniunt, ut Iulia maiestatis, Iulia de adulteriis, Cornelia de sicariis et veneficis, Pompeia parricidii, Iulia peculatus, Cornelia de testamentis, Iulia de vi privata, Iulia de vi publica, Iulia ambitus, Iulia repetundarum, Iulia de annona* ('Not all cases in which crime is involved are public, but only those which are derived from the laws relating to the prosecution of crimes, such as the Julian Law on Treason; the Julian Law on Adultery; the Cornelian Law on Assassins and Poisoners; the Pompeian Law on Parricide; the Julian Law on Peculation; the Cornelian Law on Wills; the Julian Law on Private Violence; the Julian Law on Public Violence; the Julian Law on the Bribery of Voters; the Julian Law on Extortion; and the Julian Law on *Annona*', *Dig.* 48.1.1). Not all these procedures pertained to capital offences (48.1.2). However, a public trial is annulled in the absence of the accused: *Publica accusatio reo vel rea ante defunctis permittitur* (*Dig.* 48.1.3). For further discussion see Kaser and Hackl 1996: 115–16; Crawford 1996 § 61.

pecuniary penalties: It appears that *imperium*-bearing magistrates had a certain amount of discretion when inflicting a penalty. Thus, Ulpian explained elsewhere that in legal inquiries that could lead to prosecution (i.e., in conducting *cognitiones*) presided over by prefects or provincial governors, pecuniary penalties could be replaced with other punishments if the culprit is insolvent. Justinian included both excerpts under the title *de poeniis* in the *Dig.* 48.19.1.3.

capital punishment: Capital punishment could mean execution, banishment, or enslavement: *Rei capitalis damnatum sic accipere debemus, ex qua causa damnato vel mors vel etiam civitatis amissio vel servitus contingit* ('We must see a person to have been convicted of a capital crime if he is found guilty of an offence which entails death, the loss of civil rights, or servitude', *Dig.* 48.19.2.pr).

Senatus Consultum Turpillianum: The *SC Turpillianum* (62 CE) is discussed in *CJ* 9.45. It interdicts an accuser to be absent from the proceedings he has instigated, without having first secured a dismissal (*abolitio*). An accuser who fails to secure such annulment and is still absent is subjected to infamy (*infamia*) and shall be punished further in extraordinary cognition; *CJ* 9.45.2. Rules governing dismissal are explained at *CJ* 9.44, and *Dig.* 48.16.

§ 2190
Punishment: The *lex Iulia peculatus* imposed pecuniary penalties, specifically a quadruple sum of the embezzled amount (*Dig.* 48, 13, 1 [Ulp.]; *Dig.* 48, 13, 15 [Mod.]; Sent. Paul 5, 27, 1; *Dig.* 49, 14, 46, 9 [Hermogenianus]; *CTh* 10, 24, 1 = *CJ* 10, 6, 1 [368/70]; *CTh* 9, 28, 1 [392]; Ed. Theod., 115). A pecuniary penalty is also mentioned in the municipal law of Terentius (*Roman Statutes*, n. 15. 1.4). However, Ulpian noted elsewhere that peculatus was also sanctioned with *aquae et ignis interdictio*, although the *lex peculatus* is not explicitly mentioned (*Dig.* 48, 13, 3). As argued by Mommsen et al., this was not necessarily mandatory.

The culprit's nature: By the term *qualitas*, Ulpian denoted social status. See the note on *honestiores* below.

Hanged on the gallows: An instrument of torture, shaped like a fork (V or II), was placed under the culprit's neck, with the arms fastened to the two ends. This instrument is mentioned in literary sources such as Plaut. *Pers.* 5.2.71; id. *Cas.* 2.6.37; Cic. *Div.* 1.26.55; Liv. 2.36.1; Val. Max. 1.7.4; Lact. 2.7.20. It also appears eight times in legal texts: *Dig.* 48.19.9.11 (Ulp. *de off. proc.*); *Dig.* 48.19.28 (Call. *De cogn.*); *Dig.* 48.19.28.15 (Call. *De cogn.*); *Dig.* 48.19.38.1, 2 (Paul. 5 sent.); *Dig.* 49.16.3.10 (Mod. *De poen.*); Paul. 5.21a.2.

Mines: *In metallem damnare* means condemnation to a lifetime of hard labour in a mine or a quarry. It is the second severest punishment, after death (*proxima morti*). It pertains to the loss of freedom; those subjected to it were kept in fetters.

Of noble birth: During the second century CE and onwards, Roman penal law increasingly distinguished between culprits of noble birth (*honestiores*) and those of humble descent (*humiliores*). *Honestiores* included senators, equites, decurions, and veterans. Members of these classes were exempt from torture, various forms of dishonour, hard labour, and essentially from capital punishment, as they were given the option of exile. The terms *honestiores* and *humiliores* are first attested in Ps. Paul, *Sententiae*, before becoming ubiquitous. However, no legal definition of these categories is known (Garnsey 1970; Rilinger 1988).

§ 2191
Christians: Lenel commented *ad loc.*: *verisimile est Ulpianum de Christianis aut sub titulo de sacrilegis aut ad legem Iuliam maiestatis egisse* ('it is likely that Ulpian discussed [them] under the title on Christians or of sacrilege, or under the Julian law on treason').

§ 2191
Domitius: While it is not unlikely that Ulpian addressed the legal repercussions of being a Christian, the wording Lactantius used is probably not Ulpian's.

§ 2192
Astrologers: On astrologers and soothsayers, this excerpt is from Lactant. *div. inst.* 5.11. *Verisimile est Ulpianus de Christianis aut sub titulo de sacrilegis aut ad legem Iuliam maiestatis egisse*; Lenel *ad loc.*

L. Caelius Firmianus Lactantius (c. 250–325) was a Christian author who wrote in Latin. Born in Africa and dying in Gaul, Lactantius was one of the most important Christian authors during the third and early fourth centuries. The work used here was dedicated to Constantine and reflects how embedded Christian thought was in Graeco-Roman literature.

Senatus Consultum of Pomponius' and Rufus' consulate: The consulship of Pomponius and Rufus was in the year 15 CE, under the reign of Tiberius.

Fire and water: *Aqua et igni interdictio* was originally an *ad hoc* ruling of a Roman magistrate against a fugitive, which essentially meant exile, as all essentials were denied. Later, with the establishment of permanent courts and the courts of assizes, the *aqua et igni interdictio* became a punishment in itself, which implied exile, and was applied in capital cases (Mommsen 1889: 68–73, 971–80).

It has been said by the elders: It is assumed that Ulpian alludes to the leading figures of the early Republic here (cf. Cic. *Phil.* 5.17.47; Plin. 36.7.12.§ 59; Quint. 9.3.1).

Gaius Ulpius Pacatus Prastina Messalinus was a Roman senator and a consul in 147 CE.

Lugdunensis: A Roman province in Gaul.

Avidius Cassius (c. 130–75 CE) was a Roman general and usurper. Cassius pronounced himself emperor while governor of Syria and Egypt (Fronto, *Ad Am.* 3.312ff), possibly with the support of Marcus' wife Faustina (Cass. Dio 71.27.2f.), and probably after having received false news of the emperor's death. Cassius' claim to power was well received among the soldiers in the east, particularly in Syria and Egypt. The rebellion posed a considerable threat to Marcus' reign, who was forced to make his way to the east to appease the soldiers.

The island of Syros (or Syra) is an island in the Cyclades, in the Aegean Sea.

On the Julian Law concerning treason: Sources for the *lex Iulia maiestatis* are: *Dig.* 48, 4, 1, pr.-1; 48, 4, 2; 48, 4, 3; 48, 4, 4, pr.-1; 48, 4, 3; 48, 1, 1; 48, 4, rubr.; 48, 4, 6; Sent. Pauli, 5, 29, 1 (= Sent. Paul. Leid., 9); *Inst.* 4, 18, 3; *CTh* 9, 5; *CJ* 9, 8, 3; Cic. *Phil.* 1, 9, 21–3; Tac. *Ann.* 3, 24, 2. It is impossible to ascertain whether the *leges Iuliae* were promulgated by Caesar or Augustus. Allison and Cloud 1962: 712–13, and *passim.* Cloud 1962 made a persuasive attempt at restoring the original wording of the *lex Iulia maiestatis*, which he assumed heavily relied on the earlier *lex Cornelia maiestatis*.

§ 2193

The crime closest: Mommsen, *Jur. Schrift.* III, p. 407, sensibly assumed that *Dig.* 48.4.1.pr is an interpolation, as Ulpian noted elsewhere that *sacrilegium* was subsumed under *peculatus*. Since it has been included by Justinian in the *Digest*, the pr. must have been interpolated by a later Christian hand who associated *sacrilegium* with treason.

… or their security: Beseler (1913: 164) conjectured that these words are a post-classical interpolation because the word *securitas* is rarely used by classical jurists.

Dolus malus: The *actio de dolo malo* was introduced by the praetor to provide a remedy in cases where an injured party had no other available action to seek redress for a wrong suffered due to the fraudulent actions of a second party. Lenel *EP* § 40 gives the following text: *verba autem edicti talia sunt: Quae dolo malo facta esse dicentur, si de his rebus alia actio non erit et iusta causa esse videbitur, intra annum, cum primum experiundi potestas fuerit, iudicium dabo* ('the words of the edict are the following: these things are said to have been enacted *dolo malo*, if there will be no other action pertaining to them, and it will seem right that there is an action, within a year from when the power of trying would be, I will appoint a judge'). On the applicability of the *actio de dolo malo*, see Watson (1961).

Without the emperor's command: Probably a later substitution by Ulpian (there is no reason to assume otherwise) of the original *iniussu populi Romani*; cf. Allison and Cloud (1962: 715).

Killed: Probably not part of the original law, but there is no evidence to indicate that it is not Ulpian's; cf. Kübler, *RE* XIV.1, 550.

On the Cornelian law concerning assassins: The *lex Cornelia de sicariis et veneficiis* is one of the laws promulgated by Sulla as part of his judicial reforms. See Cloud (1968) on Sulla's intention in promulgating this statute and (1969) on its primary purpose. It was already in place when Cicero defended Sextus Roscius and Cluentius. The *lex Cornelia de sicariis et veneficiis*, alongside the *lex Cornelia de iniuriis* and the *lex Cornelia de falsis*, was not replaced by a *lex Iulia* and remained the statute under which murderers were prosecuted under the Roman Empire (except in the case of parricide). For the text and sources see *RS* § 50 and, more elaborately, Ferrary (1991).

§ 2194

A praetor or a judge: The praetor or the *iudex quaestinis* presided over the tribunal.

A person: As Latin is a gendered language, I translate 'homo' as man rather than person, but the *lex Cornelia* applied to women as well.

... or commit a robbery: Bauman (1980: 122) pointed out the difficulty of including *furtum* under the *lex Cornelia de sicariis et veneficiis*. *Furtum* is an offence aimed at unlawfully acquiring profit from another's property, which could range from armed robbery to contractual violations. Furthermore, *furtum* was a private crime (*delictum*), actionable only by the injured party (cf. *Dig.* 47.2). Brasiello (1976: 254) went further, dismissing *furtive faciendi* as an interpolation. However, Ferrary (1991: 422 ff) pointed out that *furtum* is also included under the *lex Cornelia de sicariis et veneficiis* by Marcian and Paul and that Cicero never claimed to have quoted the law in its entirety. Hence, it is reasonable to assume that the meaning of *furtum* here is armed robbery and that it has been included under the *lex Cornelia de sicariis et veneficiis*.

Dolus malus: See comment *ad* § 2194.

And other things of similar nature: i.e., and similar actions of that kind. This phrase suggests that the anonymous author of the *Collatio legum Mosaicarum et Romanarum* was excerpting a longer passage from Ulpian's original work.

... has killed a man ... : This reflects a shift from an earlier law ascribed to Numa, which restricted the law's scope to killers of free people (i.e., Roman citizens) alone. Similarly, the killing of a slave was actionable under the first chapter of the *lex Aquilia*. A slave owner would have had a delictual action against his slave's killer, without needing to demonstrate dolus malus, for the maximal worth of the slave in the year before the killing.

§ 2196

A rescript of Hadrian: Cf. Marcian fr. 169 § 3 Lenel = *Dig.* 48.8.1.3. For the slight variation between the rescript, as quoted by Marcian and Ulpian, see Wieacker (1960: 402–4).

Intention to kill: The term animus has a wide variety of meanings. I translate *occidendi animo* as intention to kill, referring to the mental component of the act.

The identity of Epafroditus is perplexing: The name is not mentioned by Marcian, who also quoted this rescript in his treatise *On Institutions*, excerpted as *Dig.* 48.8.1.3. As noted by Mommsen, the two versions display slight discrepancies. I quote *Dig.* 48.8.1.3 in full: *Divus Hadrianus rescripsit eum, qui hominem occidit, si non occidendi animo hoc admisit, absolvi posse, et qui hominem non occidit, sed vulneravit, ut occidat, pro homicida damnandum: et ex re constituendum hoc: nam si gladium strinxerit et in eo percusserit, indubitate occidendi animo id eum admisisse: sed si clavi percussit aut cuccuma in rixa, quamvis ferro percusserit, tamen non occidendi animo. Leniendam poenam eius, qui in rixa casu magis quam voluntate homicidium admisit.* ('The deified Hadrian wrote in a rescript that it is possible to absolve a person who killed another person without intending to kill him, and to condemn for homicide a person who did not kill but wounded a man with the intention of killing, as if he had killed. This should be determined based on the circumstances: if he drew his sword and struck with it, it is undoubtedly clear that he did so with the intention of killing. But if he struck with a nail or a cooking vessel in a brawl, even if he attacked with a metal instrument, it was not with the intention of killing. A more lenient punishment should be inflicted on someone who, in a brawl, committed homicide more by accident than by intent').

A stab: Although the MSS has *lapis* here, Mommsen et al. print *clavis* based on a comparison with *Dig.* 48.8.1.3: *Divus Hadrianus rescripsit eum, qui hominem occidit, si non occidendi animo hoc admisit, absolvi posse, et qui hominem non occidit, sed vulneravit, ut occidat, pro homicida damnandum: et ex re constituendum hoc: nam si gladium strinxerit et in eo percusserit, indubitate occidendi animo id eum admisisse: sed si clavi percussit aut cuccuma in rixa, quamvis ferro percusserit, tamen non occidendi animo. Leniendam poenam eius, qui in rixa casu magis quam voluntate homicidium admisit.* ('The deified Hadrian wrote in a rescript that a person who kills a man, if he did so without the intention of killing, can be acquitted, and that a person who did not kill but wounded a man with the intention of killing should be condemned as a murderer. This should be determined based on the circumstances: if he drew his sword and struck with it, it is undoubtedly clear that he did so with the intention of killing. But if he struck with a nail or a pot in a brawl, even if he struck with an iron instrument, it was not with the intention of killing. The punishment should be mitigated for someone who, in a brawl, committed homicide more by accident than by intent').

§ 2197

Taurinus: Not much is known of Egnatius Taurinus, except that he was proconsul of Baetica; *PIR*[2] E 34. For the importance of the correspondence between Egnatius Taurinus and Hadrian see Millar 2016: § 4.

I have judged [Latin]: The verb *cognosco, -ere* means (in this context) to act as a judge or to preside over a dispute. Its association with the *cognitio* process is clear.

The words of the rescript: the MSS has V(erba) R(escripsi). The author/ collator of the *collatio* must have had access to both documents (the resolution of the proconsul and the rescript of Hadrian), which were included in Ulpian's seventh book.

§ 2198

My treasury: The question of whether the *fiscus* meant the public treasury or the emperor's private property stood (and perhaps still does) at the heart of a scholarly debate. Cf. Millar 1964; 1965; 1977: 175–201; Brunt 1990: 134–62, 163–87.

Absentees: Cf. § 2189 *[de absentibus]*. A possible discrepancy between the application of the *lex Cornelia de Sicariis et Veneficis* and the prohibition against prosecuting criminals in absentia could support an argument of ruling § 2189 as a later interpolation.

Clearly, if those who have suffered this injury: Hadrian hinted here at the right of slaves to approach the provincial governor on such matters. In Rome's early days slaves could not bring an action against their owners, as they were considered an object (*res*) and not a person (*persona*). However, from the age of Claudius onwards, Roman law allowed slaves to either bring an action in court or to be perceived as a person by the court. In theory, these new items of the law were not in breach of the so-called vitae *necisque potestas*, which a *paterfamilias* exercised towards his household members. See § 2213.

Medicus: While there are no explicit caveats pertaining to medical practice in the *Corpus Iuris Romani*, or in earlier Roman legal texts, some were probably included in the unabridged legal texts, as can be attested from the attitude towards physicians and medical practice in the *Visigoth Code.* The eleventh book of the *Visigothic Code* begins with eight items of law pertaining to physicians; their responsibilities; their professional conduct; and some contractual aspects of their employment (*Visigoth Code* XI. 1, 1–8). These include a prohibition to physicians from bleeding a woman in the absence of her relatives (XI. 1, 1. *Ne absentibus propinquis mulierem medicus fleotomare presumat*) and liability in case of the death of a slave induced by bleeding (XI. 1, 6. *Si per flebotomare ingenuus vel servus mortem incurrat*). The edict of Hadrian suggests that *medici* performed such procedures. For the legal status of physicians under Roman law see Below 1953 and, more broadly, Israelowich 2015. For a study of *medici* in the *Visigoth Code* see Israelowich 2021. The standard edition is Zeumer 1902.

§ 2199

And he who kidnapped a free-born boy: The offence was probably covered by the *lex Iulia de vi*. For reconstruction see *RS* § 62, with Cloud 1988/9.

A copy: *expemplum* here means a transcript. The technical term alludes to an existing taxonomy of legal documents that prevailed during the High Empire. The emperor requires a transcript of an official letter of complaint, submitted to the court by Domitius Silvanus, the paternal uncle of the victim.

petition: *libellus* (literally, a 'small book') is a letter or petition. More specifically, it is an official form of request, submitted to a magistrate or the emperor himself. In fact, the emperor had a titular official (*a libellis*) in charge of handling these petitions and presenting them to the emperor in due order.

Domitius Silvanus and Domitius Silvanus: both otherwise unattested.

scourges and torments: The often-used expression *verberibus ac tormentis quaestionem habere* means to hold examination by floggings and tortures.

Geminus: Probably Titus Prifernius Geminus, who is mentioned in Pliny's Letters (*Ep.* 8.1.; 8.5; 9.11. 10.26.1). Amongst other posts, Geminus was pro praetorian governor of the province of Achaea in 122/3 CE; Eck 1983: 157. He was later a governor of Africa, but perhaps only during Pius' reign; *CIL* viii, 7059.

§ 2200
Social status: For the distinction between the so-called *honestiores* and the *humiliores* see note *ad* § 2190, above.

Book 8

On the Julian … : The title is attested at *Coll.* 9.2. but erroneously ascribed to book nine, rather than eight: *ULPIANUS libro VIIII de officio proconsulis sub titulo ad legem Iuliam de vi publica et privata* (Ulpian, eighth book on the duty of the proconsul, under the title of the Julian law concerning public and private violence).

§ 2202
Imperium: By the time of Ulpian, unqualified *imperium* referred to the authority of the emperor. However, in a certain context, it could denote the executive power of a magistrate or a military commander.

potestas is the power of a magistrate, be it an *imperium*-bearing magistrate or not. It often inferred the right to issue edicts relevant to the magistracy (*ius edicendi*) and coercive power (*ius coercendi, ius dicendi* etc.).

something [quid]: Mommsen *ad loc.* included the following note: *eorum quae supra scripta sunt* and cited *Dig.* 48.4.3 as a parallel.

Iniuria: *iniuria* could mean 'anything outside the realm of law' (cf. *Inst.* 4.4.pr.). In the context of the Roman law of delict (the *lex Aquilia*), the phrase *damnum iniuria darun* denotes actionable delict. It could also denote bodily harm or an attack on one's reputation. In all instances, *iniuria* is a private crime, which means it can be pursued only by the injured party. In turn, there could be no voluntary (i.e., by the will of the injured party) *iniuria*; *Dig.* 39.3.9.1.

§ 2203

Coll. 9.2 and cf. *Dig.* 22.5.3.5: *Lege Iulia de vi cavetur, ne hac lege in reum testimonium dicere liceret, qui se ab eo parenteve eius liberaverit, quive impuberes erunt, quique iudicio publico damnatus erit qui eorum in integrum restitutus non erit, quive in vinculis custodiave publica erit, quive ad bestias ut depugnaret se locaverit, quaeve palam quaestum faciet feceritve, quive ob testimonium dicendum vel non dicendum pecuniam accepisse iudicatus vel convictus erit. Nam quidam propter reverentiam personarum, quidam propter lubricum consilii sui, alii vero propter notam et infamiam vitae suae admittendi non sunt ad testimonii fidem.* ('It is maintained by the Julian law concerning violence lest a person be permitted to give testimony against an accused who has been freed by him or by his father; or a minor; or anyone who has been condemned for a public crime, and has not been restored to his former condition, or who is in chains, or in prison, or has hired himself out to fight with wild beasts; or any woman who openly prostitutes herself, or has already done so; or anyone who has been sentenced or convicted of having received money for giving or withholding testimony. For, indeed, certain persons should not be allowed to testify on account of the reverence due to their position; others on account of the unreliability of their judgement; and still others because of the notorious infamy of their lives').

A public court: Cf. § 2189, above.

Condemned … : The phrase *iudicio publico damnatus est, qui* is unattested in the MSS. It was introduced into the text by its sixteenth-century editor Pithou, based on *Dig.* 22.5.3.5, and has been accepted by all editors, including Mommsen and Frakes afterward.

restitutio in integrum means reinstatement to the previous condition. A praetorian remedy, the *restitutio in integrum* aimed to cure inequity. It followed an inquiry (*causae cognitio*) and concluded in a decree (*decretum*).

[or nor giving]: This phrase is unattested in the MSS. It has been added to the text by Huschke, based on *Dig.* 22.5.3.5. Mommsen and Frakes rejected Huschke's conjecture.

And other matters: As has been noted before, the *collator* uses the phrase *et reliqua* to indicate that there is more in the source used. Cf. § 2194, above.

Concerning the Pompeian law on parricide: On the *lex Pompeia de parricidiis* see *Dig.* 48.9; *Inst.* 4.18. *Pauli Sententiae*, 5.24. Unlike homicide, which was a private crime, the offence of *parricidium* (which implied the murder of a parent or a relative) was a public crime and has instigated action on behalf of the public; cf. Thomas 1981.

§ 2204
Maecianus: Lucius Volusius Maecianus (c. 110–175) was a Roman jurist, an *amicus* of Antoninus Pius, and a tutor of the future emperor Marcus Aurelius. Maeicianus held several magistracies, including prefect of Egypt in 161 CE and a suffect consul *circa* 166 CE; Alföldy 1977: 182. His cursus honorum is recorded in an Ostian inscription: *CIL* vix, 5347 and 5348. He held the posts of *a studiis*, *a libellis*, and a *censibus*, and authored a number of legal treatises, including one *de fideicomissaria, iudicia publica* and on *the lex Rhodia de iactu.*

... should also be afflicted with the same punishment: For punishment see § 2194, above.

Concerning the punishment of the Cornelian law concerning testimonies: the title is attested by *Coll.* 8.7.

§ 2205
the crime of forgery: Paul gives a general definition of *falsum* as anything that does not exist (Paul. *Coll.* 8.6.1). A *lex Cornelia de falsis* (81 BCE) targeted all types of forgery. Furthermore, the term *falsum* has also been implied in the *lex Cornelia testamentaria*, which concerned wills.

§ 2206
knowingly and fraudulently ... : The phrase does not appear in the MSS but does in *Dig.* 48.10.9.3, citing Ulpianus, libro octavo de officio proconsulis: *Poena legis Corneliae irrogatur ei, qui quid aliud quam in testamento sciens dolo malo falsum signaverit signarive curaverit, item qui falsas testationes faciendas testimoniave falsa invicem dicenda dolo malo coierint* ('Ulpian's eighth book on the duty of the proconsul: a penalty under

the Cornelian law is inflicted upon him who fraudulently signed something other than what is in the testament, or arranged for it to be signed. Similarly, those who came together in order to make false testaments or to five false testimonies with an ill intent.'). Mommsen included it in his edition. Frakes did not. As noted in the preface, we are fortunate to have the testimony of the *Collatio*. Wieacker (1960: 396–7) argued convincingly that both the collator and the committee of Tribonian might have used an intermediary early post-classical edition of Ulpian's treatise.

Signed: The verb *signo* means, in this context, to seal (a testimony).

<by the consulship of Licinius and Taurus>: Cf. *Dig.* 48.10.9.3 (quoted above, § 2206). The confusion between the names at the beginning of the sentence and its end is part of the MSS tradition and is usually explained as a scribal error, cf. Frakes 2011: *ad loc.*

he who shall receive wages for furnishing legal assistance or advocacy: The meaning of this phrase is ambiguous. By the time of Ulpian an advocate could have received wages. Furthermore, Ulpian himself included amongst the duties of the proconsul the provision of advocates for those who were unable to secure one: see § 2152 above.

the *senatusconsultum* enacted under the consulship of Cotta and Messalla: This is not the same *SC* mentioned in § 2142, which is also associated with these two consuls.

§ 2207

an informer: The term *delator* is derived from the Latin verb *defero*. Its literal meaning is a person who reports. However, the term *delator nominis*, or sometimes just *delator*, came to mean an accuser. Being a *delator* was lucrative. If successful, the *delator* was entitled to a portion of the accused's property. This incentive was often abused and a caveat of *calumnia* (slander) to the unsuccessful accuser had to be introduced. The term of *delator* has a strong negative connotation, particularly under certain notorious emperors who were seen as keen to appropriate the property of the condemned; cf. Rivière 2002 and Robinson 2007.

Concerning witnesses: Title introduced by Lenel, based on § 2203.

§ 2208

Publicani: The term *publicani* originated from *publica*, which denotes public revenues. Those entrusted with the collection of revenues were called *publicani*. While the *publicani* no longer collected direct taxes during the Principate, they were still connected with the collection of tolls. Likewise, though *societates publicanorum*, in which they were organised, diminished in number and size, some were still active during Ulpian's time; cf. Brunt 1990: 354–432.

Of interrogations: Like the previous title, Lenel assumed the original title concerned a particular law.

§ 2209

Sennius Sabinus (*PIR*[2] S 382), otherwise unknown, was a proconsul under Hadrian.

Torture of slave: Slaves were, as a rule, liable to crime. They could have been tortured, and the court would have issued an *actio ad exhibendum* for this purpose: *Dig.* 10.4.20; Buckland 1970: 91. In fact, a *senatus consultum Silanianum* (reaffirmed by a *senatus consultum Claudianum*, a *senatus consultum Pisonianum*, and a speech of Marcus Aurelius) approved the torture of a slave suspected of the murder of his owner; cf. Buckland 1970: 95. Furthermore, from the time of Cicero onwards, the implements of torture were provided by the municipality; *AE* 1971, 88, with Bradley 1994: 165–70.

Tiberius Claudius Quartinus (*PIR*[2] C 990) was a senator of an equestrian origin. He was consul suffect in 130 CE. An inscription from Lugdunum records his *cursus honorum* (*CIL* xiii, 1802). During the reign of Hadrian he served as a legate to the proconsul of Asia, a *iuridicus* in Hispania Taraconensis, and a governor of Gallic Lugdunensis; cf. Eck 1983: 198.

Those whom the accuser has brought from his own home should not be subjected to torture … : The reasons behind this caveat are obscure. It is not unlikely that Ulpian provided more information in the unabridged version. However, the substitution of newborns was a crime. If a midwife had been present she would have been liable and, by extension, it seems from this rescript that the female household members, who would presumably have been assisting during parturition, would have been liable for substitution in all other instances. For the legal duty of the midwife see Israelowich 2017.

Quintus Cornelius Proculus (*PIR*[2] C 1421/22/23) was a senator and a consul suffect. His full name is known through *CIL* vi, 1387. A native of Hispania Baetica, he was a proconsul in Asia towards the end of the reign of Pius, in the years 161/2 CE; Alföldy 1977: 216.

Should not be interrogated about their master: Generally, slaves were not to be interrogated under torture in pursuit of evidence against their owners.

Lelianus Longinus: otherwise unknown.

A fictitious sale: The jurist Paul defines *imaginaria venditio* (in fact, *nuda et imaginaria venditio*) as an action that has not been undertaken, and therefore is of no interest to anyone: *Nuda et imaginaria venditio pro non facta est et ideo nec alienatio eius rei intellegitur*; *Dig.* 18.1.55 (Paulus *libro secundo ad edictum aedilis curulis*). Ulpian noted that a sale cannot be termed imaginary if a price has been agreed upon: *Imaginaria venditio non est pretio accedente*; *Dig.* 50.17.16. Furthermore, Ulpian's use of the term *imaginaria venditio* does not necessarily imply *mancipatio*. Although Gaius defines *mancipatio* as an *imaginaria quaedam venditio*, it does not mean that a *imaginaria venditio* is always a *mancipatio*; cf. Gai. 1.119: *Est autem mancipatio, ut supra quoque diximus, imaginaria quaedam venditio: Quod et ipsum ius proprium civium Romanorum est* (*mancipatio* is, however, as who have stated above, an imaginary sale: it is a legal institution unique of the Roman people). More generally, Roman jurists had neither a systemised theory of invalidity nor a taxonomy to match; Zimmermann 1996: chap. 22.

Corporation: Roman jurists were unaware of a legal entity distinguishable from its owner(s). Hence, a *corpus* is not a limited company *vel sim.*

Consilium: The word *consilium* is the subject of the clause and governs the verb. I have translated it as 'the resolution of the inquiry' to convey this meaning.

Religio: The term *religio* does not have any religious meaning here. Rather, it conveys a moral quality, which I have translated as 'moral obligation'.

If one would be willing to pay the price of a slave so that he could interrogate: As sale was a consensual obligation, which required intent, and agreement of price and object, this phrase might imply that an obligation has already been set.

Apud iudicem: The term *apud iudicem* could denote the second stage in a legal procedure that follows the formulaic pattern. In the process, the first stage occurs in front of a magistrate (*in iure*) who will hear the parties and decide whether the complaint merits a legal procedure. If so, he would issue a *formula*, which dictates what is it that the judge should resolve. In the second stage of the process (*apud iudicem*) an *ad hoc* appointed judge/s will inquire whether the offence described in the *formula* took place. However, during the late Republic and the Principate certain magistrates could have initiated a legal procedure and conducted what is included in both stages of the formulaic process by themselves. This legal procedure is often labelled *cognitio* or *cognitio extra ordinem*. However, there is no evidence to suggest that these were technical terms, nor that the use of the term *apud iudicem* here infers a formulaic procedure.

The state: The phrase *res publica* here does not mean Republic in the narrow sense of the form of Roman government from 509 BCE until the foundation of the Principate. Rather, it means the public interest. I have translated it as 'commonwealth' to convey this meaning.

§ 2210
Lucius Titius: A generic name. Roman jurists habitually used generic names to exemplify legal formulas.

Calpurnius Celerianus: otherwise unknown.

Pompeius Ualens: Otherwise unattested, but must have been the instigator of the petition, which led the (presumably) provincial governor Calpurnius Celerianus to consult Hadrian.

§2211
Constitutions: The term '*constitutio*' denotes imperial decisions with a force of law. Cf. Gai. 1.5: *Constitutio principis est, quod imperator decreto vel edicto vel epistula constituit.*

§ 2212

Quintus Voconius Saxa (*PIR*^{2} V 921) was a Roman senator (*inter alia*) whose *cursus honorum* is known through an inscription *IGRR* iii, 763 = *TAM* II, 1201. He was a quaestor at the province of Macedonia and later a governor of Bithynia et Pontus, and later still of Lycia et Pamphylia. A third inscription shows that he was a proconsul in Africa during the early years of the reign of Marcus and Lucius.

Of cruelty of slave owners: Lenel includes this title based on *Coll.* 3.3.

§ 2213

Slaves: Servos *Dig.*, servum *Coll.* The plural is attested by *Inst.* 1.8.2 and by *Bas* 31.1.2.

Unchasteness: Honoré has argued that Ulpian perceived this edict of Pius and a further Severan law, which granted a slaveowner an *actio iniuriarum* against a person who sexually assaulted his slaves, as an indication of Ulpian's attentiveness to human rights (Honoré 2002: 86–7). The Severan law was included in Ulpian's work on the duties of the Urban Prefect. *Dig.* 47.10.9.4 (Ulp. 57 ed.): *Si quis tam feminam quam masculum, sive ingenuos sive libertinos, impudicos facere adtemptavit, iniuriarum tenebitur. Sed et si servi pudicitia adtemptata sit, iniuriarum locum habet* ('If someone has attempted to make a woman or a man, either free or manumitted, impudent, he is accountable for *iniuria*. If he would attempt to make a slave impudent, there are also grounds for an accusation of *iniuria*').

A rescript of Pius: This rescript, which curtailed the power of a master to harm his slaves without cause, is also mentioned in *Inst.* 1.8.2 and by Gai. 1.48–53 in a general exposition of the division between persons who are *sui iuris* and those *iuris alieni*: *Sequitur de iure personarum alia divisio. Nam quaedam personae sui iuris sunt, quaedam alieno iuri sunt subiectae ... . Sed hoc tempore neque civibus Romanis nec ullis aliis hominibus, qui sub imperio populi Romani sunt, licet supra modum et sine causa in servos suos saevire: Nam ex constitutione sacratissimi imperatoris Antonini, qui sine causa servum suum occiderit, non minus teneri iubetur quam qui alienum servum occiderit. Sed et maior quoque asperitas dominorum per eiusdem principis constitutionem coercetur: Nam consultus a quibusdam praesidibus provinciarum de his servis, qui ad fana deorum vel ad statuas principum confugiunt, praecepit, ut si intolerabilis videatur dominorum saevitia, cogantur servos* *suos vendere. Et utrumque recte fit: Male enim nostro iure uti non debemus; qua ratione et prodigis interdicitur bonorum suorum administratio.* (There is another division with reference to the law of persons, for some persons are their own masters, and some are subject to the authority of others … . But at the present time neither Roman citizens nor any other persons who are under the empire of the Roman people are permitted to employ harshness towards their slaves beyond what is due or to treat them cruelly without cause; for by a constitution of the Most Holy Emperor Antoninus, anyone who kills his slave without good reason is no less liable than one who kills the slave of another; and the excessive severity of masters is restrained by another constitution of the same Emperor; for he, having been consulted by certain governors of provinces with reference to slaves who flee for refuge to the temples of the gods or the statues of the Emperor, ordered that if the cruelty of masters appeared to be intolerable, they should be compelled to sell their slaves; and in both cases, he acted justly, for we should not make a bad use of our rights, in accordance with which principle the administration of their own property is forbidden to spendthrifts.) In *Dig.* 1.6.2 it is discussed under the rubric '*De his qui sui vel alieni iuris sunt*'. A fuller quote of this passage appears in *Coll.* 3.3.2–3 under the heading Ulpianus, *libro octavo de officio proconsulis* sub titulo de dominorum saevitia.

Aurelius Marcianus: The identity of Aurelius Marcianus is otherwise unknown. However, two other proconsuls of Baetica had the same cognomen: the first was M. Granius Marcianus, who was governor of Baetica c. 22 CE (*CIL* IX, 2335 = *ILS* 961 = *AE* 1990: 222). The second was a Severan jurist whose works are included in the *Digest.*

The power of the masters: The *potestas* of a slaveowner is often discussed under the more general title of *vitae necisque potestas*. This unique Roman institution bestowed upon a *paterfamilias* the utmost power over the members of his *familia*, which some scholars understood to include the right to sentence them to death. Scholarship on the *vitae necisque potestas* is vast. See, particularly, Yaron 1962; Crook 1967; Thomas 1984; Harris 1986; Westbrook 1999; Nótári 2013.

The interest of the masters: I have suggested elsewhere that the intention of Pius was not necessarily (or exclusively) moral, and that the prohibition of inexplicable brutality toward one's slaves was meant to protect the interests of his *sui heredes*. This is why this edict is delictual and not criminal. It also explains the nature of the remedy: to sell the slave under the caveat that he/she cannot go back under the *potestas* of the abusing owner. There is no punishment or even loss. Furthermore, the association of such abuse of one's slaves with the damaging of another person's slaves alludes to the *Lex Aquilia*, which pertains to damages caused by the fault of another (*damnum iniuria datum*) without addressing the question of *dolus malus*. Pius equated the killing of one's own slave to the killing of another's: *qui sine causa servum suum occiderit, non minus teneri iubetur quam qui alienum servum occiderit* ('who kills his slave without good reason is no less liable than one who kills the slave of another'). More specifically, when juxtaposed with the *Lex Aquilia* on the one hand and the nature, extent, and raison d'être of the *cura furiosi* on the other hand, this rescript should be seen as a mechanism set by Pius to protect slaveowners – as well as heirs under the paternal power of the deceased (*sui heredes*) – from self-imposed delict (Israelowich 2023).

Therefore, investigate … : The use of the verb *cognosco* means to hold an inquiry. It is used here not as a technical term, which could suggest what some modern scholars entitle *cognitio* or *cognitio extra ordinem* process.

Family: The Latin term '*familia*' referred predominantly to a collection of slaves and freedmen attached to a married couple (*Dig.* 50.16.195; Thomas 1976: 411–12; Dixon 1992: 2).

§ 2214
Alfius Iulius: The otherwise unknown Alfius Iulius appears to have been the author of a petition sent to the emperor, Antoninus Pius, presumably concerning an unfavourable judicial decision of a lower order.

On shipwrecks and arsonists: Lenel included the title based on *Coll.* 12.5.

§ 2216
Cornelian law: Probably the *lex Cornelia de sicariis et veneficis*.

Lowly status: For the *humiliores* (and *honestiores*) see § 2190, above.

The lex Cornelia … : This phrase is also quoted in *Dig.* 47.9.12.1; cf. *Bas* 60.39.6, but the *Digest* has *puniri*. For the variation between the text of the *Digest* and the *Collatio* see Wieacker 1960: 401–2.

§ 2217

Annona: The term *annona* initially alluded to a yearly product. During the Republic, Roman authorities attended to the provision and guarantee of food supply for the people of Rome. This vital care was known as *cura annonae*. It later developed into the collection of tax in kind (predominantly in Egypt and North Africa), in the form of basic nutrients, such as grains, oil, and, later on, wine, and their transport to the city of Rome. Gaius Gracchus went further and set fixed prices for the sale of grains, founded storehouses within the city to prevent shortages, and banned speculators. Augustus went further still and founded a senior magistracy in charge of the care of the *annona*, the *praefectus annonae*. This allowed Augustus and future emperors to distribute these commodities to the city's population (cf. Garnsey 1988; Pavis D'Escurac 1976; Sirks 1991).

Dardanarii: This term appears only twice elsewhere in the legal sources, both bearing the same meaning of speculators (*Dig.* 48.19.37 [Paul. 1 Sent.]; Paul. 1.20a).

The negotiatores were tradesmen of commodities on a large scale (cf. Andreau 1987: 123–8).

Humiliores and honestiores: For the legal distinction between humiliores and honestiores see § 2190.

Counterfeit: For counterfeit money see also § 2205.

The Cornelian law: Probably the *lex Cornelia de falsis*.

Counterfeit scales: By 'false measurement' Ulpian refers to the incorrect measurement of land, either for a commercial contract (i.e., *emptio-venditio* or *locatio-conductio*) or for tax purposes. It complements an *actio finium regundorum* (*Dig.* 10.1). The measurement of land, and its official approval by the state, was handled by professional and, at times, official land surveyors. See Israelowich 2020.

On cattle thieves: Lenel suggested this title based on *Coll.* 11.7. On the slight discrepancies between *Coll.* 11.7 and *Dig.* 47.14 see Wieacker 1960: 396–401.

§ 2218
Sentenced to the sword [Latin]: *Gladius* as a symbol of the death penalty is common, as in the case of the *ius gladii*, which is the power to sentence a person to death, cf. § 2144.

Opus: The meaning of *opus* is labour, i.e., hard labour.

Relegation to the mines: This was a particularly severe punishment: cf. Millar 1984 and Gustafson 1984.

Condemnation to the arena: Frakes *ad loc.* assumes that the distinction between five and three years meant that a person who was condemned to fight in the arena as a gladiator fought for a period of three years but was not altogether free until he completed a period of five years.

§ 2220
In Rome: Ulpian presumably included this clarification because a weaponised attack could have been pursued under other laws as well, such as the *lex Iulia de vi*.

§ 2221
Q. Venuleius Saturninus: A Roman jurist active under the Antonines. Known works of Saturninus, other than the treatise *de officio proconsulis*, include *De stipulationibus*, *Actiones*, and *De interdictis*. All existing fragments of his work are collected in Lenel, *Palingenesia*, vol. 2, 1207–24.

Civil examination [*examinationem civilem*]: I translate into 'civil scrutiny', although a literal translation would render it as legal scrutiny under civil law (*ius civile*), under which questions of ownership are resolved.

On thieves: Lenel concludes the title based on *Coll.* 7.4.

§ 2222.
Extra ordinem: Literally, outside the order, which means not under the formulaic procedure.

Causa cognita: This ablative absolute expression means 'after a study of the case has been concluded'.

§ 2223
Aemilius Tiro: *PIR*[2] A 410, otherwise unattested.

Expilator(es): This is not a common term. In fact, this is its only appearance in any legal text.

Saccularius: The noun *saccularius* appears only in Ulp. *de off. proc.* within the Roman legal corpus.

Derectarius: The noun *derectarius* appears only in Ulp. *de off. proc.* within the Roman legal corpus.

§ 2224
Stellionites: Much like the *actio de dolo malo*, an action against a *stellionatus* is subsidiary, meaning that it applies only if no other action is available.

Datio in solutum: This is a mechanism by which a debtor under contract is absolved by giving an object other than the one agreed upon in the contract, with the consent of the creditor (Zimmermann 1996: 753–4).

Extra ordinem: I translate '*extra ordinem*' here as 'outside the realm of the formulaic system'. As Turpin 1999, following Millar 1968, has noted, the term *extra ordinem*, or *extraordinarius*, is an adjective and therefore cannot denote a legal institution. Habitually, it is associated with the *cognitio* of a Roman magistrate, like a provincial governor, who conducted legal procedures from beginning to end.

Book 9

§ 2225
Manus intulit: Literally 'to carry a hand', but I translate idiomatically as 'was violent'.

Calumnia: In private law, the groundless or slanderous accusation known as *calumnia* brought upon the *calumniator* considerable pecuniary penalty. In criminal law, an accuser (*delator*) who failed to convince the court of his case was liable for a loss of his civic status under the late Republican *lex Remnia*.

Informer (Delator): See § 2207, above.

§ 2226
derectarii: As noted above (§ 2223), this term is used only by Ulpian in this treatise.

Guilty of prevarication: Cf. *Dig.* 47.15 *De praevaricatione.* Ulpian defined the *praevaricator* elsewhere as an advocate who betrays his client by collaborating with the other party: *Praevaricator est quasi varicator, qui diversam partem adiuvat prodita causa sua. Quod nomen Labeo a varia certatione tractum ait: nam qui praevaricatur, ex utraque parte constitit, quin immo ex altera.* ('A prevaricator is a person who supports opposite parties in their case. This name, Labeo says, is derived from a varying contest, for he acts in this manner who, apparently being on one side, actually favours the other', *Dig.* 47.15.1.pr.) Cf. *Dig.* 3.2.4.4; 47.15.1; 47.15.4; 47.15.6; 48.16.1.6; *CJ* 9.9.10; *Nov.* 6 caput 8; *Nov.* 7 caput 12.

§ 2227
extraordinaria: I translate as 'extraordinary', avoiding unwarranted association to an extraordinarily judicial process (cf. *cognitio*).

§ 2228
Theft: Roman law perceived *furtum* (theft) as a delict. As such, *furtum* was a civil wrong, not a criminal one. From the late Republic onwards *furtum* was associated with *contrectatio* (literally 'handling'), which implied forbidden or excessive handling of another person's object. The delict of *furtum* required a mental component, often described as *animus furandi.* Likewise, *furtum* could only occur against the owner's will. The remedy procured through an *actio furti* was a multiplication of the value of the object stolen; cf. Watson 1965: 221.

A charge for spoliation of an inheritance: A *crimen expilatae hereditatis* filled a void in the Roman criminal law concerning the illegal appropriation of an inheritance. It was necessary, as an inheritance was the property of no one before an heir made an *aditio hereditatis* (i.e., the entering upon an inheritance), thus making an *actio furti* inapplicable. It was Julian who first identified this legal void (*Dig.* 9.4.40) and Gaius who provided an explanation: '*nam res hereditariae, antequam aliquis heres existat, nullius* *in bonis sunt*' ('for the inheritance, before a certain heir is present, is in no one's possession', *Dig.* 1.8.1.pr); cf. Lemosse 1998.

Before the inheritance is entered upon: The term *aditio hereditatis* means entering upon an inheritance; cf. *Dig.* 50.17.77.

On boundary lines removed: Lenel assumed title based on *Coll.* 13.3.

§ 2229
The regulation of boundary disputes: Boundary disputes habitually occupied the Roman judicial system. Two actions included in the *Digest* affirm both how commonplace these contentions were and how dependent the judiciary system was on professional land surveyors. The first is the *actio finium regundorum*, included in *Dig.* 10.1. This action delineates how the court should preside over such disputes (*Dig.* 10.1.1). The second is the *actio si mensor falsum modum dixerit* ('action if a land surveyor would declare false measurements'). This action assumes that the involvement of a professional surveyor in such disputes was indispensable and offered a safety mechanism against possible deception by the surveyor (*Dig.* 11.6). On the involvement of surveyors in legal disputes pertaining to boundaries, see Israelowich 2020.

Decimus Terentius Gentianus: (*PIR*^{2} T 71) was a Roman senator and magistrate under the reign of Hadrian. His *cursus honorum* is recorded in *CIL* iii, 1463. He is mentioned by the author of the *Historia Augusta* as one of the persons involved in Hadrian's death (SHA *vit. Hadr.* 23.5). For the date of his consulate see Eck 2013.

... and his state of mind: Like the delict of *furtum* (civil, not criminal), *mens rea* was necessary for liability.

§ 2230
By the Julian law concerning grain supply: The *lex Iulia de annona* was enacted by Augustus. The law criminalised magistrates and merchants who raised the price of basic goods either by storing and manipulating market prices or by disturbing the transportation of these goods to Rome (initially, and later also to Constantinople).

The Fabian law: Lenel assumed this title based on *Coll.* 14.3.

§ 2231

The Fabian law: A *lex Fabia de plagiariis* (a Fabian law against kidnapping) is first attested by Cicero in 63 BCE (Cic. *Rab. perd.* 8.7). This law is discussed in *Dig.* 48.15; *Coll.* 14.2–3; Paul. Sent. 5.37.1–2 (ed. Liebs). For the text and discussion of the original wording see Crawford, *RS* § 51. For dating see Kantor 2013, who argued for a late Republican provenance.

The term *tribunal, -alis*: Alluded to in this context as the court; cf. *OLD* s.v., 1.

... provincial governors: A papyrus recording the cases reserved for the legal scrutiny of the Egyptian prefect, M. Petronius Mamertinus, and dated to 133–7 CE includes (alongside the *lex Fabia de plagiariis*) the leges *de vi, de iniuriis, testamentaria nummaria*, and *de abigeis*. For the text, see *SB* XII, 10929 with Jördens 2011; cf. § 2233.

Urban prefect: This magistrature dates to the regal era. Tradition has it that, under the kings, the *praefectus urbi* was a senior magistrate in charge of the business of the state. The urban prefect then ceased to exist before being reintroduced by Augustus as a senior figure (habitually *consularis*) and a representative of the emperor, mainly in matters of jurisdiction.

The praetorian prefect: Was one of the most important magistratures from the Antonine era onwards. Initially set by Augustus in 2 CE, the praetorian prefect was originally in charge of the praetorian guard. However, the praetorian guard soon lost its military duties for civilian ones. The praetorian prefect oversaw the administration of justice and various other key administrative duties.

Capital cases: The meaning of capital cases here is intriguing. Kantor 2013 demonstrated, based on *SEG* lv, 1452, ll. 32–4, that by the late Republic the punishment under the first chapter of the *lex Fabia de plagiariis* was not pecuniary but capital.

Preside over cases: Although the literal meaning of *quaestionem accepit* is 'to hold an inquiry', the phrase *accipere quaestionem* means, in this context, to hold court.

§ 2232

The senatus consultum: This must have been mentioned at the beginning of this excerpt. Ulpian probably referred to the *senatus consultum Silanianum*, which is recorded in *Dig.* 29.5 and mentioned by Tacitus in *Ann.* 14.42–5. See further Buckland 1970: 94–7 and Fuhrmann 2012: 23, n. 15.

§ 2233

There are also crimes that pertain to the jurisdiction of the provincial governor: *SB* XII, 10929 gives a list of all charges which belong under the jurisdiction of the provincial governor: ὁ ἡγεμὼν διαγνώσεται περὶ φόνου περὶ ληστειῶν περὶ φαρμακείας περὶ πλαγιαρίας περὶ ἀπελατῶν περὶ βίας σὺν ὅπλοις γεγενημένης περὶ πλαστογραφίας καὶ ῥᾳδιουργίας περὶ ἀνῃρημένων διαθηκῶν περὶ ὕβρεως ἀνηκέστου περὶ ὧν ἐὰν μέμφωνται οἱ ἐλευθερώσαντες ἀπελευθέρους ἢ γονεῖς παῖδας οἱ λοιποὶ οὐκ ἄλλως ὑπ' ἐμοῦ ἀκουσθήσονται εἰ μὴ ἐπικαλεσάμενοι καὶ παραβόλιον θέντες τὸ τέταρτον μέρος ἐκ τιμήματος περὶ οὗ ἐδικάσθη. (The prefect will hear cases of homicide (φόνος = homicidium), brigandage (λῃστεία = latrocinium), poisoning (φαρμακεία = veneficium), kidnapping (πλαγιαρία = plagium), rustling of livestock (ἀπελατῶν = abigeatus), armed assault (βία σὺν ὅπλοις = vis armata), counterfeit and forgery (πλαστογραφία = falsum) and fraud (ῥᾳδιουργία = fraus), the destruction of testaments (ἀνῃρημέναι διαθῆκαι = testamenta rescissa), grave personal injury (ὕβρις ἀνήκεστος = de iniuria atroci), and all accusations that patrons bring against their freedmen or parents against their children. To all others I will not grant a hearing unless they have lodged appeals and have made a deposit of one-fourth of the estimated value of the case). This papyrus is quoted and discussed by Oliver 1979: 550; Lewis 1981; Jördens 2011; and Dolganov 2019.

Records: *Instrumentum* means, in this context, a document or a record; cf. Quint. 12.8.12; Suet. *Vesp.* 8; *Dig.* 24.1.58; Paul. Sent. 5.7.2; 2.17.13.

§ 2234

The custom of the provinces: It is noteworthy that Ulpian composed his treatise on the duty of the proconsul after the enactment of the so-called *Constitutio Antoniniana*. However, this example, which agrees with various others, shows that the bestowal of Roman citizenship did not imply an immediate codification of law (criminal or civil).

σκοπελισμὸν: This noun, like the associated verb σκοπελίζειν, is otherwise unattested. *L&S* give s.v. 'plant boundary-stones on a man's land to warn him against tilling it, Ulp. in *Dig.* 47.11.9: hence σκοπελισμός, ὁ, ibid.'

§ 2235
Choma is a transliteration of the Greek χῶμα, -ατος, τό, which means here a riverbank.

aeque plectitur extra ordinem: I translate this as 'equally punished by the governor'. The term *extra ordinem* or *extraordinarius* alludes to a legal process that is managed from beginning to end by the provincial governor (if in the provinces), unlike the formulaic procedure. As the context here is various crimes or charges which are tried by the provincial governor, the phrase *plectitur extra ordinem* emphasises just that.

Dams (for leading off the water): A transliteration of the Greek διάκοπος, which means an opening or sluice in a dam for leading off the water.

§ 2236
For whom he provided security: *Satisdatio* is a security given to a creditor through the person of a surety (*sponsor* or *fideiussor*). Cf. *Inst.* 4.11. pr.: *Olim enim si in rem agebatur, satisdare possessor compellebatur, ut, si victus nec rem ipsam restitueret nec litis aestimationem, potestas esset petitori aut cum eo agendi aut cum fideiussoribus eius. Quae satisdatio appellabatur iudicatum solvi: unde autem sic appellabatur, facile est intellegere* ('Formerly, where an action *in rem* was brought, the possessor of the property was obliged to provide security, and if he was declared compelled and did not surrender the property itself or pay its appraised value, power was granted to the plaintiff to proceed either against him or his sureties'). Hence, it aimed to offer the creditor security even if the debtor is unavailable or insolvent. However, this institution did not originally mean to target fraudulent creditors. Ulpian, therefore, assumed that an absent creditor required particular attention by the governor, hence an extraordinary conviction.

Sureties: Originally a form of *cautio* (habitually translated into English as a pledge), which is an obligation to offer a guarantee for a pre-existing obligation or duty.

§ 2239
***Infamia*:** A social demotion due to a legal process. It had significant implications in various aspects of life, from the ability to hold certain magistracies to certain restrictions as debtors for civilians and a dishonourable discharge from the army for soldiers.

§ 2240
Must be executed by sword: The expression *animadvertere in acc.* means to punish by death; cf. *L&S* 1 c.

But it is necessary ... : Syntax here is obscure. Mommsen added the following marginalia: *oportet: non securi vel telo vel fusti vel laqueo vel quo alio modo, multo minus venendo, necandi, proinde nec liberam mortis facultatem concedendi ius praesides habent?*

The bodies ... : According to Tac. *Ann.* 6.23.2. this was the general rule, and various examples mark deviation from this pattern as illicit, cruel, and lawless.

§ 2241
Lucius Fabius Cilo Septiminus Catinius Acilianus Lepidus Fulcinianus: A Roman consul and a member of Severus' inner circle. His *cursus honorum* is given in two inscriptions from the near vicinity of Rome (*CIL* vi, 1408 = *ILS* 1141; *CIL* vi, 1409 = *ILS* 1142). Cilo was a quaestor of the province of Crete and Cyrenaica, a proconsul of Gallia Narbonensis, and urban prefect, a *praefectus aerarii militaris*, and a governor of Galatia. For all biographical information see Dietz 1983.

Et si in *decem annos damnatus sit, aut perpetuari ei debet poena aut in opus metalli transmitti* ('and if anyone is sentenced to ten years, or the penalty to him should continue indefinitely, or if he is transmitted to public work in a mine'). These words, which are printed in Lenel's *Palingenesia* and in Mommsen's edition of the *Digest*, are dismissed by both as a gloss.

Salt mines: The distinction between unqualified mines and salt mines is also made by Pomponius, who used the term *opus in salinarum*; *Dig.* 49.15.6.

§ 2242

Deportation: Two types of exile existed under the Roman punitive law, *relegatio* and the more severe *deportatio.* Fergus Millar has noted that 'in the developed system deportatio was the harshest penalty applicable to upper-class persons, except for particularly offensive or dangerous crimes, such as parricide, treason, and later arson'. Millar 1984: 125.

Cilo: For the person and career of Fabius Cilo see § 2241.

Jail (carcer): Yet another instance of the meaning of the *carcer* as a jail, not a prison, where an accused awaits verdict.

The municipal decurions: Either members of the municipal curia (i.e., the senate) or, more broadly speaking, members of the social tier which provides members to the municipal curia.

Book 10

§ 2243

Relegation: A second distinction between the milder *relegatio* and the harsher *deportatio* was also that the latter was the most severe punishment for upper-class Romans, except for the most heinous crimes, such as *parricidium*, *maiestas*, and arson; cf. Millar 1984: 125.

Oasis: Roman emperors habitually relegated criminals to the great oasis in Upper Egypt, *Dig.* 48.22.7; *CJ* 9.47.26.

Someone to stay in a certain part of the province: *domicilium* denotes one's place of residence either permanently or temporarily, or where his place of business is located, cf. *Dig.* 50.16.203, *Dig.* 50.1.27.1, *Dig.* 11.5.1.2, 23.2.5, *CJ* 10.40.7.1. A settled *domicilium* was imperative for tax purposes, as well as jurisdiction. More relevant here is that a person could be a citizen of one place and have *domicilium* in another. The legal status in the second place is *incola*; *Dig.* 50.16.239.2.

Patria: Unlike the terms province, Italy, Rome, named cities, etc., the term *patria* had no strict legal meaning. It meant provenance but could refer to Rome (city, or empire), one's hometown, province, region, etc. I, therefore, leave the term *patria* untranslated.

It should be examined whether they are also banned from their … : This phrase seems incoherent, which led Beseler (1931: 43) to question its authenticity.

The province of Syria was originally created by Pompey in 64 BCE, but later divided into two provinces, Coele Syria and Syria Phoenice.

The province of Dacia was created in 106 CE but soon after divided into Dacia Superior and Dacia Inferior.

The term *urbs*, *-is* habitually referred to Rome.

libellus*, *-i is a small letter or a pamphlet, but the term is often used to denote a petition (dispatched to a governor or the emperor himself).

§ 2246
Advocacy: Cf. § 2152, where Ulpian discusses the duties of the provincial governor towards the *advocationes*, but also his obligation to provide an *advocatio* to anyone who cannot provide one for himself. It appears that at least some *advocationes* were employed by the provincial governor, which implies a certain amount of regulation.

Nec non (Latin): This double negative expression means 'and also'.

Thus, a person may be prohibited from pleading before the governor's tribunal but still allowed … : This is a similar pattern to the one Ulpian offered in § 2244, pertaining to a hierarchy of honours, where he explained that a prohibition by punishment of a certain honour implies the prohibition of all higher honours, but not necessarily all lesser ones.

The forum was the place where public matters were undertaken. Exclusion from the forum equates to an exclusion from public affairs, in the broadest sense.

Law students, advocates, notaries, and those skilled in business: The elaborated taxonomy, which includes the legal scholar (*iuris peritus*, or *iuris studiosus*), the advocate, the scrivener (*tabellio*), and the businessman, who is skilled in matters of law (the *pragmaticus*, which is a Latinised form of the Greek term πραγματικός, which was used by the like of Cicero, Quintilian, and Juvenal, as well as by jurists; Cic. *de Or.* 1.59.253; 1.59.253 (1.45.198, written as Greek); Quint. 12.3.4, all indicate a high level of professionalisation and differentiation in the legal field. Mommsen SZ 25 (1904), 53, n. 5 assumed that *sive pragmaticis* is a later gloss.

Grammatophylacium: A Latinised form of γραμματοφυλάκιον, which is a place for keeping records. It is the only appearance of this term in Roman legal texts.

§ 2247
Negotiatio is a term denoting either a large-scale commercial activity or banking. The *negotiatores* were those pursuing this activity, either for themselves or on behalf of the Roman state as tax collectors. Cicero often referred to them as those who *negotia gerunt*. During the late Republic the *negotiatores* were high-ranking equestrians. Cicero noted in passing (*Font.* 46) that the *negotiatores* were indistinguishable from the *publicani*. Some *negotiatores*, like the *negotiatores vinarii* (wine merchants), pursued a particular branch of commerce, while other records (cf. *ILS* 7273) qualify the *negotiatoes* as *mercatores* who practise commerce; cf. Rougé 1966; D'Arms 1981; Brunt 1988: 144 ff.

Vectigal essentially denoted income generated from public land, mines, saltworks, and similar sources, including the rents obtained from state-owned property. These were the fundamental sources of revenue of the early Republic and continued to be the primary form of income for the *municipia* and *civitates* during the empire period.

Generaliter, and its opposite *specialiter* are used to denote a general argument and a particular exception.

§ 2248
***Dig.* 48.22.11; cf. *Bas* 60.54.12.** As noted by Mommsen and Lenel *ad loc.*, this excerpt is omitted in *F* and is found only in *Bas* 60.54.10: 'Εστιν, ὅτε καταδικάζονται χρηματικωῶς οἱ τούς ἐξορίστους ὑποδεχόμενοι B (*Anon.*) ἔσθ' ὅτε δέ καί αὐτοί ἐξορίζονται, ὅτε διὰ μέγα ἐγκλημα ἐξωρίσθησαν ἔκεῖνοι. *SB.* ('it occurs, that those convicted in pecuniary cases welcome banishment B (Anon) at times they relegated themselves, when they are banished for a major charge.')

§ 2249

Salvius Marcianus: *PIR*² S 139; otherwise unknown.

§ 2250

Aquilius Bradua: *PIR*² A 987; otherwise unknown, but perhaps to be identified with M. Metilius Bradua, *cos.* 108 CE.

Ventralis is a bellyband or a small purse; cf. Plin. *HN* 8.48.73, 193; 27.7.28, 52.

Sardonychica: A precious stone; cf. Plin. 37.6.23

***Chirographum*:** In this context, means a surety; cf. *Inst.* 3.134; *Dig.* 20.1.26; 49.14.3; *Gell.* 14.2.7.

The *speculatores* were special soldiers who gathered military intelligence. The term was also applied to denote elite soldiers entrusted with the guard of the emperor or carriers of delicate information. However, the term speculator(es) could have also meant an executioner. Jones 1949: 44 ff.

For the fisc, and whether it should be translated as treasury or the imperial purse, see § 2148.

§ 2251

The *lex Iulia de pecuniis reperundis* (not to be confused with the *lex Calpurnia de repetundis* of 149 BCE) was enacted at 101 BCE and curtailed the propensity of provincial magistrates and their staff to extort the provincials. The law is known from Cic. *Rab. Post.* and is summarised by Marcian (*Dig.* 48.11). Although the original law must have been extensive, it was not created *ex nihilo*. Rather, at least some of its contents appeared in previous laws; cf. *RS* § 55, p. 769–70.

Publius Calpurnius Macer Caulius Rufus was a prominent senator and held a number of senior posts, such as consul suffect at 103 CE. Two letters of him to Pliny survived (Plin. *Ep.* 5.18; 6.24). Pliny himself mentioned Rufus in a letter to Trajan (10.42). On the evidence of *CIL* iii, 777 we know that Rufus was a governor of Lower Moesia, probably between 110 and 113 CE; Eck 1982.

APPENDIX

Three known works bore the title *de officio proconsulis* (Ulpian, Aemilius Macer, and Venuleius Saturninus), and a fourth is entitled *de officio praesidis* (Iulius Paulus). For convenience, I include the remaining excerpts, following Lenel's collation and paragraph numbers.

Iulius Paulus

De officio proconsulis

LIBRI II.

LIBER I.

1061.[1] [furioso et prodigo …] Sed et aliis dabit proconsul curatores, qui rebus suis superesse non possunt, vel dari iubebit, nec dubitabit filium quoque patri curatorem dari.

1061.[2] Ob casum, quem civitas passa est, si quis promiserit se quid facturum: etsi non inchoaverit, omnimodo tenetur, ut divus Severus Dioni rescripsit.

LIBER II.

1063.[3] Senatus censuit, ne quis ob idem crimen pluribus legibus reus fieret.

1064.[4] Hi quoque, qui thlibias faciunt, ex constitutione divi Hadriani ad Ninnium Hastam in eadem causa sunt, qua hi qui castrant.

1065.[5] Etiamsi redhibitus[6] fuerit servus, in caput emptoris non torquebitur.

Book 1

---

1 *Dig.* 27.10.2; cf. *Bas* 38.10.2. See Ulp. *De Off. Proc.* § 2158.

2 *Dig.* 50.12.7.

3 *Dig.* 48.2.14; cf. *Bas* 60.34.14.

4 *Dig.* 48.8.5; cf. *Nomocanon*, p. 470, Cap. XIV. Ed. Pitrae. See Ulp. *De Off. Proc.* § 2198.

5 *Dig.* 48.18.11; cf. *Bas* 60.50.10.

6 An *actio redhibitoria* was given to a buyer who was sold a slave with concealed ailments or defects, under the aedilian edict; cf. *Dig.* 21.1.1.1 with Watson 1971.

Julius Paulus

On the Duty of the Proconsul

BOOKS II.

BOOK I.

1061. [Concerning lunatics and spendthrifts] The proconsul will also appoint curators for those who cannot manage their affairs, or order that a curator be appointed, nor will he hesitate to appoint a son as a curator to his father.

1062. If, due to a calamity suffered by the city, someone promised to do something: even if he has not started, he is nonetheless obligated, as the deified Severus wrote in a rescript to Dio.

BOOK II.

1063. The Senate decreed that no one should be charged under multiple laws for the same crime.

1064. According to a constitution of the deified Hadrian addressed to Ninnius Hasta, those who perform castration by bruising (thlibias) are in the same legal position as those who castrate.

1065. Even if a slave has been returned to the seller, he cannot be tortured regarding his buyer.

Aemilius Macer

De officio praesidis

LIBRI II.

LIBER I.

[De praeside eiusque comitibus.]

50.[7] Praesidis nomen generale est eoque et proconsules et legati Caesaris et omnes provincias regentes, licet senatores sint, praesides appellantur: proconsulis appellatio specialis est.

51.[8] Si eadem provincia postea divisa sub duobus praesidibus constituta est, velut Germania, Mysia, ex altera ortus in altera adsidebit nec videtur in sua provincia adsedisse.

52.[9] Senatus consulto cavetur, ut de his, quae provincias regentes, comites aut libertini eorum, antequam in provinciam venerint, contraxerunt, parcissime ius dicatur, ita ut actiones, quae ob eam causam institutae non essent, posteaquam quis eorum ea provincia excesserit, restituerentur. Si quid tamen invito accidit, veluti si iniuriam aut furtum passus est, hactenus ei ius dicendum est, ut litem contestetur resque ablata exhibeatur et deponatur aut sisti exhiberive satisdato promittatur.

[De mandata iurisdictione].

53.[10] Cognitio de suspectis tutoribus mandari potest. Immo etiam ex mandata generali iurisdictione propter utilitatem pupillorum eam contingere constitutum est in haec verba: 'Imperatores Severus et Antoninus Braduae proconsuli Africae. Cum propriam iurisdictionem legatis tuis dederis, consequens est, ut

---

7 *Dig.* 1.18.1; cf. *Bas* 6.1.35.
8 *Dig.* 1.22.3; cf. *Bas* 6.24.9.
9 *Dig.* 1.18.16; *Bas* 6.1.40.
10 *Dig.* 1.21.4; cf. *Bas* 6.24.5.

Book 1.

50. The title of governor (praeses) is a general one and includes proconsuls, imperial legates, and all those governing provinces, even if they are senators; the title of proconsul is more specific.

51. If the same province is later divided and placed under two governors, as in the case of Germany and Mysia, one originating from one part will sit in the other without it appearing that he has settled in his own province.

52. A senate resolution provides that legal actions concerning contracts made by governors, their entourage, or their freedmen before they arrived in the province, should be conducted sparingly. This applies provided these cases were not initiated before their departure and will be resumed after they leave the province. However, if something occurs without their consent, such as injury or theft, jurisdiction must be offered to the extent of contesting the case and producing or depositing the allegedly stolen goods or securing the other party's appearance and the return of the items.

[On delegated jurisdiction.]

53. An inquiry into suspected tutors can be delegated. It is contained in the general delegation of jurisdiction for the benefit of the wards, constituted in these words: 'Emperors Severus and Antoninus to Braduas, proconsul of Africa. As you have given proper jurisdiction to your legates, it follows that

etiam de suspectis tutoribus possint cognoscere'. Ut possessio bonorum detur, vel si cui damni infecti non caveatur ut is possidere iubeatur, aut ventris nomine in possessionem mulier, vel is cui legatum est legatorum servandorum causa in possessionem mittatur, mandari potest.

[De restitutionibus.]

54.[11] De aetate eius, qui se maiorem annis viginti quinque dicit, causa cognita probandum est, quia per eam probationem in integrum restitutioni eiusdem adulescentis et aliis causis praeiudicatur.

55.[12] Si minor annis, posteaquam ex parte heres exstitit, in integrum restitutus est, divus Severus constituit, ut eius partis onus coheres suscipere non cogatur, sed bonorum possessio creditoribus detur.

LIBER II.

[De criminibus].

56.[13] Solent praesides provinciarum, in quibus delictum est, scribere ad collegas suos, ubi factores agere dicuntur, et desiderare, ut cum prosecutoribus ad se remittantur: et id quoque quibusdam rescriptis declaratur.

57.[14] Quod ad statum damnatorum pertinet, nihil interest, iudicium publicum fuerit nec ne: nam sola sententia, non genus criminis spectatur. Itaque hi, in quos animadverti iubetur quive ad bestias dantur, confestim poenae servi fiunt.

[De municipiis].

58.[15] A decurionatu, quamvis hic quoque honor est, ad alium honorem nullam vacationem tribuendam Ulpianus respondit.

---

11 *Dig.* 4.4.43; cf. *Bas* 10.4.43. Marcellus libro primo de officio praesidis inscr. F. Macer *dett.*

12 *Dig.* 29.2.61; cf. *Bas* 35.14.6.

13 *Dig.* 48.3.7; cf. *Bas* 60.35.7.

14 *Dig.* 48.19.12; cf. *Bas* 60.51.12.

15 *Dig.* 50.5.5.

they can also investigate suspected tutors. Possession of goods may be given, or if someone does not provide security against potential damage, they may be ordered to possess, or a woman may be placed in possession on behalf of an unborn child, or someone may be sent into possession to safeguard a legacy.'

[On restitutions.]

54. The age of a person who claims to be older than twenty-five must be verified through an inquiry because this verification prejudices the restitution to the same youth and other causes.

55. If a person under the age of twenty-five is reinstated after being named heir to his father, the deified Severus decreed that his co-heir is not obliged to assume the burden of that portion, but possession of the property of his part only will be given to the creditors.

Book 2.

[On crimes.]

56. Provincial governors customarily write to their colleagues concerning those accused of crimes, indicating their whereabouts and requesting that they be sent back with guards. This is also declared in some rescripts.

57. Regarding the status of the condemned, it does not matter if it is a public trial because only the sentence, not the nature of the crime, is considered. Therefore, those sentenced to be exposed to wild beasts must serve their sentence without delay.

[On municipalities.]

58. Concerning the decurionate, although it is an honour, Ulpian responded that it does not provide exemption from any other honour.

59.[16] Opus novum privato etiam sine principis auctoritate facere licet, praeterquam si ad aemulationem alterius civitatis pertineat vel materiam seditionis praebeat vel circum theatrum vel amphitheatrum sit. Publico vero sumptu opus novum sine principis auctoritate fieri non licere constitutionibus declaratur. Inscribi autem nomen operi publico alterius quam principis aut eius, cuius pecunia id opus factum sit, non licet.

16 *Dig.* 50.10.3.

59. An individual is allowed to undertake a new project even without the authority of the emperor, except if it pertains to rivalry with another city or incites sedition or involves a circus, theatre, or amphitheater. It is declared by constitutions that a new project undertaken with public funds is not allowed without the emperor's authority. Moreover, it is not permitted to inscribe the name of anyone other than the emperor or the person whose money funded the project on a public monument.

Venuleius Saturninus

De officio proconsuli

LIBRI IV.

LIBER I.

[De cognitionibus].

42.[17] Qui se venire passus esset maiorem, scilicet ut pretium ad ipsum perveniret, prohibendum de libertate contendere divus Hadrianus constituit: sed interdum ita contendendum permisit, si pretium suum reddidisset. Qui se ex libertinitate ingenuitati adserant, non ultra quinquennium, quam manumissi fuissent, audientur. Qui post quinquennium repperisse instrumenta ingenuitatis suae adseverant, de ea re ipsos principes adire oportere cognituros.[18]

43.[19] *Qui pecora, de quorum proprietate faciebat controversiam, abegit, ut Saturninus quidem scribit, ad examinationem civilem remittendus est. Sed hoc ita demum probandum est, si non color abigeatus quaesitus est, sed vere putavit sua iustis rationibus ductus.*

44.[20] De militibus ita servatur, ut ad eum remittantur, si quid deliquerint, sub quo militabunt: is autem, qui exercitum accipit, etiam ius animadvertendi in milites caligatos habet.

45.[21] Is, qui servum castrandum tradiderit, pro parte dimidia bonorum multatur ex senatus consulto, quod Neratio Prisco et annio vero consulibus factum est.

---

17 *Dig.* 40.14.2.

18 Cf. *Bas* 48.10.2.

19 *Dig.* 47.14.1.4. Lenel printed this excerpt as § 43, but it is attributed to Ulp. *De Off. Proc.* in the *Digest* and is found in the main text at § 2221.

20 *Dig.* 48.3.9; cf. *Bas* 60.35.9.

21 *Dig.* 48.8.6; cf. *Nomocanon*, p. 470, Cap. XIV. Ed. Pitrae. See Ulp. *De Off. Proc.* § 2198.

Book 1.

42. The deified Hadrian decreed that a person who allowed himself to be sold, intending to receive the price, is prohibited from contending for his liberty. However, at times he is permitted to do so if he returns the price he received. Freedmen who assert their claim to freeborn status shall not be heard after five years from the date of their manumission. Those who, after five years, claim to have discovered documents establishing their freeborn status, must have recourse to the princeps, who will examine their claims.

43. A person who drove away livestock, about the ownership of which there was a dispute, must be referred to a civil examination, as Saturninus writes. However, this is to be approved only if it is not a case of theft under the guise of ownership, but he truly believed he had rightful reasons.

44. Regarding soldiers, it is observed that if they have committed a crime, they must be sent back to their commanding officer. The one who commands the army also has the right to punish the rank-and-file soldiers.

45. He who has given a slave to be castrated must be punished by losing half of his property, according to a senatus consultum passed during the consulship of Neratius Priscus and Annius Verus.

46.[22] Divus Hadrianus eos, qui in numero decurionum essent, capite puniri prohibuit, nisi si qui parentem occidissent: verum poena legis Corneliae puniendos mandatis plenissime cautum est.

LIBER II.

[De officio legati].

47.[23] Si quid erit quod maiorem animadversionem exigat, reicere legatus apud proconsulem debet: neque enim animadvertendi coercendi vel atrociter verberandi ius habet.

48.[24] Appellari a legatis proconsul potest, et, si multam dixerit, potest de iniquitate eius proconsul cognoscere et quod optimum putaverit statuere.

[De magistratibus municipalibus].

49.[25] In testimoniis autem dignitas fides mores gravitas examinanda est: et ideo testes, qui adversus fidem suae testationis vacillant, audiendi non sunt.

50.[26] Ne quis receptam custodiam sine causa dimittat, mandatis ita cavetur: 'Si quos ex his, qui in civitatibus sunt, celeriter et sine causa solutos a magistratibus cognoveris, vinciri iubebis et his, qui solverint, multam dices. Nam cum scierint sibi quoque molestiae futurum magistratus, si facile solverint vinctos, non indifferenter de cetero facient.'

22 *Dig.* 48.19.15.
23 *Dig.* 1.16.11; cf. *Bas* 6.2.13.
24 *Dig.* 49.3.2; cf. *Bas* 9.1.31.
25 *Dig.* 22.5.2; cf. *Bas* 21.1.2.
26 *Dig.* 48.3.10; cf. *Bas* 60.35.3.

46. The deified Hadrian prohibited capital punishment for those who are decurions, unless they have killed a parent. However, it is clearly mandated that they should be punished according to the lex Cornelia.

Book 2.

[On the duty of the legate].

47. If there is a case requiring greater attention, the legate must refer it to the proconsul, as he does not have the power of severe punishment or harsh whipping.

48. The proconsul can be appealed after a decision by the legate, and if a fine has been imposed, the proconsul can review its fairness and decide what he thinks is best.

[On municipal magistrates].

49. In testimonies, the dignity, trustworthiness, character, and seriousness of the witness must be examined; therefore, witnesses who waver in their faithfulness to their testimony should not be heard.

50. To prevent anyone from dismissing prisoners without sufficient reason, it is provided as follows by the imperial mandates: 'If you learn that prisoners have been released too soon and without good cause by the magistrates, you will order them to be placed back in custody, and you will impose a fine on those who released them. For when the magistrates know that they themselves will face trouble if they release prisoners too easily, they will not do so indiscriminately in the future.'

EX LIBRO INCERTO.

51.[27] *De his, qui carcere effracto evaserunt, sumendum supplicium divi fratres Aemilio Tironi rescripserunt. Saturninus etiam probat in eos, qui de carcere eruperunt sive effractis foribus sive conspiratione cum ceteris, qui in eadem custodia erant, capite puniendos: quod si per neglegentiam custodum evaserunt, levius puniendos.*

27 *Dig.* 47.18.1.pr. Lenel printed this excerpt as § 43, but it is attributed to Ulp. *De Off. Proc.* In the *Digest* and is found in the main text § 2223.

From an uncertain book.

51. The deified brothers wrote in a rescript to Aemilius Tiro that punishment should be inflicted on those who have escaped from prison by breaking out. Saturninus also approves that those who break out of prison, whether by breaking doors or by conspiring with others in the same custody, should be punished with death. If they escaped through the negligence of their guards, they should be punished more leniently.

Uncertain book

51. See § 2223.

BIBLIOGRAPHY

Abbott, F.F. and Johnson, A.C. 1921. *Municipal Administration in the Roman Empire*. Princeton, NJ.

Absil, M. 1997. *Les préfets du prétoire d'Auguste à Commode. 2 av. J.-C.-192 ap. J.-C.* Paris.

Alföldy, G. 1967. *Die Legionslegaten der römischen Rheinarmeen*. Cologne.

Alföldy, G. 1977. *Konsulat und Senatorenstand unter den Antoninen*. Bonn.

Allison, J.E. and Cloud, J.D. 1962. 'The Lex Julia Maiestatis', *Latomus* 21: 711–31.

Alonso, J.L. 2013. 'The Status of Peregrine Law in Egypt: "Customary Law" and Legal Pluralism in the Roman Empire', *Journal of Juristic Papyrology* 43: 351–404.

Alonso, J.L. 2020. 'The Constitutio Antoniniana and Private Legal Practice in the Eastern Empire', in K. Czajkowski, B. Eckhardt, and M. Strothmann (eds) *Law in the Roman Provinces*. Oxford, 44–64.

Amundsen, D.W., and G.B. Ferngren. 1978. 'The Forensic Role of Physicians in Ptolemaic and Roman Egypt', *BHM* 52: 336–53.

Ando, C. 2000. *Imperial Ideology and Provincial Loyalty in the Roman Empire*. Berkeley, CA.

Ando, C. 2006. 'The Administration of the Provinces', in D.S. Potter (ed.) *A Companion to the Roman Empire*. Oxford, 193–205.

Andreau, J. 1987. *La Vie financière dans le monde romain: les métiers de manieurs d'argent (IVe siècle av. J.-C–IIIe siècle ap. J.-C)*. Rome.

Barnes, T. 1968. 'Legislation against the Christians', *Journal of Roman Studies* 58: 32–50.

Bauman, R.A. 1980. 'The "Leges iudiciorum publicorum" and their Interpretation in the Republic, Principate and Later Empire', in H. Temporini (ed.) *Band 13 Recht (Normen, Verbreitung, Materien)*. Berlin and Boston, 103–233.

Baumbach, L. 1983. 'Quacks then as Now? An Examination of Medical Practice, Theory and Superstition in Plautus' Menaechmi', *Acta Classica* 26: 99–104.

Baviera, J. 1940. 'Sententiarum receptarum libri quinque qui vulgo Iulio Paulo adhuc tribuuntur', in S. Riccobono et al. (eds) *Fontes Iuris Romani Anteiustiniani*, vol. II *Auctores*. 2nd ed. Florence, 317–417.

Below, K.H.O. 1953. *Der Arzt im römischen Recht*. Munich.

Bérenger, A. 2014. *Le métier de gouverneur dans l'Empire romain de César à Dioclétien*. Paris.
Beseler, G. 1911. *Beiträge zur Kritik der römischen Rechtsquellen*, vol. I. Tübingen.
Beseler, G. 1913. *Beiträge zur Kritik der römischen Rechtsquellen*, vol. III. Tübingen.
Beseler, G. 1926. 'Einzelne Stellen', *Zeitschrift der Savigny-Stiftung für Rechtsgeschichte* 46: 267–75.
Beseler, G. 1930. 'Romanistische Studien', *Zeitschrift der Savigny-Stiftung für Rechtsgeschichte* 50.1: 18–77.
Beseler, G. 1931. *Beiträge zur Kritik der römischen Rechtsquellen*. Leipzig.
Biondi, B. 1957. 'Ius Novum', *Novissimo Digesto Italiano* 9: 385–6.
Birks, P. 1983. 'Honoré's Ulpian', *The Irish Jurist* 18: 151–81.
Birley, A.R. 1999. *Septimius Severus: The African Emperor*. 2nd ed. London.
Bluhme, F. 1960 [1820]. 'Die Ordnung der Fragmente in den Pandektentiteln', *ZGR* 4: 257 (= Labeo 6: 50–96).
Bluhme, F. ed. 1833. *Lex Dei, sive Mosaicarum et Romanarum legum collatio: e codicibus manuscriptis vindobonensi et vercellensi nuper repertis, auctam atque emendatam*. Bonnae.
Bradley, K.R. 1994. *Slavery and Society at Rome*. Cambridge.
Brasiello, U. 1976. 'Sulla ricostruzione dei crimini in dirrito romano. Cenni sulla evoluzione dell'omicidio', *SDHI* 42: 246–64.
Brélaz, C. 2005. *La securité publique en Asie mineure sous le principat (Ier–IIIème s. ap. J.-C.): institutions municipales et institutions imperiales dans l'Orient romain*. Basel.
Bringmann, K. 1983. 'Edikt der Triumvirn oder Senatsbeschluss? Zu einem Neufund aus ephesos', *Epigraphica Anatolica* 2: 47–76.
Brunt, P.A. 1975. 'The Administrators of Roman Egypt', *Journal of Roman Studies* 65: 124–47.
Brunt, P.A. 1988. *The Fall of the Roman Republic and Related Essays*. Oxford.
Brunt, P.A. 1990. *Roman Imperial Themes*. Oxford.
Bryen, A.Z. 2012. 'Judging Empire: Courts and Culture in Rome's Eastern Provinces', *Law and History Review* 30: 771–811.
Buckland, W.W. 1908. *The Roman Law of Slavery: The Condition of the Slave in Private Law from Augustus to Justinian*. Cambridge.
Buckland, W.W. 1924. 'Gaius and the liber singularis regularum', *Law Quarterly Review* 40: 185–201.

Buckland, W.W. 1934. 'L'Edictum provinciale', *Revue Historique de Droit Français et Étranger* 13: 81–96.
Burton, G.P. 1975. 'Proconsuls, Assizes and the Administration of Justice under the Empire', *Journal of Roman Studies* 65: 92–106.
Burton, G.P. 1996. 'The Lex Irnitana, ch. 84, the Promise of Vadimonium and the Jurisdiction of Proconsuls', *Classical Quarterly* 46: 217–21.
Buti, I. 1982. 'La "cognitio extra ordinem": da Augusto a Diocleziano', *Aufstieg und Niedergang der Romischen Welt* II.14: 29–59.
Cloud, J.D. 1963. 'The Text of Digest XLVIII,4 ad legem Iuliam maiestatis', *Zeitschrift der Savigny-Stiftung für Rechtsgeschichte* 80: 206–32.
Cloud, J.D. 1968. 'How Did Sulla Style His Law de Sicariis?' *Classical Review* 18: 140–3.
Cloud, J.D. 1969. 'The primary purpose of the lex Cornelio de sicariis', *Zeitschrift der Savigny-Stiftung für Rechtsgeschichte* 86: 258–86.
Cloud, J.D. 1988/9. 'Lex Iulia de vi: Part I–II', *Athenaeum* 76: 579–95 and 77: 427–65.
Cohn-Haft, L. 1956. *The Public Physicians of Ancient Greece.* Northampton.
Coriat, J.P. 1997. *Le Prince législateur. La technique législative des Sévères et les méthodes de création du droit impérial à la fin du principat.* [No publisher listed.]
Cornu Ténard, N. 2011. 'La notion de fait dans la jurisprudence classique: Étude sur les principes de la distinction entre fait et droit', PhD diss., Université Paris II.
Connolly, S. 2010. *Lives behind the Laws: The World of the Codex Hermogenianus.* 1st ed. Bloomington.
Crawford, M.H. 1988. 'The laws of the Romans: knowledge and diffusion', in J. Gonzalez and X. Arce (eds) *Estudios sobre la Tabula Siarensis.* Madrid, 127–40.
Crawford, M.H. 1996. *Roman Statutes.* London.
Crews, R.B. 2016. 'The Handbooks de Officio Proconsulis: Authorship and Audience', PhD diss, University of North Carolina at Chapel Hill Graduate School.
Crifò, G. 1976. 'Ulpiano. Esperienze e responsabilità del giurista', *ANRW* II.15: 708–89.
Crook, J. 1967. 'Patria Potestas', *Classical Quarterly* 17: 113–22.
Cyrielle, L. 2011. 'M. Aurelius Cotta Maximus Messallinus: un noble sous les julio-claudiens', *Mélanges de l'École française de Rome. Antiquité* 123–2: 557–79.

D'Arms, J.H. 1981. *Commerce and Social Standing in Ancient Rome.* Cambridge.

de Ste Croix, G.E.M. 1963. 'Why Were the Early Christians Persecuted?' *Past & Present* 26: 6–38.

Dell'Oro, A. 1960. *I libri de officio nella giurisprudenza romana.* Milan.

Derow, P.S. 1989. 'Rome, the fall of Macedon and the sack of Corinth', *Cambridge Ancient History* 8^2: 290–323.

D'Escurac, P.H. 1976. *La préfecture de l'annone, service administratif impérial d'Auguste à Constantin.* Rome.

Dietz, K. 1983. 'Caracalla, Fabius Cilo und die Urbaniciani', *Chiron* 13: 381–404.

Dixon, S. 1992. *The Roman Family.* Baltimore, MD.

Dolganov, A. 2019. 'Reichsrecht and Volksrecht in Theory and Practice: Roman Justice in the Province of Egypt (P.Oxy. II 237, P.Oxy. IV 706, SB XII 10929)', *Tyche* 34: 27–60.

Dolganov, A. 2022. 'Imperialism and social engineering: Augustan social legislation in the Gnomon of the Idios Logos', *Klio* 104: 656–92.

Dolganov, A. 2023. 'Law as performance: performative aspects of the legal process in Roman courts', in C. Bubb and M. Peachin (eds) *Medicine and Law under the Roman Empire.* Oxford, 67–123.

Dyck, A.D. 2010. *Pro Sexto Roscio.* Cambridge.

Eck, W. 1982. 'Jahres- und Provinzialfasten der senatorischen Statthalter von 69/70 bis 138/139', *Chiron* 12: 349–53.

Eck, W. 1983. 'Jahres- und Provinzialfasten der senatorischen Statthalter von 69/70 bis 138/139', *Chiron* 13: 281–362.

Eck, W. 2013. 'Konsuln des Jahres 117 in Militärdiplomen Traians mit tribunicia potestas XX', *Zeitschrift für Papyrologie und Epigraphik* 185: 235–8.

Fanizza, R. 1977. 'Il senato e la prevenzione del crimen repetundarum in età tiberiana', *Labeo* 23: 199–214.

Fanizza, L. 1994. 'Iurisdictio mandata', *Studia et documenta historiae et iuris* 60: 303–59.

Ferrary, J.-L. 1991. 'La lex Cornelia de sicariis et ueneficis', *Athenæum* 1991: 417–34.

Ferrary, J.-L. 2001. 'À propos des pouvoirs d'Auguste', *Cahiers du Centre Gustave Glotz* 12: 101–54.

Ferrary, J.-L. 2007. 'Loi Iulia *peculatus* – Loi Iulia *de residuis*', in J.-L. Ferrary and P. Moreau (eds) *Lepor. Leges Populi Romani.* Paris. URL: http://www.cn-telma.fr/lepor/notice454/. Accessed 16 October 2024.

Fournier, J. 2010. *Entre tutelle romaine et autonomie civique. L'administration judiciaire dans les provinces hellénophones de l'Empire romain (129 av. J.-C.–235 apr. J.-C.)*. Athens.

Frakes, R.M. 2011. *Compiling the Collatio Legum Mosaicarum et Romanarum in Late Antiquity*. Oxford.

Frier, B. 2023. 'Juristic Literature and the Law: Competition and Cooperation', in C. Bubb and M. Peachin (eds) *Medicine and Law under the Roman Empire*. Oxford, 177–95.

Frier, B.W. and McGinn, H.F. 2004. *A Casebook in Roman Family Law*. Oxford.

Fuhrmann, C.J. 2012. *Policing the Roman Empire: Soldiers, Administration, and Public Order*. Oxford.

Galsterer, H. 1986. 'Roman Law in the Provinces: Some Problems of Transmission', in M.H. Crawford (ed.) *L'Impero romano e le strutture economiche e sociali delle provincie*. Como, 13–27.

Galsterer, H. 1987. 'La loi municipale des Romains', *Revue d'Histoire du Droit* 65: 181–203.

Galsterer, H. 1988. 'Municipium Flavium Irnitanum: A Latin Town in Spain', *Journal of Roman Studies* 78: 78–90.

Galsterer, H. 1996. 'The administration of justice', *Cambridge Ancient History* X^2: 397–413.

Gamauf, R. 1999. *Ad statuam licet confugere: Untersuchungen zum Asylrecht im römischen Prinzipat*. Frankfurt.

Garnsey, P. 1968. 'The Criminal Jurisdiction of Roman Governors', *Journal of Roman Studies* 58: 51–9.

Garnsey, P. 1970. *Social Status and Legal Privilege in the Roman Empire*. Oxford.

Garnsey, P. 1971. 'Taxatio and Pollicitatio in Roman Africa', *Journal of Roman Studies* 61: 116–29.

Garnsey, P. 1988. *Famine and Food Supply in the Graeco-Roman World: Responses to Risk and Crisis*. Cambridge.

Garnsey, P. and Scheidel, W. 1998. *Cities, Peasants and Food in Classical Antiquity: Essays in Social and Economic History*. Cambridge.

Gaudemet, J. 1956. 'La coutume au Bas-Empire. Rôle pratique et notion théorique', *Labeo* 2: 147–59.

Georgescu, V.-Al. 1948. 'L'opposition entre "ius" et "factum" en droit romain et en droit moderne: Contribution à l'étude des styles de la pensée juridique', in *Scritti in onore di C. Ferrini pubblicati in occasione della sua beatifcazione*. Milan, 3:144–65.

Gibbs, M. 2012. 'Collegia', In R.S. Bagnall, K. Brodersen, C.B. Champion, A. Erskine, and S.R. Huebner (eds) *The Encyclopedia of Ancient History*. Chichester, 381–4.

Gleason, M.W. 2006. 'Greek Cities Under Roman Rule', in D.S. Potter (ed.) *A Companion to the Roman Empire*. Oxford, 228–49.

Gnoli, Fr. 1973. 'Cic., Nat. deor. 3, 74 e l'origine della quaestio perpetua peculatus', *Rendiconti Istituto Lombardo* 109: 331–41.

Gnoli, Fr. 1974. 'Rem priuatam de sacro surripere. Contributo allo studio della repressione del sacrilegium in diritto romano', *Studia et documenta historiae et iuris* 40: 151–204.

González, J., and Crawford, M. 1986. 'The lex Irnitana', *Journal of Roman Studies* 76: 147–243.

Grodzynski, D. 1974. 'Superstitio', *Revue des études anciennes* 76: 36–60.

Gruen, E.S. 1974. *The Last Generation of the Roman Republic*. Berkeley, CA.

Gustafson, M. 1994. 'Condemnation to the Mines in the Later Roman Empire', *The Harvard Theological Review* 87: 421–33.

Habicht, C. 1975. 'New Evidence on the Province of Asia', *Journal of Roman Studies* 65: 64–91.

Hackl, K. 1997. 'Der Zivilprozeß des frühen Prinzipats in den Provinzen', *Zeitschrift der Savigny-Stiftung für Rechtsgeschichte* 114: 141–59.

Haensch, R. 1997a. 'Zur Konventsordnung in Aegyptus und den übrigen Provinzen des römischen Reiches', in B. Kramer et al. (eds), *Akten des 21. internationalen Papyrologenkongresses Berlin, 13.–19.8.1995*. Stuttgart and Leipzig, 320–91.

Haensch, R. 1997b. *Capita Provinciarum: Statthaltersitze und Provinzialverwaltung in der Römischen Kaiserzeit*. Mainz Am Rhein.

Halfmann, H. 1979. *Die Senatoren aus dem östlichen Teil des Imperium Romanum: Bis zum Ende des 2. Jahrhunderts N. Chr.* Göttingen, Hft. 58.

Hanson, W.S. 1988. 'Administration, urbanisation and acculturation in the Roman West', in D. Braund (ed.) *The Administration of the Roman Empire: 241BC–AD193*. Exeter, 53–68.

Harmon, D.P. 1978. 'The Public Festivals of Rome', *Aufstieg und Niedergang der Romischen Welt* II.16.2: 1440–68.

Harris, W.V. 1986. 'The Roman father's power of life and death', in R.S. Bagnall and W.V. Harris (eds) *Studies in Roman Law in Memory of Arthur Schiller*. Leiden, 81–96.

Hemelrijk, E.A. 2004. 'City Patronesses in the Roman Empire', *Historia* 53: 209–45.

Hemelrijk, E.A. 2006. 'Priestesses of the Imperial Cult in the Latin West: Benefactions and Public Honour', *L'Antiquité Classique* 75: 85–117.

Hemelrijk, E.A. 2012. 'Public roles for women in the cities of the Latin West', in S.L. James and S. Dillon (eds) *A Companion to Women in the Ancient World*. Oxford, 478–90.

Herzog, R. 1935. 'Urkunden zur hochschulpolitik der römischen Kaiser', *Sitzungsberichte der preussischen Akademie der Wissenschaft, phil.-hist. Klasse*: 967–1019.

Hirschfeld, H.O. 1877. *Die kaiserlichen Verwaltungsbeamten bis auf Diocletian*. Berlin.

Honoré, T. 1978. *Tribonian*. London.

Honoré, T. 1994. *Emperors and Lawyers*. 2nd ed., completely rev., with a palingenesia of third-century imperial rescripts, 193–305 AD. Oxford.

Honoré, T. 2002. *Ulpian*. Oxford.

Honoré, T. 2010. *Justinian's Digest: Character and Compilation*. Oxford.

Howe, L.L. 1942. *The Praetorian Prefect from Commodus to Diocletian (A.D. 180–305)*. London.

Humfress, C. 2012. 'Law and Custom under Rome', in A. Rio (ed.) *Custom in the Middle Ages*. London, 23–47.

Hurlet, F. 2006. *Le Proconsul et le Prince D'Auguste à Dioclétien*. Paris.

Huschke, N. 1888. 'XII. Weitere Beiträge zur Pandektenkritik', *Zeitschrift der Savigny-Stiftung für Rechtsgeschichte* 9: 331–65.

Huschke, P.E. 1860. 'Lex Dei sive Mosaicarum et Romanarum Legum Collatio', in his *Iurisprudentia Anteiustiniana*, II.2. Leipzig, 325–94.

Israelowich, I. 2014. 'Identifications of Physicians during the High Empire', in M. Depauw and S. Coussement (eds) *Identifiers and Identification Methods in the Ancient World*. Leuven, 233–52.

Israelowich, I. 2015. *Patients and Healers in the High Empire*. Baltimore, MD.

Israelowich, I. 2017. 'The extent of the patria potestas during the High Empire: the decision of non tollere as a case in point', *Museum Helveticum* 47: 237–54.

Israelowich, I. 2020. 'Land surveyors and the Roman court', *Revue Internationale des Droits de l'Antiquite* 66: 135–53.

Israelowich, I. 2021. 'Visigoth *medici*: a legal and genealogical study', *Studies in Late Antiquity* 5: 618–38.

Israelowich, I. 2023. 'Brutality towards Slaves: Delictual or Criminal? Re-reading a Rescript of Antoninus Pius', *Studia et documenta historiae et iuris* 77: 138–52.

Israelowich, I. 2025. 'An outline of social change: the long life of an action against a fraudulent land surveyor', *RIDA* 71 (forthcoming).

Janssen, L.F. 1979. 'Superstitio and the Persecution of the Christians', *Vigiliae Christianae* 33: 131–59.

Johnston, D. 1987. 'Three Thoughts on Roman Private Law and the Lex Irnitana', *Journal of Roman Studies* 77: 62–77.

Johnston, D. 1989. 'Justinian's Digest: The Interpretation of Interpolation', *Oxford Journal of Legal Studies* 9: 149–66.

Jolowicz, H.F. and Nicholas, B. 1972. *Historical Introduction to the Study of Roman Law*. Cambridge.

Jones, A.H.M. 1949. 'The Roman Civil Service (Clerical and Sub-Clerical Grades)', *Journal of Roman Studies* 39: 38–55.

Jones, A.H.M. 1950. 'The Aerarium and the Fiscus', *Journal of Roman Studies* 40: 22–9.

Jones, A.H.M. 1964. *The Later Roman Empire, 284–602: A Social, Economic and Administrative Survey*. Oxford.

Jones, A.H.M. 1968. *Studies in Roman Government and Law*. New York.

Jones, C.P. 1978. *The Roman World of Dio Chrysostom*. Cambridge, MA.

Jördens, A. 2011. 'Eine kaiserliche Konstitution zu den Rechtsprechungskompetenzen der Statthalter', *Chiron* 41: 327–56.

Kantor, G. 2013. 'SEG LV 1452, ll. 32–34, and the Crime of plagium in the Late Republic', *Zeitschrift für Papyrologie und Epigraphik* 184: 219–24.

Kaser, M. 1939. 'Mores maiorum und Gewohnheitsrecht', *Zeitschrift der Savigny-Stiftung für Rechtsgeschichte* 59: 52–101.

Kaser, M. 1967. 'The Changing Face of Roman Jurisdiction', *Irish Jurist* 2: 129–43.

Kaser, M. and Hackl, K. 1996. *Das römische Zivilprozessrecht*. Munich.

Katzoff, R. 1969. 'The Provincial Edict in Egypt', *Tijdschrift voor Rechtsgeschiedenis* 37: 415–37.

Knibbe, D. 1981. 'Quandocumque quis trium virum rei publicae constituendae … : ein neuer text aus ephesos', *Zeitschrift für Papyrologie und Epigraphik* 44: 1–10.

Koschaker, P. 1919. 'Moriz Wlassak, Anklage und Streitbefestigung im Kriminalrecht der Römer', *Zeitschrift der Savigny-Stiftung für Rechtsgeschichte* 40: 364–70.

Krueger, P. and Mommsen, T. 1872. *Corpus iuris civilis. Editio stereotypa*. Berolini.

Kübler, B. n.d. 'Maiestas', *RE* XIV.1: 542–60.

Kunkel, W. 1973. *An Introduction to Roman Legal and Constitutional History*. 2nd ed. Oxford.

Le Roux, P. 2022. 'Chapitre XX. L'*ordo decurionum* à l'horizon municipal', in Y. Maligorne, S. Armani, and N. Mathieu (eds) *L'Empire romain. Histoire et modèles: Scripta varia III*. Renne, 357–72.

Lemosse, M. 1998. 'Crimen Expilatae Hereditatis', *Revue Historique de Droit Français et Étranger* 76: 255–60.

Lenel, O. 1889 (repr. 1960). *Palingenesia Iuris Civilis*. 2 vols., with supplement by L.E. Sierl. [No publisher listed.]

Lewis, N. 1981. 'On Judicial Appeals in Roman Egypt', *The American Journal of Philology* 102: 340–3.

Liebs, D. 1964. *Hermogenians Iuris Epitome*. Göttingen.

Liebs, D. 1984. 'Review of Honoré (1982)', *Gnomon* 56: 441–50.

Liebs, D. 1996. 'Die pseudopaulinischen Sentenzen II: Versuch einer neuen Palingenesie, Ausführung', *Zeitschrift der Savigny-Stiftung für Rechtsgeschichte* 113: 132–242.

Liebs, D. 1997. 'Jurisprudenz', *HLL* 4 §§410–31.

McCrum, M. and Woodhead, A.G. 1961. *Select Documents of the Principates of the Flavian Emperors, A.D. 68–96*. Cambridge.

Magie, D. 1950. *Roman Rule in Asia Minor: To the End of the Third Century after Christ*. Princeton, NJ.

Manthe, U. 1989. 'Bemerkungen zur Cura Furiosi', *Tijdschrift voor Rechtsgeschiedenis* 57: 157–68.

Mantovani, D. 1993–4. 'Il "bonus praeses" secondo Ulpiano. Studi su contenuto e forma dei "Libri de officio proconsulis"', *Bullettino dell'Istituto di Diritto Romano* 35–6: 203–67.

Mantovani, D. 2021. 'Aspects of the Critical Edition of Roman Juristic Works. The Example of Ulpian's De Officio Proconsulis', in A. Schiavone and F. Nasti (eds) *Jurists and Legal Science in the History of Roman Law*. London, 235–60.

Marotta, V. 2000. *Ulpiano e l'impero*. Loffredo.

Marotta, V. 2004. *Ulpiano e l'impero*. Napoli.

Marshall, A.J. 1964. 'The structure of Cicero's edict', *American Journal of Philology* 85: 185–91.

Marshall, A.J. 1966. 'Governors on the Move', *Phoenix* 20.3: 231–46.

Marshall, A.J. 1972. 'The Lex Pompeia de provinciis (52 B.C.) and Cicero's Imperium in 51–50 B.C.: Constitutional Aspects', *Aufstieg und Niedergang der Romischen Welt* 1.1: 887–921.

Marshall, A.J. 1975. 'Roman Women and the Provinces', *Ancient History* 6: 109–28.

Mayer, P.M. 1910. *Griechische Papyri im Museum des Oberhessischen Geschichtsvereins zu Giessen*. Berlin.

Méleze Modrzejewski, J. 1970. 'La règle de droit dans l'Égypte Romaine', in *Proceedings of the Twelfth International Congress of Papyrology*. Toronto, 317–77.

Méleze Modrzejewski, J. 2014. 'Loi et coutume dans l'Égypte grecque et romaine: les facteurs de formation du droit en Égypte d'Alexandre le Grand à la conquête arabe', *Journal of Juristic Papyrology* supplement 21.

Merkelbach, R. 1978. 'Der Rangstreit der Städte Asiens und die Rede des Aelius Aristides über die Eintracht', *Zeitschrift für Papyrologie und Epigraphik* 32: 287–96.

Meyer-Zwiffelhoffer, E. 2002. *Politikōs archein: zum Regierungsstil der senatorischen Statthalter in den kaiserzeitlichen griechischen Provinzen*. Stuttgart.

Millar, F. 1963. 'The Fiscus in the First Two Centuries', *Journal of Roman Studies* 53: 29–42.

Millar, F. 1964. 'Some Evidence on the Meaning of Tacitus "Annals XII". 60', *Historia* 13.2: 180–7.

Millar, F. 1965. 'The Development of Jurisdiction by Imperial Procurators; Further Evidence', *Historia* 14: 362–7.

Millar, F. 1968. 'Review of A.N. Sherwin-White, The Letters of Pliny', *Journal of Roman Studies* 58: 218–24.

Millar, F. 1977. *The Emperor in the Roman World: 31 BC–AD 337*. London.

Millar, F. 1984. 'Condemnation to Hard Labour in the Roman Empire, from the Julio-Claudians to Constantine', *Papers of the British School at Rome* 52: 124–47.

Millar, F. 1986. 'A New Approach to the Roman Jurists', *Journal of Roman Studies* 76: 272–80.

Millar, F. 2002. *Rome, the Greek world, and the east. 1. The Roman Republic and the Augustan Revolution*, eds H. Cotton and G.M. Rogers. Chapel Hill, NC.

Millar, F. 2005. *Rome, the Greek World, and the East. 2. Government, Society, and Culture in the Roman Empire*. Chapel Hill, NC.

Millar, F. 2016. 'Imperial Letters in Latin: Pliny and Trajan, Egnatius Taurinus and Hadrian', *Scripta Classica Israelica* 35: 65–83.

Mitteis, L. 1891. *Reichsrecht und Volksrecht in den östlichen Provinzen des römischen Kaiserreichs*. Leipzig.

Mitteis, L. 1912. 'Ueber den Ausdruck "Potentiores" in den Digesten', in *Mélanger P.F. Girard*. Paris, 225–35.

Mommsen, T. 1887/8. *Römisches Staatsrecht*. Leipzig.

Mommsen, T. 1889. *Römisches Strafrecht*. Leipzig.

Mommsen, T. 1890. *Fragmenta Vaticana: Mosaicarvm et Romanarvm Legvm Collatio*, ed. P. Krueger. Berlin.

Mommsen, T. and Krueger, P. 1870. *Digesta Iustiniani Augusti recognouit adsumpto in operis societatem*. Berolini.

Nagy, À. 2002. 'Superstitio et coniuratio', *Numen* 49: 178–92.

Nelis-Clément, J. 2000. *Les beneficiarii: militaires et administrateurs au service de l'Empire* (1 ers. a.C.–VIe s. p.C.). Paris.

Nicholls, M. 2005. 'Roman public libraries'. DPhil thesis, University of Oxford.

Nicolet, C. 1991. *Space, Geography, and Politics in the Early Roman Empire*. Ann Arbor, MI.

Nicols, J. 1988. 'On the Standard Size of the Ordo Decurionum', *Zeitschrift der Savigny-Stiftung für Rechtsgeschichte* 105: 712–19.

Nogrady, A. 2006. *Römisches Strafrecht nach Ulpian: Buch 7 bis 9 De officio proconsulis*. Berlin.

Nörr, D. 1969. 'Zur Entstehung der gewohnheitsrechtlichen Theorie', in M. Kaser et al. (eds) *Festschrift für Wilhelm Felgentraeger zum 70. Geburtstag*. Göttingen, 353–66.

Nörr, D. 1981. 'Zur Reskriptenpraxis in der hohen Prinzipatszeit', *Zeitschrift der Savigny-Stiftung für Rechtsgeschichte* 98: 1–46.

Nörr, D. 1987. *Causa mortis: Auf den Spuren einer Redewendung*. Munich.

Nótári, T. 2013. 'Remarks on two aspects of the patria potestas in Roman law', *Fiat Iustitia* 2: 29–49.

Nutton, V. 1977. 'Archiatri and the Medical Profession', *Papers of the British School at Rome* 32: 191–226.

Oliver, J.H. 1966. 'A Roman governor visits Samothrace', *American Journal of Philology* 87: 75–80.

Oliver, J.H. 1979. 'Greek Applications for Roman Trials', *American Journal of Philology* 100: 543–58.

Oliver, J. 1989. *Greek Constitutions of the Early Roman Emperors from Inscriptions and Papyri*. Philadelphia, PA.

Orestano, R. 1980. 'La "cognitio extra ordinem": una chimera', *Studia et documenta historiae et iuris* 46: 236–7.

Ovadiah, A. and Mucznik, S. 2014. 'Deisidaimonia, Superstitio and Religio: Graeco-Roman, Jewish and Early Christian Concepts', *Liber Annuus* 64: 417–40.

Pavis D'Escurac, H. 1976. *La préfecture de l'annone. Service impérial d'Auguste à Constantin*. Paris.

Peachin, M. 1996. *Iudex Vice Caesaris: Deputy Emperors and the Administration of Justice during the Principate*. Stuttgart.

Perozzi, S. 1906. *Istituzioni di Diritto Romano*. Florence.

Pflaum, H.G. 1950. *Les Procurateurs équestres sous le Haut Empire Romain*. Paris.

Pflaum, H.-G. 1952. 'La fortification de la ville d'Adraha d'Arabie', *Syria* 29: 307–30.

Pithou, P. 1573. *Fragmenta Quaedam Papiniani, Pauli, Ulpiani, Gaii, Modestini, aliorumque veterum Iuris auctorum ex integris ipsorum libris ante Iustiniani Imp. tempora collecta, et cum Moysis legibus collata*. Paris.

Pohl, R. 1905. *De graecorum medicis publicis*. Berlin.

Pottier, B. 2003. *Banditisme et ordre public dans les campagnes de l'Empire romain*. Paris.

Price, S.R.F. 1984. *Rituals and Power: The Roman Imperial Cult in Asia Minor*. Cambridge.

Purcell, N. 1983. 'The Apparitores: A Study in Social Mobility', *Papers of the British School at Rome* 51: 125–73.

Riccobono, S. 1949. 'Cognitio extra ordinem: Nozione e caratteri del "ius novum"', *Revue Internationale des Droits de l'Antiquite* 3: 277–93.

Rilinger, R. 1988. *Humiliores – honestiores: zu einer sozialen Dichotomie im Strafrecht der romischen Kaiserzeit*. Munich.

Rivière, Y. 1994. '*Carcer et uincula*: la détention publique à Rome (sous la République et le Haut-Empire)', in *Mélanges de l'École française de Rome. Antiquité*, tome 106: 579–652.

Rivière, Y. 2002. *Les délateurs sous l'empire romain*. Rome.

Rivière, Y. 2004. *Le cachot et les fers. Détention et coercition à Rome*. Paris.

Robert, L. 1967. 'Sur les inscriptions d'Éphèse', *Rev. Phil.* 41: 1–84.

Robert, L. 1977. 'La titulature de Nicée et de Nicomédie: la gloire et la haine', *Harvard Studies in Classical Philology* 81: 1–39.

Robinson, O.F. 2007. 'The Role of Delators', in J.W. Cairns and P.J. du Plessis (eds) *Beyond Dogmatics: Law and Society in the Roman World*. Edinburgh, 206–20.

Rodger, A. 1983. 'Behind the Scenes in Roman Law', *Oxford Journal of Legal Studies* 3: 382–404.

Rodger, A. 1990. 'The Jurisdiction of Local Magistrates: Chapter 84 of the Lex Irnitana', *Zeitschrift für Papyrologie und Epigraphik* 84: 147–61.

Rodger, A. 1991. 'The Lex Irnitana and Procedure in the Civil Courts', *Journal of Roman Studies* 81: 74–90.

Rodger, A. 1996. 'Jurisdictional Limits in the Lex Irnitana and the Lex de Gallia Cisalpina', *Zeitschrift für Papyrologie und Epigraphik* 110: 189–206.

Rougé, J. 1966. *Recherches Sur l'organisation du commerce maritime en Mediterranée sous l'empire romain*. Paris.

Rüfner, T. 2016. 'Imperial *Cognitio* Process', in P.J. du Plessis, C. Ando, and K. Tuori (eds) *The Oxford Handbook of Roman Law and Society*. Oxford, 257–69.

Salzman, M.R. 1987. 'Superstitio in the Codex Theodosianus and the Persecution of Pagans', *Vigiliae Christianae* 41: 172–88.

Sartre, M. 1991. *L'Orient romain: provinces et sociétés provinciales en Méditerranée orientale d'Auguste aux Sévères 31 avant J.-C.–235 après J.-C.* Paris.

Schiller, A.A. 1938. 'Custom in Classical Roman Law', *Virginia Law Review* 24: 268–82.

Schiller, A.A. 1953. 'The jurists and the prefects in Rome', *Bullettino dell'Istituto di Diritto Romano* 57: 60–97.

Schiller, S.S. 1978. *Roman Law: Mechanisms of Development*. Berlin.

Schulz, F. 1951. 'The Manuscripts of the Collatio Legum Mosaicarum et Romanarum', *Bullettino dell'Istituto di Diritto Romano* 55: 50–69.

Sherwin-White, A.N. 1966. *The Letters of Pliny: A Historical and Social Commentary*. Oxford.

Simshäuser, W. 1989. 'La juridiction municipale à la lumière de la lex Irnitana', *Revue Historique de Droit Français et Étranger* 67: 619–50.

Sirks, A.J.B. 2001. 'Making a request to the emperor: rescripts in the Roman Empire', in L. de Blois (ed.) *Administration, Prosopography and Appointment Policies in the Roman Empire*. Leiden, 121–35.

Sirks, B. 1991. *Food for Rome: The Legal Structure of the Transportation and Processing of Supplies for the Imperial Distributions in Rome and Constantinople*. Amsterdam.

Speidel, M. 1974. 'Stablesiani. The Raising of New Cavalry Units during the Crisis of the Roman Empire', *Chiron* 4: 541–46.

Steel, C. 2012. 'The Lex Pompeia de Provinciis of 52 B.C: a reconsideration', *Historia* 61: 83–93.

Stein, E. 1922. *Untersuchungen über das Officium der Prätorianerpräfektur seit Diokletian*. Berlin.

Stein, P. 1995. 'Custom in Roman and medieval civil law', *Continuity and Change* 10: 337–44.

Sutherland, C.H.V. 1945. 'Aerarium and Fiscus during the Early Empire', *American Journal of Philology* 66: 151–70.

Syme, R. 1958. 'Consulates in Absence', *Journal of Roman Studies* 48: 1–9.

Syme, R. 1972. 'Lawyers in Government: The Case of Ulpian', *Proceedings of the American Philosophical Society* 116: 406–9.

Syme, R. 1978. *History in Ovid*. Oxford.

Syme, R. 1980. 'Fiction about Roman Jurists', *SZ* 97: 78–104.

Syme, R. 1982. 'The Career of Arrian', *Harvard Studies in Classical Philology* 86: 181–211.

Syme, R. 1983. 'The Proconsuls of Asia under Antoninus Pius', *Zeitschrift für Papyrologie und Epigraphik* 51: 271–90.

Syme, R. 1984. 'P. Calvisius Ruso. One Person or Two?' *Zeitschrift für Papyrologie und Epigraphik* 56: 173–92.

Syme, R. 1989a. 'A Lost Legate of Aquitania', *Zeitschrift für Papyrologie und Epigraphik* 79: 181–7.

Syme, R. 1989b. 'A Dozen Early Priesthoods', *Zeitschrift für Papyrologie und Epigraphik* 77: 241–59.

Thomas, J.A.C. 1963. 'Custom and Roman Law', *Tijdschrift voor Rechtsgeschiedenis* 31: 39–53.

Thomas, J.A.C. 1976. *Textbook of Roman Law*. Amsterdam.

Thomas, Y. 1984. 'Vitae necisque potestas. Le père, la cité, la mort', in *Du châtiment dans la cité. Supplices corporels et peine de mort dans le monde antique. Table ronde de Rome (9–11 novembre 1982)*. Rome, 499–548.

Thomas, Y. 1986. 'Le "ventre". Corps maternel, droit paternel', *Le Genre humain* 14: 211–36.

Thomas, Y. 2007. 'L'enfant à naître et l'"héritier sien": Sujet de pouvoir et sujet de vie en droit romain', *Annales. Histoire, Sciences Sociales* 62.1: 29–68.

Tuori, K.T. 2004. 'The ius respondendi and the Freedom of Roman Jurisprudence', *Revue Internationale des Droits de l'Antiquite* 51: 295–337.

Turpin, W. 1999. 'Formula, cognitio, and proceedings extra ordinem', *Revue Internationale des Droits de l'Antiquite* 46: 499–574.

van Minnen, P. 2020. 'Three Edicts of Caracalla? A New Reading of P.Giss. 40', *Chiron* 46: 205–21.

Veyne, P. 1958. 'La table des Ligures Baebiani et l'institution alimentaire de Trajan', *Mélanges de l'école française de Rome* 70: 177–241.

Veyne, P. 1976. *Le Pain Et Le Cirque: Sociologie Historique d'un Pluralisme Politique*. Paris.

Villers, R. 1939. 'Essai sur la "pollicitatio" à une "res publica"', *Revue Historique de Droit Français et Étranger* 18: 1–38.

Visscher, Fernand de. 1964. *Les édits d'Auguste découverts à Cyrène*. Osnabrück.

Ward Perkins, J.B. 1937. 'The Career of Sex. Julius Frontinus', *Classical Quarterly* 31: 102–5.

Watson, A. 1961. 'Actio de dolo and actiones in factum', *Zeitschrift der Savigny-Stiftung für Rechtsgeschichte* 78: 392–402.

Watson, A. 1967. *The Law of Persons in the Later Roman Republic*. Oxford.

Watson, A. 1971. 'The imperatives of the aedilician edict', *Tijdschrift voor Rechtsgeschiedenis* 39: 73–84.

Westbrook, R. 1999. 'Vitae necisque potestas', *Historia* 48: 203–23.

Wieacker, F. 1960. *Textstufen klassischer Juristen*. Göttingen.

Wolff, C. 2003. *Les brigands en Orient sous le Haut-Empire romain*. Rome.

Yaron, R. 1962. 'Vitae necisque potestas', *Tijdschrift voor Rechtsgeschiedenis* 30: 243–51.

Yiftach-Firanko, U. 2009. 'Law in Greco-Roman Egypt: Hellenization, Fusion, Romanization', in R.S. Bagnall (ed.) *The Oxford Handbook of Papyrology*. Oxford, 541–60.

Youtie, H. 1964. 'A reconsideration of P. *Oxy.* 1.40', in H. Braunert (ed.) *Studien zur Papyrologie und Antiken Wirtschaftsgeschichte*. Bonn, 20–9.

Zeumer, K., ed. 1902. *Leges Visigothorum*, MGH Legum sectio i.1. Hannover.

Zimmermann, R. 1996. *The Law of Obligations: Roman Foundations of the Civilian Tradition*. Oxford.

INDEX